Empire of Defense

Empire of Defense

Race and the Cultural Politics
of Permanent War

JOSEPH DARDA

THE UNIVERSITY OF CHICAGO PRESS   CHICAGO AND LONDON

The University of Chicago Press, Chicago 60637
The University of Chicago Press, Ltd., London
© 2019 by The University of Chicago
Published 2019
Printed in the United States of America

28 27 26 25 24 23 22 21 20 19   1 2 3 4 5

ISBN-13: 978-0-226-63289-6 (cloth)
ISBN-13: 978-0-226-63292-6 (paper)
ISBN-13: 978-0-226-63308-4 (e-book)
DOI: https://doi.org/10.7208/chicago/9780226633084.001.0001

Library of Congress Cataloging-in-Publication Data

Names: Darda, Joseph, author.
Title: Empire of defense : race and the cultural politics of permanent war / Joseph Darda.
Description: Chicago ; London : The University of Chicago Press, 2019. | Includes
    bibliographical references and index.
Identifiers: LCCN 2018049439 | ISBN 9780226632896 (cloth : alk. paper) |
    ISBN 9780226632926 (pbk. : alk. paper) | ISBN 9780226633084 (e-book)
Subjects: LCSH: United States—History, Military—20th century. | United States—
    History, Military—21st century. | Racism—United States.
Classification: LCC E745 .D373 2019 | DDC 355.0097309/04—dc23
LC record available at https://lccn.loc.gov/2018049439

♾ This paper meets the requirements of ANSI/NISO z39.48-1992 (Permanence of Paper).

FOR MY PARENTS

I still think today as yesterday that the color-line is a great problem of this century. But today I see more clearly than yesterday that back of the problem of race and color, lies a greater problem that both obscures and implements it: and that is the fact that so many civilized persons are willing to live in comfort even if the price of this is poverty, ignorance and disease of the majority of their fellowmen; that to maintain this privilege men have waged war until today war tends to become universal and continuous, and the excuse for this war continues to be color and race.

W. E. B. DU BOIS, Preface to the 1953 Fiftieth Anniversary Edition of *The Souls of Black Folk*

Contents

Introduction: A Perpetual Wartime Footing   1

CHAPTER 1.   How to Tell a Permanent War Story   28

CHAPTER 2.   Antiwar Liberalism against Liberal War   60

CHAPTER 3.   Dispatches from the Drug Wars   92

CHAPTER 4.   Kicking the Vietnam Syndrome with Human Rights   123

CHAPTER 5.   The Craft of Counterinsurgent Whiteness   155

Epilogue: Defense in the Fifth Domain   186

Acknowledgments   203

Notes   207

Bibliography   233

Index   255

Introduction: A Perpetual Wartime Footing

The war was over, again. In the first months of his second term, President Barack Obama announced plans to end the war on terror. From an auditorium at Fort McNair in Washington, he acknowledged that the United States had, for more than a decade, stood on "a perpetual wartime footing" and declared that it was time to change course.[1] For close to an hour, Obama outlined an agenda for winding down the war that included training and arming militaries in the Middle East and Central Asia, distributing aid to combat anti-Western attitudes, adding new checks on his administration's drone program, and closing the prison at Guantánamo Bay, where detainees were staging yet another months-long hunger strike. The ideas weren't new. Obama had been reciting some since 2002, when he made headlines as an Illinois state senator for declaring the invasion of Iraq "dumb," "rash," and "cynical."[2] But liberal news media praised him for fulfilling the promise he had made years earlier as an antiwar presidential candidate. The *New York Times* editorial board hailed the speech as "a momentous turning point in post-9/11 America," welcoming it as the beginning of the end of the war on terror.[3]

That day, May 23, 2013, turned out to be one more false ending to an unending war. Weeks later, NSA contractor Edward Snowden leaked classified information detailing the government's far-reaching global surveillance programs, leaving the Obama administration scrambling to defend itself. A year later, the Islamic State captured Mosul, defeating the US-trained Iraqi Army, and proclaimed a caliphate. The president answered with airstrikes, launching a new war in Iraq that his successor, Donald Trump, despite having campaigned as an "America first" isolationist, would escalate three years later. The long war got longer. Perhaps, standing at the podium at Fort McNair, Obama couldn't have anticipated the trials ahead, or that he would end his second term as he had his first: at war. But his plan for ending the war on terror—that momentous turning point—was also a plan to continue it. He heralded the end of the war on terror by introducing a new "comprehensive counterterrorism strategy" that entailed the continuous flow of advisers, planes, tanks, surveillance technologies, and humanitarian aid to the Middle East, Central Asia, and North Africa. "Our systematic effort to dismantle terrorist organizations must continue," the president told the crowded auditorium. "But this war, like all wars, must end. That's what history advises. That's what our democracy demands." His plan to end the war amounted to a plan to redefine it as something other than war. The war would go on—the state would continue dismantling terrorist organizations with force—but under a different name. His war on terror was not a war, he argued, but "a series of persistent, targeted efforts to dismantle specific networks of violent extremists that threaten America."[4] It was strategic nonwar. It was defense.

War, Obama claimed, must end. It was antithetical to all that the United States stood for as the leader of the free world. That belief originated in the years after World War II, the last one waged with an official declaration of war. President Harry Truman faced a changing world in 1945, the year he took office, with mass migrations, the decline of colonialism across Asia and Africa, the erosion of Jim Crow at home, and the rise of antiracist movements the world over. He also faced an ascendant Soviet Union that, under Premier Joseph Stalin, moved to consolidate a Communist Eastern bloc.[5] The Truman administration responded with force, building a national security state that, with some seven hundred bases dotting the globe, would wage a Cold War and police the postcolonial world. It built an empire as others crumbled by incorporating the language of anticolonialism and antiracism, by reframing war against nonwhite, non-Western enemies as the defense of humanity from illiberal beliefs.[6] With the National Security Act of 1947 and the amendments of 1949, the Truman administration dissolved the Department of War, a cabinet-level office since 1789, and formed the Department of Defense. The United States no longer waged war but, the legislation announced, safeguarded the world from the fluid threats of communism, crime, authoritarianism, and terrorism. It waged defense. It created the conditions for endless war by framing the invasion of Asian countries as an antiracist defense against deracinated beliefs and behaviors. In 1945, the Truman administration faced twinned crises of race and war that it managed with the idea of defense, giving a future president the language to describe a globe-spanning war as "a series of persistent, targeted efforts to dismantle specific networks of violent extremists that threaten America."[7]

This book tells the story of how the United States turned war into defense. The formation of the Department of Defense inaugurated an era of contradiction for the rising American empire. That empire has waged permanent war while calling it something else—a police action, a humanitarian intervention, a counterinsurgency campaign—and declared itself an antiracist leader in the world while designating whole societies as illegitimate, backward, and deserving of destruction. From the Cold War to the war on terror, it has concealed the contradictions of race and war through the idea of defense, with which it governs who can and can't execute legitimate violence and who does and doesn't deserve to be defended. Defense is a racial regime. It separates those with the right to self-defense from those to be integrated or "saved" and those to be contained or killed. It denies the state's enemies the right to conduct legitimate violence, or wage war. The idea of defense is sustained through race, which turns war into a mere safeguard against illegitimate enemies, and itself *makes race* by assigning value and valuelessness to bodies and beliefs. The shifts in the idea of defense since the late 1940s make it difficult to see the continuities between the Cold War, the drug wars, the humanitarian wars, and the counterterror wars. But the empire of defense surfaces in the consistent failure of officials, writers, filmmakers, and journalists to give narrative form to war that neither begins nor ends. It is this failure that tells the story of permanent war. And it is this failure that this book is about.[8]

W. E. B. Du Bois, the historian and activist, recognized the new racial regime in the first years of the Cold War. In 1953, Blue Heron Press published a fiftieth anniversary edition of *The Souls of Black Folk*, in which Du Bois declared, famously and prophetically, that "the problem of the Twentieth Century is the problem of the color-line."[9] Du Bois, eighty-five and under mounting pressure from the FBI for his antiwar and anticapitalist beliefs, contributed a preface to the new edition in which he amended his original claim. "I still think today as yesterday that the color-line is a great problem of this century," he wrote. "But today I see more clearly than yesterday that back of the problem of race and color, lies a greater problem which both obscures and implements it." This "greater problem," he concluded, was the West's effort to maintain racial rule through war "until today war tends to become universal and continuous, and the excuse for this war continues to be color and race."[10] The problem of the twentieth century was the problem of the color line, and the perpetuation of that problem depended on the perpetuation of war. Du Bois argued that war served to maintain the uneven distribution of resources and life chances along racial lines. Race excused war, and war made race. Writing at the height of the Korean War, which officials branded a police action, he knew that war had not ended. It had become "universal and continuous" because war alone could contain the crisis of race brought on by the fall of colonialism. The problem of the twentieth century was the problem of the color line, drawn and policed through permanent war.

This was not the story that Obama, the first black president, told at Fort McNair, where he sketched a history of triumph and progress. "From the Civil War to our struggle against fascism, on through the long twilight struggle of the Cold War, battlefields have changed and technology has evolved. But our commitment to constitutional principles has weathered every war, and every war has come to an end," he stated. "By staying true to the values of our founding, and by using our constitutional compass, we have overcome slavery and Civil War and fascism and communism." The United States, Obama suggested, had fought wars as a last resort and for brief intervals to protect the nation and the world from illiberal beliefs and behaviors, including its own. The war on terror was no different, he concluded; it too had been fought for the greater good, and it too would end. But that end would be definitional. Obama insisted that "we must define our effort not as a boundless 'global war on terror,'" distancing himself from the term used by his predecessor, George W. Bush. His press secretary even placed "global war on terror" in scare quotes in the official transcript.

The president had been attacked from the right and the left for the hundreds of lethal drone strikes his administration had ordered. In Washington, he defended the program by asking Americans to "remember that the terrorists we are after target civilians, and the death toll from their acts of terrorism against Muslims dwarfs any estimate of civilian casualties from drone strikes." His administration's drone attacks in Pakistan, Yemen, and elsewhere were justified, he argued, because it conducted them in countries *already* defined by violence against Muslims and with "no functioning law."[11] Obama described al-Qaeda's and the Taliban's violence as illegitimate and racist and his own government's as legitimate and antiracist. The United States couldn't be accused of anti-Muslim racism because Muslims were killing each other in greater numbers. The president declared his plan to end the war on terror and then, by invoking an ethic of defense and delegitimizing the state's declared enemies, denied that a war had ever begun or therefore needed to end.

Obama's own story lent weight to the one he told about the war. Years earlier, in his keynote address at the 2004 Democratic National Convention, Obama, then a candidate for the US Senate, introduced himself to America by presenting his achievements—born the son of a Kenyan villager and a working-class Midwesterner and now a rising star on the world's biggest stage—as evidence of the nation's tolerance and egalitarianism that had made it "the envy of the world." He concluded his life story, a story on which he would build his future presidential run, by telling the crowd, "Tonight, we gather to affirm the greatness of our nation" not because of "the power of our military" but because it was founded on the idea that "all men are created equal."[12] Massachusetts Senator John Kerry headed that year's Democratic ticket, and his team had some misgivings about letting an Illinois state senator best known for his opposition to the Iraq War deliver the keynote when Kerry had voted for the 2001 and 2002 AUMFs (Authorizations for Use of Military Force). Nine years and two conventions later, that antiwar state senator had become a war president. Obama recognized, it seems, that "the power of our military" rests on the state's claim to model the liberal idea that "all men are created equal"—a claim reinforced, he later suggested, by his election as the first black man to lead it.

But the president, as eloquent as ever at Fort McNair, couldn't hide the holes in his speech from at least one person in the audience. As he recounted his efforts to transfer the remaining detainees from Guantánamo, Medea Benjamin, a cofounder of the feminist antiwar organization Code Pink, stood up and reminded him of their hunger strike, asking that he "release them today." She went on to demand answers for the death of Abdulrahman al-Awlaki, a sixteen-year-old American killed by a CIA drone strike in Yemen. "Is that the way we treat a sixteen-year-old American?" she asked. "Can you tell us why Abdulrahman al-Awlaki was killed? Can you tell the Muslim people their lives are as precious as our lives?"[13] Secret service agents removed Benjamin from the audience. But Obama acknowledged her protest and the hunger strike she had called attention to, a strike that included 103 of the 166 remaining detainees and built on a series of strikes dating back to 2002.[14] Medical officers had, he admitted, resorted to force-feeding the prisoners to keep them alive.

The detainees were contesting their indefinite incarceration by threatening to introduce a different order of time by the most dramatic means
available: by ending their own lives.[15] Although the United Nations Office
of the Commissioner for Human Rights had issued a statement earlier
that month declaring the force-feeding carried out at Guantánamo "cruel,
inhuman, and degrading,"[16] the president suggested that it reflected his
administration's commitment to caring for the men until he could secure
their transfer. Obama never set out to end war but to make it seem more
methodical, humane, and sensitive to cultural difference—to make a perpetual wartime footing look like a stand for justice. Benjamin recognized
this, as Du Bois had of Truman before her. Defense is not the end of war;
it is the transformation of war from an event to a norm.

Defense Is the Health of the State

"War is the health of the State," Randolph Bourne, the radical journalist,
argued in 1918.[17] He wrote this, his most quoted phrase, in the waning
months of World War I, not long before he died in the flu pandemic at
the age of thirty-two. Friends, sorting through the journalist's apartment
after his death, found the unpublished manuscript in a wastebasket by his
desk. War strengthened the state, Bourne wrote in the discarded pages,
by wedding it to the nation and encouraging Americans to think of themselves as amateur agents of the state responsible for policing what can and
can't be thought and said. The patriot, who gives no thought to the state
in peacetime, identifies with the state at war. Its actions are his. "Wartime
brings the ideal of the State out into very clear relief, and reveals attitudes
and tendencies that were hidden," Bourne observed. "In times of peace
the sense of the State flags in a republic that is not militarized. For war is
essentially the health of the State."[18] War demands that Americans conform in thought and behavior to the ideals of the state, but it also divides
the nation, Bourne determined, because it unifies some as patriots and
"outlaws the rest."[19] It introduces human divisions by naming legitimate
enemies elsewhere and illegitimate enemies at home; the nonconformists
in the United States are "outlaws." This changed after World War II as
all of the state's enemies, within and without, were treated as illegitimate
through a racial regime of defense. The ideological conformities of the
state were imposed on the world. North Korea was an outlaw state that
needed to be policed, not a legitimate antagonist. The idea of defense al-

lowed the state to grow stronger than ever by creating the conditions for permanent war without having to acknowledge it as war at all. Defense is the health of the state.

The Truman administration inaugurated the shift from war to defense with the National Security Act of 1947. Signed into law after months of heated negotiations between the army, the navy, and the White House, the act unified the branches of the armed forces under the direction of the new National Military Establishment and created the Air Force, the National Security Council, the Central Intelligence Agency, and the Joint Chiefs of Staff. Truman first made the plan public in his State of the Union address earlier that year, in which he presented the new department as a safeguard against another Pearl Harbor. "This is an age when unforeseen attack could come with unprecedented speed. We must be strong enough to defeat, and thus forestall, any such attack," the president stated, making the case for "a single Department of National Defense" that blurred the line between war ("strong enough to defeat") and defense ("and thus forestall").[20] Truman appointed James Forrestal, then the secretary of the navy, to head the new NME as the first secretary of defense. Hanson Baldwin, the *New York Times* military affairs editor, while praising Forrestal, worried that the National Security Act set a dangerous course for the nation. "In seeking security we must be careful that we do not lose freedom," he wrote, days after the first defense secretary assumed office. "For there can be a trend—given the threat of the atomic bomb—to increase military power in all fields more and more to such a degree that the ultimate end would be the 'garrison state.'"[21] The tension between militarism and liberal rights that Baldwin identified was not lost on the Truman administration, which resolved it by building a garrison state in the name of defending freedom, a fortress of civil liberties.

Historians describe the National Security Act as the founding document of the defense establishment, "the Magna Charta of the national security state."[22] And it is. But the first defense secretary had almost no power. Forrestal directed the NME with a skeleton staff and had limited control over the secretaries of the services. The job exhausted Forrestal, and he ended his tenure at the Bethesda Naval Hospital in a deep depression. To address the limitations of the office, the Truman administration amended the act in 1949, restructuring the financial management of the department by appointing a comptroller to distribute the budgets of the army, navy, air force, and intelligence agencies under the direction of the secretary. The president described the restructuring as a transition to a "performance-type" budget that ensured the defense secretary greater "flexibility in the control and use of funds."[23] The amendments allowed the two-year-old department to make its own allocation decisions without internal oversight from the legislative branch. Along with the financial reforms that readied it for massive growth, growth that arrived with the escalation of the Korean War in 1950, the department received a new name. The National Military Establishment became the Department of Defense.

The National Security Act Amendments of 1949 instituted the idea of defense that would govern the state's conduct in the world for decades to come, from Korea to Vietnam, Iraq, and Afghanistan. Officials use the term to name wars against enemies they consider illiberal and illegitimate— not adversaries but threats to the liberal democratic values for which the United States stands. Defense is the idea with which the state assigns value to some forms of being and denies it to others. Some are worth defending; some are worth saving; and some must be abolished. This is the idea of defense. It depends on the delegitimization of others to make war. It racializes the state's enemies. Baldwin had it right in 1947 when he acknowledged that the United States had embraced defense "in an age when to defend is to attack" and to attack is never to wage war.[24] When Truman announced his administration's plan to restructure the armed forces, he stressed that it was about more than defending the nation. "National security does not consist only of an army, a navy, and an air force," he stated. It also rests on "civil liberties and human freedoms" and the achievement of "collective security for all mankind." With a unified defense establishment, he imagined, "the faith of our citizens in freedom and democracy will be spread over the whole earth and free men everywhere will share our devotion to those ideals."[25] Truman had Soviet Communism on his mind, but he framed national defense in more general terms as a commitment to defending liberal values by convincing the unaligned world, whether by consent or through a show of force, to adopt them. The president described "free men" as a universal that must be defended from illiberal beings living at the limits of or outside the human world. He sketched a liberal idea not limited to anticommunism that would long outlast him and his Cold War.

The French philosopher Michel Foucault delivered what may be the most sweeping pronouncement on permanent war. In a 1976 lecture at the Collège de France, where he held the chair in the History of Systems of Thought from 1971 until his death in 1984, Foucault wondered whether Prussian General Carl von Clausewitz had it backward when he claimed that war is the continuation of politics by other means. Perhaps politics is the continuation of war by other means, Foucault mused. He argued that the modern state tamed war by internalizing it and the uneven distribution of power it founded. Politics does not form the basis for war. War forms the basis for politics. "The role of political power is perpetually to use a sort of silent war to reinscribe that relationship of force, and to reinscribe it in institutions, economic inequalities, language, and even the bodies of individuals," he argued. "Politics, in other words, sanctions and reproduces the disequilibrium of forces manifested in war."[26] Foucault believed that modern hierarchies of human value were formed through war and maintained by the state. The state ended war by internalizing the racial hierarchies it established. Modern politics transformed race war into state racism. Beneath the state institutions that order our lives, he concluded, rages "a sort of primitive and permanent war."[27] Foucault inverted Clausewitz's dictum in his first lecture of the year. Ten weeks later, in his last lecture of the term, he gave a name to the permanent war he identified as the substructure of the state: *biopolitics*. But Foucault's argument that biopolitics ended war by incorporating it into the modern institution doesn't hold for the United States, where the state did not replace race war with a warlike politics but reframed it as deracinated defense. It made war permanent by turning it into politics as usual.

The empire of defense has endured through change. It has managed crisis after crisis by inventing new enemies derived from earlier ones. When the anticommunist consensus that allowed Truman and his successors to build the world's largest armed forces came apart in Vietnam, officials launched a war on drugs that, they argued, emerged from the same Asian countries and black neighborhoods that they had earlier identified as hotbeds of communism. Racial anticommunism waned, and the idea of defense reemerged as racial criminalization. Since the first years of the Cold War, the defense establishment has shifted from anticommunism to anticrime, humanitarianism, and counterterrorism, waging a long war against illiberalism in whatever form it takes. This can be difficult to see because we think of war as a discrete event that begins and ends, a break in the normal time of the nation. "Wartime is not merely a regulation of the clock; it is the calibration of an era," legal historian Mary Dudziak writes. "Once we enter it we expect the rules to change. Some burdens are more tolerable because we think of war as important and exceptional, and also because, by definition, wartime comes to an end."[28] The belief that wartime is an abnormal form of time brought about by a historical crisis has survived because presidents, while they won't declare war, are more than willing to declare it over. In 2003, President Bush announced from the deck of the *USS Abraham Lincoln*, with a "Mission Accomplished" banner hanging from the aircraft carrier's bridge, that "major combat operations in Iraq have ended."[29] In 2010, President Obama, echoing his predecessor, told a national audience that "the American combat operation in Iraq has ended."[30] The Iraq War outlasted both of their presidencies. Wartime is normal time in the United States, but it is an ever-changing normal, with new justifications, new enemies, and familiar results.[31]

The Color-Blind Color Line

The decline of colonialism and the rise of antiracist movements forced the United States, which emerged from World War II victorious and more visible on the world stage, to embrace racial reform. Pearl S. Buck, the Nobel Prize–winning author of *The Good Earth* (1931), argued in 1942 that racism threatened the war effort, noting that Japan was using stories of racial segregation and extralegal violence to encourage anti-American attitudes across Asia. "Every lynching, every race riot gives joy to Japan," she wrote. "'Look at America,' Japan is saying to millions of listening ears. 'Will white America give you equality?'"[32] The United States could not fight fascism abroad without addressing racism at home. It could not win hearts and minds in decolonizing Asia if it had not won them in Harlem and Montgomery. It could not win a Cold War with the Soviet Union without first defeating Jim Crow. The end of World War II and the launch of the Cold War led to the consolidation of racial liberalism, a limited form of antiracism that sees race as cultural rather than biological and racism as moral rather than material, an effect of wrong-headed ideas. Racial liberals achieved dominance in the years after the war by defeating biological racists on the right and material antiracists on the left. Race was "constructed," they argued, not through the misdistribution of resources and life chances but through the learned mental habits of white Americans. White America needed a moral education—they needed to get to know difference—and racial liberals could teach them.[33]

The bible of racial liberalism is the sociological tome *An American Dilemma: The Negro Problem and Modern Democracy*, which, running more than a thousand pages, was the unlikeliest of bestsellers in 1944. The Carnegie Corporation commissioned the book in 1937. Frederick Keppel, the president of the corporation, overlooking black scholars—Du Bois, for example, was pursuing funding at the time for his ambitious *Encyclopedia of the Negro*, a project he never completed—invited Swedish sociologist Gunnar Myrdal to direct what Keppel described as "a comprehensive study of the Negro in the United States, to be undertaken in a wholly objective and dispassionate way as a social phenomenon."[34] Myrdal agreed and, in collaboration with political scientist Ralph Bunche and sociologist E. Franklin Frazier, his silent black coauthors, delivered two volumes and fifteen hundred pages of research that framed the "Negro problem" as a white moral problem. Americans, Myrdal determined, are rational and moral beings; they subscribe to the highest Enlightenment values, an "American creed." The American dilemma of the book's title refers to the "ever-raging conflict" between the national creed and antiblack racism. "The American Negro problem is a problem in the heart of the American," Myrdal wrote. "It is there that the interracial tension has its focus. It is there that the decisive struggle goes on."[35] The heart that concerned him was the heart of the white American, whose misguided ideas about race contradicted the American creed. The white American's racial attitudes needed to be brought into line with the nation's high moral values. Mydral didn't address black life at all until the forty-third chapter, in which he described black culture as "a distorted development, or a pathological condition, of the general American culture."[36] Black culture needed to be integrated into white national culture, he concluded, and the obstacle to integration was the white American mind that had distorted it. Sociologist Robert Lynd distilled the book's message in an admiring review for the *Saturday Review of Literature*. "The 'Negro problem,'" he wrote of *An American Dilemma*, "is found to be basically a moral problem in us white Americans."[37]

The Carnegie Corporation turned to Myrdal not despite but because of his foreign passport. The corporation, Keppel wrote, wanted "someone who could approach his task with a fresh mind, uninfluenced by traditional attitudes or by earlier conclusions" and who hailed from a nation "with no background or traditions of imperialism."[38] It wanted someone who could recognize American racism as an international problem and who could, as a dispassionate, non-imperialist European, assure the rest of the world that the United States could be trusted to lead it. Myrdal delivered. "The Negro problem," he insisted, "is not only America's greatest failure but also America's incomparably great opportunity for the future." The United States could demonstrate for the world how to transcend the color line by enfranchising and integrating the descendants of those it had enslaved—by turning its greatest failure into evidence of its deep-rooted, if inconsistent, commitment to racial justice. "America feels itself to be the world in miniature," Myrdal wrote in the final pages of *An American Dilemma*. "When in this crucial time the international leadership passes to America, the great reason for hope is that this country has a national experience of uniting racial and cultural diversities and a national theory, if not a consistent practice, of freedom and equality for all."[39] The former colonies of Asia and Africa could feel confident, he argued, that progress in the United States moved in one direction toward the inevitable realization of the American creed. Myrdal believed that if the United States could unite racial and cultural diversities at home, it could do the same abroad and that if it embraced racial liberalism, it could build an empire with the consent of the decolonizing world. With the Negro problem solved, the United States could launch an antiracist empire—an empire against imperialism, an empire of defense.[40]

But liberalism, including racial liberalism, is never universal. It does not mend breaks in humanity. It forms them. Myrdal treated the exclusion of black Americans as an aberration, a divergence from the liberal national creed. But liberalism, far from universal, founds the exclusions and differentiations on which the modern nation is built and that we come to know as racial. There is nothing aberrational about racism in the United States. It is woven into the American creed. Liberalism defines the human by universalizing the characteristics of white Western man and valuing all others based on their adoption of, or failure to adopt, his characteristics. It defines humanity through inclusion but also through the violence of assimilation and exclusion, securing the liberal freedoms of some by looting the land and labor of others. Ethnic studies scholar Lisa Lowe describes race as the "trace" left by liberal violence. "*Race* as a mark of colonial difference," she writes, "is an enduring remainder of the processes through which the human is universalized and freed by liberal forms, while the peoples who created the conditions of possibility for that freedom are assimilated or forgotten. The genealogy of modern liberalism is thus also a genealogy of modern race."[41] Liberalism is not universal but normative. It treats some as universal; it promises to assimilate others; and it forgets those it deems nonhuman, ineligible for liberal selfhood. The fall of colonialism and the devastation of World War II shook the foundation of Western liberal governance, threatening to reveal liberal universalism as a fiction, an Enlightenment mask for white colonialists. The United States managed the crisis of colonialism through reform, shifting from a color-line racial regime to a belief-based one. It waged war against and devalued not Africans, Arabs, Asians, and Latin Americans, it contended, but communists, drug traffickers, authoritarians, and terrorists. It introduced new racial categories through which it could do the old work of racial sorting—of constructing and perpetuating hierarchies of human value—without reference to skin color.[42]

The liberal state, facing a rising anticolonial tide, constructed a color-blind color line through the idea of defense. When the Truman administration dissolved the Department of War and formed the Department of Defense, it set out to defend more than the nation. It set out, as Truman put it in his 1947 State of the Union address, to achieve "collective security for all mankind."[43] But defense also means defining who does and doesn't count as mankind. Defense is a racial regime through which the state distinguishes between the human with the right to self-defense, the deferred human to be assimilated, and the nonhuman to be killed. The invention of the deferred human allows the United States to declare victories in what it reimagines, after the fact, as small wars (the "liberation" of anticommunist Korea, the "rescue" of refugees), while the construction of the nonhuman enables it to turn unending war into a defense against illegitimate enemies (the containment of communist Korea). Defense is an artifact of racial liberalism. Racial liberals argued that racism was moral rather than material, a problem of the white American mind. The architects of the defense establishment contended that communism and other illiberal ideologies were also distortions of the mind, learned mental habits that needed to be unlearned. The United States was not, they maintained, waging war against raced bodies but defending mankind against deracinated beliefs. The first article of the Universal Declaration of Human Rights, which the United Nations General Assembly adopted in 1948 at the urging of American delegate Eleanor Roosevelt, holds that all humans are "born free" and "endowed with reason and consciousness."[44] Defense forms the boundaries of the human by determining what counts as reason and consciousness and who therefore has *human* rights. It turns color-line racial categories into new belief-based ones that hide how the liberal state continues to divide humanity along racial lines. The idea of defense detaches race from the color line while all the while toeing it.

Not all Americans could overlook the color of defense. Black writers and artists, from Du Bois and William Patterson to Alice Childress and

Ollie Harrington, refused to ignore the continuities between European colonialism, antiblack racism, and American imperialism. Their refusal threatened the emerging racial liberal consensus, which Myrdal acknowledged in *An American Dilemma*, dismissing Du Bois's internationalism as "a frustrated effort to view [antiblack racism] in a wider setting as an ordinary American and as a human being." Du Bois's writing, Myrdal argued, takes on "a queer touch of unreality as soon as he leaves *his* problem, which is the American Negro problem."[45] The ascendance of racial liberalism and the second red scare diminished but did not silence the black internationalist left. In his 1957 poem "Memo to Non-White Peoples," Langston Hughes, who was himself brought before Senator Joseph McCarthy's Permanent Subcommittee on Investigations in 1953, denounces the idea of a reformed antiracist state. Western governments, he writes, "are quite willing / to pauperize you—/ Or use your kids as labor boys / For army, air force, or uranium mine," continuing,

> It's the same from Cairo to Chicago,
> Cape Town to the Caribbean,
> Do you travel the Stork Club circuit
> To dear old Shepherd's Hotel?
> (Somebody burnt Shepherd's up.)
> I'm sorry but it is
> The same from Cairo to Chicago,
> Cape Town to the Carib Hilton,
> Exactly the same.[46]

Hughes identifies how war secures white wealth through the theft of nonwhite land and labor in the United States, the Middle East, South Africa, and the Caribbean, drawing a line from elite hotels in New York (the Stork Club), Cairo (Shepherd's Hotel, a British colonial hub burned down by anti-British resisters in 1952), and San Juan (the Caribe Hilton) to segregation in Chicago and apartheid in Cape Town. There is nothing that distinguishes the new imperialism from the old, he concludes; it is "exactly the same." Hughes, who maintained correspondences with anti-apartheid activists throughout the 1950s and 1960s, first published the poem in the Cape Town journal *Africa South*. His title suggests that revealing defense for what it is—a new but all-too-familiar racial regime—could lead to transnational coalitions uniting nonwhite peoples, from Chicago to South Africa, against an empire never built to defend them.[47]

A Few Good White Men

In 1948, President Truman issued Executive Order 9981, mandating "equality of treatment and opportunity" in the armed forces.[48] The order, celebrated as a forerunner to later civil rights legislation, led to the gradual desegregation of the army, navy, and air force. But the president's order wasn't just about upholding principles. It was also a political calculation. The military needed more men, and the promise of better treatment encouraged black men, who faced an anemic and segregated job market, to enlist. A disproportionate number of black, Latino, and American Indian soldiers served in the Korean War two years later and then in Vietnam, Iraq, Afghanistan, and elsewhere. More and more women served and died. Millions of Koreans, Southeast Asians, Iraqis, and Afghans lost their lives, their families, and their homes, some resettling in the United States. But war culture in the United States has remained dominated by stories about white men, who star in best-selling books and blockbuster movies, from James Michener's *The Bridges at Toko-Ri* (1953) to Tim O'Brien's *The Things They Carried* (1990) and from *Platoon* (1986) to *The Hurt Locker* (2008). The most acclaimed, the winners of book awards and Oscars, tell stories about good liberal white men, men who befriend their comrades of color and show no hatred toward, and sometimes come to love, civilians. "To advertise bad American race relations by maintaining them in the armed forces sent overseas is, under present circumstances, highly detrimental to American interests," Myrdal wrote in *An American Dilemma*, making an argument that, it seems, resonated with Truman. He added that if change were to come, it would better serve the nation if it came not "as a result of outside pressure from Negroes" but from the moral decision making of white leaders.[49] The armed forces should integrate soldiers of color, but this should not, he advised, decenter the liberal consciousness of white men. In the decades since, war culture has conformed to Myrdal's recommendation, turning combat into a moral trial for white men that weds liberal whiteness to American nationalism.

War is hell, we know, but for the white soldier it is also existential and sometimes enlightening. In a 1925 letter to F. Scott Fitzgerald, Ernest Hemingway, who drove an ambulance for the Red Cross in World War I, wrote, "Well the reason you are so sore you missed the war is because war is the best subject of all. It groups the maximum of material and speeds up the action and brings out all sorts of stuff that normally you have to wait a lifetime to get."[50] Hemingway, whose stature grew as the United States mobilized for the next world war, served as a model for future generations of war writers, who subscribed to his argument that war could be a source of great wisdom for a young man and great material for a young writer. In 1994, Tim O'Brien, who had just published his fifth Vietnam War novel, explained to an interviewer that he kept writing about his time in the army because war threw life into relief. "The environment of war is the environment of life, magnified," he said. "The stakes of living in a war are enhanced only because of the awareness of the proximity of death. That is to say, I'm almost dead with every step I take as opposed to fifty steps to the day I get cancer or have a first heart attack. We are all living in a war. It's just that the wolf isn't quite at the door."[51] War forces the liberal warrior to reckon with who he is and what it means to live and die. It gives him a heightened plane—the maximum of material, the environment of life magnified—from which to consider life lived in the shadow of death. Most soldier and veteran stories, including antiwar stories, turn war into an existential struggle for the white American, who achieves a kind of liberal enlightenment through an encounter with death. The sensitive white soldier, from Hemingway's Frederic Henry to Joseph Heller's John Yossarian and O'Brien's Paul Berlin, though celebrated for shaking off ideological constraints, defends, above all else, himself and his own liberal consciousness.

The ideal white hero embodies the ethic of racial liberalism. He demonstrates for the world that the United States can be trusted not to act out of colonial self-interest in Asia and Africa, that it is different from Britain and France. William Lederer, a naval officer, and Eugene Burdick, a political scientist, delivered the definitive how-to guide for Cold War racial liberals with their 1958 novel *The Ugly American*. The novel, a series of vignettes about Americans living and working in Southeast Asia, some bad and some "ugly" (meaning liberal, resourceful, and committed to the slow, hard work of nation building), resonated with the young Massachusetts Senator John Kennedy, who bought it for all of his Senate colleagues, seeing the novel as a model for how the United States should combat communism in Asia. One of novel's good ugly Americans, major James "Tex" Wolchek, embeds with a regiment of the French Foreign Legion in Vietnam, observing the regiment in the final months before the French defeat. Tex notices a black man named Jim Davis among the Legionnaires. He knows Davis must be an American when he sees "the trace of an unfriendly smile" cross the man's face at hearing his Texas accent. With the international Legionnaires looking on, Tex makes a show of greeting Davis. "There's a tradition among Americans that they shake hands whenever they meet one another," he announces to the men, offering his hand to the black Legionnaire. Davis is won over by Tex's kindness, and, after shaking hands, "the two Americans spoke briefly and with enthusiasm."[52] Tex stages his racial liberal feeling for the international regiment, demonstrating for them, and for the broader world for which they stand, that the United States is committed to racial justice at home and abroad. Davis, who doesn't speak in the interaction, is a minor character in a drama of white liberal antiracism. Tex modeled for Lederer and Burdick what the United States needed in Asia: "a small force of well-trained, well-chosen, hard-working, and dedicated professionals" that could "show by example that America is still the America of freedom and hope."[53] It needed a few good white men.

Most white liberal war stories are not color blind. Nor do they exclude soldiers of color. War is an education in cultural difference for the white soldier, and his black, Latino, and American Indian comrades are his teachers and his textbooks. Though evident in earlier war stories, including *The Ugly American*, the idea of war as a racial liberal education for the young white man found a wide audience in the post–civil rights era. Black studies scholar Roderick Ferguson argues that universities and colleges contained antiracist student movements, movements demanding structural changes to their institutions, by incorporating students of color without decentering their white classmates. Student activists demanded redistribution, and the institution instead gave them representation. The civil rights era, he writes, "was not only constituted by the upheaval of prior racist formations and the insurgency of minority difference but also by the reconstitution of racial domination—this time through an ostensible reformed mode of whiteness invested in its own centrality rather than the material redistribution of resources."[54] The reformed institution, modeling a broader shift in post–civil rights America, enrolled more diverse classes and taught more diverse materials for the benefit of the white liberal collegian, whose investment in cultural difference readied her to enter the managerial classes after graduation.

The liberal war film substitutes combat for the diverse liberal arts college. The white hero, hailing from a sheltered middle-class suburb, suffers with his young black, Latino, and American Indian comrades. He gets to know poor men, men from cities, and men from small towns. He receives counsel from a kind black comrade, who welcomes him, a newcomer, into the soldiering life. "I tell you what, you be cool, I introduce you around to some of the heads," King (Keith David), a good-humored black soldier, tells his new white comrade Chris Taylor (Charlie Sheen) in Oliver

Stone's Vietnam War film *Platoon*, inviting Chris to join the circle of ston-
ers who comprise the platoon's liberal wing.[55] Brian De Palma's *Casualties
of War* (1989) includes an almost identical mentoring session, with black
specialist "Brownie" Brown (Erik King) showing an interest in white new
arrival Max Eriksson (Michael J. Fox), putting an arm around Eriksson
and inviting him to think of him as his "priest," someone he can confide
in.[56] The diverse casts of Stone's and De Palma's films never decenter the
white liberal hero. Instead, they show him to be a good white man, close
with his comrades of color, sensitive to his social environment, and getting
a liberal education in cultural difference through war.

But not all white war culture is about getting to know difference. Some
of it sees the white soldier as an embodiment of difference in his own right.
Since the defeat in Vietnam, the wounded white vet has emerged as a figure through which white men imagine themselves as aggrieved and even
minoritized in the post–civil rights era. White men have suffered, too, they
argue, and the mistreatment of Vietnam veterans is their evidence. John
Wheeler, the chairman of the Vietnam Veterans Memorial Fund, which
planned and financed the memorial on the Washington Mall, distilled this
argument in his 1984 book, *Touched with Fire*, about his and others' struggles as veterans of the war in Southeast Asia. "We soldiers were prepared for
the war zone. We were not prepared for our return to America," he wrote.
"The most searing part of our lives was deemed not to have happened. The
country's cultural energy poured instead into the needs of blacks, of women,
[and] of less developed counties and countries." Wheeler, a well-connected
white West Point graduate who went on to serve in three presidential administrations, having cataloged his grievances, concluded that "the Vietnam
veteran was the nigger of the 1970s."[57] He imagined the Vietnam veteran as
a middle-class white man defined against black people, women, and poor
communities. His white vet had suffered twice over, first in Vietnam and now
in an America that put the needs of people of color ahead of his. Somehow
white men emerged from the Vietnam War as universal norm and minoritized other—the star of the movie and the forgotten warrior—dominating
the center and margin of national culture. The white hero returned from war
enlightened, wounded, and more American than ever.[58]

Policing the Crisis

National defense does not conform to national borders. It invents them.
In the decades since Truman unified the armed forces under the banner

of defense, presidents have adopted the language of policing to describe wars and the language of war to describe policing, ordering "police actions" in Asia and declaring wars on crime and drugs in the United States. Their administrations have retreated from the idea of war in Korea, Vietnam, Iraq, and Afghanistan but embraced it at home. Days after the escalation of the Korean War, Truman stated that South Korea had been "unlawfully attacked by a bunch of bandits" and that the US-led United Nations Command was "going to the relief of the Korean Republic to suppress a bandit raid."[59] This was not a war but, he concluded, a police action. Fifteen years later, President Lyndon Johnson, announcing the establishment of the President's Commission on Law Enforcement and Administration of Justice, declared his hope that "1965 will be the year when this country began in earnest a thorough, intelligent, and effective war against crime."[60] Johnson had yet to acknowledge the conflict in Vietnam as a war. A few years later, his successor, Richard Nixon, reflected, "We have heard a great deal of overblown rhetoric during the sixties in which the word 'war' has perhaps too often been used—the war on poverty, the war on misery, the war on disease, the war on hunger. But if there is one area where the word 'war' is appropriate it is in the fight against crime."[61] Describing war as policing has allowed presidents to intervene in other countries without congressional authorization, while describing policing as war has enabled them to exercise their authority as commanders in chief to federalize law enforcement. From Truman on, they have blurred the line between war and policing, merging them into a broader defense against lawlessness, whether bandits in Korea or criminals in America, that transcends borders and divides the nation.

Defense descends from colonial policing. In the early republic, white settlers justified the theft of indigenous lands and black bodies by declaring the ownership and protection of property, including the ownership and protection of a person's own body and labor, to be the exclusive right of white men. Settlers, having denied American Indians and black people property rights, imagined them to be a preeminent threat to their own lives and property, a threat that needed to be policed.[62] Whiteness, critical race theorist Nikhil Singh writes, "emerged from the protection of private property and the interests of its holders in relation to those who were thought to have no property and thus no calculable interests, and who were therefore imagined to harbor a potentially criminal disregard for a social order organized on this basis."[63] Policing defined the boundaries between the righted and the rightless, those who deserved to be protected and those who, having nothing to protect, must be policed. It did not set out to define and punish crime. It set out to define and punish *criminals*, people who could not, no matter their behavior, be law-abiding. Colonial policing did not racialize crime. It criminalized race. Defense ties internal colonial policing to external imperial policing, constructing enemies that threaten the nation from within and without. In 1955, Charles Sloane, a senior official in the New York State Department of Civil Service, where he developed and implemented police professionalization programs, identified war as a form of police work. "If one gives some thought to the subject, there is but little difference between fighting an enemy in a declared war and fighting an enemy, the criminal, at home on the crime front," he wrote. "Both are comparable battles for the very existence of civilization, for without the thin wall of police protecting the people from criminal depredation, the world would soon revert to savagery and bestiality."[64] Sloane, arguing that police departments should institute military-style K-9 units, believed that war and policing shared a lineage in defending a deserving, civilized people from an undeserving, criminal people. The soldier and the policeman did the hard work of distinguishing the former from the latter. Later that year, Sloane left Albany for Saigon, where he worked with the State Department and the South Vietnamese government to build the first police academy in the new capital and repel enemies on the other crime front.

The Marine Corps put a name to wars conducted as imperial policing. It called them *small wars*. In 1940, the Corps published the *Small Wars Manual*, a five-hundred-page catalog of "lessons learned" from the wars in the Philippines, Cuba, Haiti, the Dominican Republic, and Nicaragua. The manual defined small wars as operations in which "military force is combined with diplomatic pressure in the internal or external affairs of another state whose government is unstable, inadequate, or unsatisfactory." Small wars were not real wars, the authors maintained, but acts of defense in which the United States intervened to protect the property of Americans living abroad in countries that could not be trusted to protect it themselves. "The use of the forces of the United States in foreign countries to protect the lives and property of American citizens resident in those countries does not necessarily constitute an act of war, and is, therefore, not equivalent to a declaration of war," they argued. "Military operations are actually police functions."[65] The property rights of Americans trumped the sovereignty of the countries in which they were living, and the invasion of these countries did not constitute an act of war, because their governments were too unstable to be considered legitimate in the first place. The wars in the Philippines, Cuba, Haiti, the Dominican Republic, and Nicaragua were not wars at all but police actions to impose law and order on lawless regimes.

The Corps did not see the darker skin of the people it policed in the Pacific, the Caribbean, and Central America as a coincidence. The authors of the manual devoted almost half of their introduction to the "racial psychology" of small wars. "The influence of racial psychology on the destiny of a people appears plainly in the history of those subject to perpetual revolution," they wrote. "Among primitive people not far removed from an oppressed or enslaved existence, it is easy to understand the people's fear of being again enslaved; fear of political subjugation causes violent opposition to any movement which apparently threatens political or personal liberty."[66] Filipinos, Cubans, Haitians, Dominicans, and Nicaraguans needed to be policed, they concluded, because their racial identities predisposed them to revolution and precluded them from stable self-government. The manual anticipated Cold War racial liberalism by acknowledging race as something constructed by white racists, who had imposed an "oppressed or enslaved existence" on people of color, which it then used to explain why black and brown people were prone to violence and needed to be policed by reformed white men.

The *Small Wars Manual*, though set aside the year after its publication when the United States entered World War II, resurfaced as a go-to handbook for policing the postcolonial world in the Truman, Reagan, and second Bush administrations. Its language—"military interventions in the fullest sense, short of war," "measures short of war"—reappeared in National Security Council Report 68, a blueprint for imperial defense, in 1950.[67] In 1987, as President Reagan continued to escalate the Cold War and the drug wars, the Department of the Navy republished the manual in full and without revision as a resource for marines engaged in "low-intensity conflicts" in the Middle East and Latin America. In a new foreword, Lieutenant General John Phillips declared it "one of the best books on military operations in peacekeeping and counterinsurgency."[68] In 2006, the celebrated Army/Marine Corps field manual *Counterinsurgency*, the brainchild of General David Petraeus, drew on the 1940 manual, which it acknowledged as a "classic" and a must-read for all counterinsurgents.[69] All wars were now small wars. All wars were police functions. All wars were defense.

While the soldier fought crime, the policeman went to war. The summer of 1943 brought a wave of race riots in which white policeman allied

with white rioters, killing and arresting black and Latino men in south-
eastern Texas, Los Angeles, Detroit, and Harlem. White racial liberals
responded by advocating not less policing but more professional policing,
and more of it. Policeman, they argued, should be trained like soldiers,
whom they admired for their dispassionate professionalism. In 1945, the
American Council on Race Relations, a Chicago-based civil rights group,
published a pamphlet by sociologist Alfred McClung Lee in which Lee
encouraged the formation of local committees that could anticipate, prevent, and respond to race riots in their communities. The sociologist outlined a ten-step plan for preparing for a riot, the first of which was to
"see that the mayor of your town knows how to bring in the state militia
or, better, the U.S. Army with the least possible delay." The good racial
liberal could not depend on the local police, Lee believed, because policemen "too often make common cause with the white rioters." The town
should "get out the state militia or the U.S. Army—and fast!" because
the "disinterested efficiency of the Army is far more discouraging to white
rioters than the anti-Negro tactics of some police departments."[70] The
United States would be a more peaceful and less racist place, Lee suggested, if the local police department could be more like the army. The
White House agreed. In 1946, Truman created the President's Committee
on Civil Rights, which delivered a report the next year recommending
federal aid and training to achieve "increased professionalization of state
and local police forces" and "the improvement of civil rights protection"
through "more aggressive and efficient enforcement techniques."[71] Lee
and the president's advisers believed that to build an antiracist America,
the federal government needed to transform the racist local policeman
into an antiracist national soldier. Their call for police professionalization
amounted to a call for police militarization.[72]

Twenty years later, after another summer of riots, President Johnson
adopted the recommendations of his predecessor's civil rights committee
by signing the Law Enforcement Assistance Act of 1965 into law. The
act created the Office of Law Enforcement Assistance, which funded,
trained, and distributed military-grade equipment to local police departments. Johnson, a month after signing the Voting Rights Act, announced
the Law Enforcement Assistance Act as another civil rights achievement.
"The Great Society we are striving to build cannot become a reality unless
we strike at the roots of crime," he stated, announcing new federal support for police professionalization programs. "The policeman," he added,
"is the frontline soldier in our war against crime."[73] The Law Enforcement

Assistance Act marked the beginning of a legislative movement to federalize policing, and Johnson launched that movement by presenting himself as the commander in chief of an army of policemen waging a war on crime. While his Department of Defense policed Southeast Asia, the president declared war at home. While soldiers walked the beat in Asia, policeman patrolled black and brown neighborhoods in America. But Truman, Johnson, and later Nixon were never policing crime—not in Korea or Vietnam and not in Los Angeles, Detroit, or Harlem—but a crisis. The collapse of colonialism and the erosion of Jim Crow threatened to undo a world long governed by white Western men. The empire of defense contained the emerging crisis by criminalizing those threatening to change that world, turning Asia and Africa into a crime front and black and brown America into a war front. It policed the crisis through repression but also by reform and, by preaching anticolonialism and antiracism, made it difficult to tell the difference.[74]

Permanent War Stories

We know wars through the stories we tell about them. We assign meaning to them; we mark their beginnings and endings; we celebrate and condemn them—all through stories. This is nothing new. The war story is an old genre. But something changed after World War II. The crises of race and war triggered by the decline of colonialism surfaced in national culture as a crisis of narrative form. The story of defense with which the state contained rising anticolonial and antiracist movements is a difficult one to tell. It neither begins nor ends. It treats beliefs rather than beings as enemies of the state. It combats racism with a new racial regime. It ends war by making it normal. Writers have struggled to find a form with which they can tell that story—a story of permanent war, which isn't a story that most people want to hear. Instead, stories of soldiers and veterans have piled up, allowing readers to treat the soldier's harrowing twelve-month tour and the vet's alienating homecoming as stand-ins for a war that never ends. High school students learn about the Vietnam War by reading Tim O'Brien's *The Things They Carried*. Moviegoers learn about the Iraq War by watching *American Sniper* (2014). Most never learn about the wars in Korea, Laos, Cambodia, Lebanon, Grenada, Bosnia, Kosovo, and elsewhere.[75]

In stories about soldiers and veterans, war is an event. The hero goes to war, innocent and naive. Twelve months later, he returns, shaken by his encounter with death and wise to the realities of the world. Sometimes memories of combat follow him home, haunting his life as a vet, but the war itself fades into the past. Soldier stories, for all their gore and sorrow, can be comforting because they turn unending war into a discrete event, obscuring how war does not end when the hero comes home. Cultural theorist Lauren Berlant argues that "the conventional genres of event," including the war story, discourage us from seeing how some crises do not disrupt normal life but constitute it. "'Trauma' has become the primary genre of the last eighty years for describing the historical present as the scene of an exception that has just shattered some ongoing, uneventful ordinary life," she writes. But trauma fails to capture how "crisis is not exceptional to history or consciousness but a process embedded in the ordinary that unfolds in stories about navigating what's overwhelming."[76] Crisis is ordinary. War is normal. This awareness comes not just from the invention of new genres and new kinds of war stories but also from critical attention to how older genres fail. The story of permanent war gets told where the war story breaks down, where it fails to hide the ordinariness of war. When President Obama announced his plan to end the war on terror in May 2013, for example, he insisted that his administration was not waging a war against terrorism but executing a targeted "comprehensive counterterrorism strategy" to defend against "extremists that threaten America." Five minutes later, though, he stated, "Under domestic law, and international law, the United States is at war with al-Qaeda, the Taliban, and their associated forces." The president declared his intention to end a war that he then claimed had never begun and yet also constituted "a just war—a war waged proportionately, in last resort, and in self-defense."[77] The empire of defense emerges in the margins of war stories, including those told by presidents, where the idea of defense falls apart and shows itself to be permanent war by a different name.

More hawkish war stories unravel under pressure, too. In Lederer and Burdick's anticommunist novel *The Ugly American*, Tex, the white liberal major, is acting as an adviser to the French Foreign Legion in Vietnam. He is a noncombatant, one of Lederer and Burdick's "ugly" American diplomats charged with winning hearts and minds, not killing Viet Minh. Tex lands in Southeast Asia with "the iron of two wars" in his legs and back from wounds suffered in combat in France and Korea. Weeks later, fighting with the Legionnaires in the Battle of Dien Bien Phu, the French colonialists' last and ill-fated stand, the American hero is wounded by hand-grenade fragments in a desperate firefight with the Viet Minh. Tex now has "the iron of three wars in his body," and, he admits, "he had expected to all along."[78] Lederer and Burdick intended their novel as an argument for fighting communism with diplomatic know-how rather than military might. The two men, a naval officer and a political scientist, understood the Cold War as an ideological struggle that the United States would lose without more diplomatic-minded, rugged men like Tex. But their hero's career maps the informal imperial routes of the defense establishment, taking him from Normandy to Pork Chop Hill to Dien Bien Phu. Tex is not a diplomat. He is a soldier, who, at thirty, has already served in three wars. The novel also fails to explain why Jim Davis, the black American Legionnaire, joined the French Foreign Legion rather than his own country's army, where he, despite attending college, would have faced obstacles to advancement as a black man. The regiment enlists local Vietnamese as guides, and Davis, a French officer tells Tex, "is the only man they'll make a night patrol with."[79] The Vietnamese, with good reason, do not trust the French or the white American advisers. Davis and the Vietnamese guides seem to know that they are engaged in a war not about communism but race—not about what can be thought but *who* can think it. Lederer and Burdick's liberal anticommunist novel shows, if against the authors' intentions, how defense makes rather than mends racial divisions and hierarchies.

Not all stories of defense obscure more than they reveal. Some draw attention to the uneven racial distribution of state violence and connect one iteration of defense to another, tracing the continuities that unite the Cold War, the drug wars, the humanitarian wars, and the counterterror wars. In his 1973 novel *The Revolt of the Cockroach People*, Oscar Zeta Acosta, the Chicano movement activist, links the policing of Chicano neighborhoods in East Los Angeles, including increasing arrests for low-level drug crimes, to the war in Southeast Asia. "We may be the last generation of Chicanos if we don't stop the war," his alter ego Buffalo Zeta Brown declares at an antiwar march. "We are the Viet Cong of America."[80] Acosta ties the fate of the Chicano movement to the fate of Vietnamese independence, arguing that racist policing in Los Angeles is not just analogous to the war but part of the same racial regime of defense. Pan-Asian political activism grew out of the same impulse. In the late 1960s, students at the University of California, Berkeley, founded the Asian American Political Alliance to mobilize students against the war in Southeast Asia, making it the first national group to use the term *Asian American* to unite Americans from different Asian ethnic backgrounds. "We identified with the struggles of the oppressed peoples of the world," founding member Vicci Wong remembered. "We fought harder because we didn't see it as just our own fight."[81] The Vietnam War, Wong and her coorganizers maintained, was a racist war that could not be separated from anti-Asian racism in the United States. Combating one meant combating the other. Martin Luther King Jr. knew this, too. On April 4, 1967, one year to the day before his assassination, he came out against the war at Riverside Church in the Manhattan neighborhood of Morningside Heights. "The war in Vietnam is but a symptom of a far deeper malady within the American spirit," the civil rights leader said, "and if we ignore this sobering reality we will find ourselves organizing clergy- and layman-concerned committees for the next generation. They will be concerned about Guatemala and Peru. They will be concerned about Thailand and Cambodia. They will be concerned about Mozambique and South Africa."[82] Acosta, Wong, and King could all see the bigger picture: that fighting racism at home meant resisting the Vietnam War and that resisting the Vietnam War meant fighting their government's unending march to war in the name of defending some against those it deemed undeserving and dangerous.

Other writers tell permanent war stories by challenging the limits of the war novel and film. Independent filmmaker Trinh T. Minh-ha, a refugee of the war, made her third film, *Surname Viet Given Name Nam* (1989), as Brian De Palma, Stanley Kubrick, and Oliver Stone collected Oscars and big box-office returns for their soldier-centered Vietnam War movies. Trinh's film, which features amateur Vietnamese actors in California reenacting interviews with Vietnamese women in Vietnam, unsettles the truth claims of the realist war movie. "If the war is the continuation of politics by other means, then media images are the continuation of war by other means," Trinh reflects in a voiceover, alluding to Clausewitz. "It is said that if Americans lost the other [war], they have certainly won this one."[83] Media images, she concludes, extend the war, allowing the United States to redeem itself through stories of good-hearted but misguided young white men, and they condition the nation to consent to the next one. The camera pans across black-and-white photographs of American soldiers and Vietnamese civilians as Trinh speaks, demonstrating how images offer not unmediated but selective truth; the photographer, editor, and filmmaker choose and frame them for their audience. Soldier stories, whether hawkish or antiwar, offer comfort by reinforcing the idea that, as Trinh puts it, "'this begins there,' 'this ends here,' while the scene keeps on recurring, as unchangeable as change itself."[84] The soldier comes home;

the president declares the end of combat operations; and the war goes on. This is the story Trinh tells, and it is the story that emerges from the failure of those told by Obama, Lederer and Burdick, De Palma, Kubrick, and Stone.

The United States has sustained the fiction of antiracist defense by continually naming new deracinated beliefs and behaviors as the foremost threat to the nation and the world, from communism and crime to authoritarianism and terrorism. This book, by treating the Cold War, the drug wars, the humanitarian wars, and the counterterror wars as stages in one long imperial campaign, asks not what but *who* we are defending against. Huey Newton, the cofounder of the Black Panther Party, asked this long ago. He and Bobby Seale formed the Black Panther Party for Self-Defense—the full, original name—in 1966, with Newton serving as the party's minister of defense. "When we used 'for Self-Defense,'" he explained in 1970, "we realized that all oppressed people or legitimate revolutionary oppressed people never are the aggressors." Newton believed that defense belonged not to the state but to oppressed people, who most needed it, often from the state itself. But defense also meant something more. It meant, the Panther leader added, "defending ourselves against poor medical care, against unemployment, against poor housing and all the other things that poor and oppressed people the world over suffer."[85] Defense is all of these things. It determines who receives medical care, who works and who doesn't, and who lives where. It separates the deserving from the undeserving, the righted from the rightless, the human from the nonhuman. The idea of defense has kept the United States on a perpetual wartime footing. Perhaps, revised and reclaimed, it could also be the idea that ends it.

CHAPTER ONE

How to Tell a Permanent War Story

O n October 5, 1951, with casualties mounting and a cease-fire agreement still two years off, *U.S. News and World Report* declared the Korean War forgotten. "Far off in Korea, 2,200 American men were killed or badly shot up last week in a war that seemed all but forgotten at home. War that was supposed to end in a deal with Communists instead is growing in intensity," the unnamed author wrote. "Men are dying at an increasing rate in the war almost forgotten at home, with no end in sight."[1] The conflict had stabilized earlier that year along the thirty-eighth parallel, but the fighting would not slacken until July 1953, when the US-led United Nations Command, the Republic of Korea Army (South Korea), the Korean People's Army (North Korea), and the Chinese People's Volunteer Army signed an armistice agreement that ended conventional combat. The *U.S. News* article, titled "Korea: The 'Forgotten' War," marked the first time that the Korean War was defined by its absence from national consciousness, a forgotten war that, while "being paid for at big-war rates," did not register in the minds of most Americans at home. This continues to be how the war is discussed, when it is discussed at all, in the United States. The Korean War was the first "hot war" of the long Cold War. It lasted thirty-eight months, from June 1950 to July 1953. Then it was forgotten. But how could a war that was still being fought with rising casualties and a big-war price tag be forgotten? What made Americans turn their attention elsewhere as the war on the Korean Peninsula raged on? What was so forgettable about the forgotten war?

The Korean War has been subsumed in American culture by the more legible wars bookending it. It is treated either as an aftershock of World War II, a minor front in the Cold War, or a forerunner to the war in Southeast Asia. Journalist David Halberstam, in his bestseller *The Coldest Win-*

ter: America and the Korean War (2007), for example, writes, "Korea would not prove a great national war of unifying singular purpose, as World War II had been, nor would it, like Vietnam a generation later, divide and thus haunt the nation. It was simply a puzzling, gray, very distant conflict, a war that went on and on and on, seemingly without hope or resolution, about which most Americans, save the men who fought there and their immediate families, preferred to know as little as possible." In the decades since, he adds, the war has been "orphaned by history."[2] Halberstam's book, his last, although it received a nomination for the Pulitzer Prize for History, overlooks the extensive research undertaken by historians and Asian American studies scholars to remember the forgotten war, to correct for its erasure from official histories.[3] The meaning of the Korean War in the United States has been articulated as a battle for memory between an amnesiac national culture and a movement to remember a war that most Americans would rather forget. But the war has also endured in the margins of national culture, framing such bestselling books and blockbuster films as *The Bridges at Toko-Ri* (novella 1953; film 1954), *The Manchurian Candidate* (novel 1959; film 1962), and *MASH* (novel 1968; film 1970; television show 1972–83), even as these books and films are often described as about something other than the Korean War. The forgotten war *has* been remembered, but it has been remembered as forgettable.

The *U.S. News* article hints at how that memory first emerged. The author wrote that "ground battles, for the area involved, are as intense as those of any war," yet, "at home, meanwhile, the big headlines concern a growing shortage of beef, graft scandals in the Government, strikes as usual, [and] prospects of a new-car scarcity."[4] A war was on, but news media, including *U.S. News*, were devoting fewer and fewer column inches to the fighting. Americans, the writer concluded, weren't interested, and the reason they weren't interested was the war's unendingness. "Korea, half forgotten, is receding in the minds of many to the status of an experimental war, one being fought back and forth for the purpose of testing men, weapons, materials and methods, on a continuing basis," the author observed of domestic attitudes toward the war. "No effort is being made or planned to win a clear military victory. New U.S. ground forces, which could help drive the enemy out of Korea, are being sent to Europe. . . . [The] U.S., faced with a third-rate enemy, has fought for 15 months with no prospect of a military victory in sight."[5] The author reasoned that the Korean War was being ignored by Americans *because of its continuation*. The defense establishment was settling into other countries and continents, relocating ground forces from Korea to the West and, although the author doesn't mention it, Southeast Asia. It was building the national security state, from Korea outward. But Americans, with no end in sight on the Korean Peninsula, had lost track of the war, concerning themselves instead with commercial goods and Washington scandals. Somehow a war that was bleeding over into other parts of the world and that showed no signs of slowing was attracting less rather than more attention from those in whose name it was being fought.

The Korean War inaugurated a new kind of war that necessitated a new kind of war story. The *U.S. News* writer determined that the war had been forgotten because it was permanent and experimental. The United States was waging war on the Korean Peninsula to test "men, weapons, materials and methods, on a continuing basis." But it was also testing a new idea about its role in the world. While Americans know the Korean War as part of a long Cold War between the United States and the Soviet Union, the "free world" versus communism, Koreans know it as a civil war motivated by the desire of leaders in the North and the South to reunite the country on their own terms and as an anticolonial war that dates back to 1910, when Japan annexed the peninsula, and that the United States and the USSR aggravated after World War II by dividing it along the thirty-eighth parallel and governing it by force. Halted by an armistice agreement in 1953, the Korean War has never ended. The country remains partitioned along the demilitarized zone that the agreement established. These histories fall away when the war is submerged within the Cold War and the nuclear arms race and ideological struggle between Americans and Soviets. But the Korean War launched the Cold War as much as the Cold War framed it. The American planners of the forgotten war constructed the enduring, if conflicting, idea that the government would, from then on, wage continuous nonwar (defense; the containment of North Korea and China) constituted of a series of discrete, winnable emergencies (small wars; the "liberation" of South Korea). That structuring idea has instead confined the Korean War to thirty-eight months of harrowing combat that curbed the encroachment of an illiberal, unredeemable social world (communism) and saved a convertible one (anticommunist Korea).

The architects of the Korean War remade the American empire for an anticolonial age by designating its enemies illegitimate for ideological rather than racial reasons, reframing wars fought along the color line as antiracist defense. While World War II formed the industrial and economic backbone of the national security state—through, for example, a reformed tax structure that could fund vast military growth[6]—the Korean War introduced the idea that transformed war into the defense of humanity from illiberal beliefs and behaviors. Since the onset of conventional combat on the peninsula, officials have shuttled back and forth between describing the government's modern wars as nonwars, or defense, and moderating them as small wars with definitive endings, committing the nation to permanent war while guaranteeing and often declaring conclusive victories. The Korean War has, at different times, been treated as both a nonwar and a small war. It has been remembered as forgettable, whether as an act of defense or as a discrete minor conflict on a remote peninsula.

This story begins with the National Security Council, which, three years after its formation, in the spring of 1950, drafted National Security Council Report 68 and delivered it to President Harry Truman. The writing team, a State–Defense Policy Review Group chaired by Paul Nitze, struggled to resolve the internal tensions of imperial defense by dividing the world into human, deferred human, and nonhuman categories of being—reframing war as either the endless policing of illegitimate societies or the conversion of "friendlies" to the West's liberal democratic values. NSC 68 formalized what became known as the containment doctrine and, as historian Walter LaFeber writes, established "the blueprint for waging the Cold War during the next twenty years."[7] It was a blueprint for the Cold War, and it was a blueprint for imperial defense then and long after. But NSC 68 did not receive the president's authorization until after June 25, 1950, when the Korean War turned hot. Dean Acheson, then the secretary of state, later remarked that the war on the peninsula "prove[d] our thesis" and "created the stimulus which made action."[8] One of his aides, Robert Feis, added, "We were sweating over it—with regard to NSC 68—thank God Korea came along."[9] The histories of NSC 68 and the Korean War were intertwined from the beginning and gave ideological form to an empire of defense that has outlasted the Cold War.

In his much-anthologized short story "How to Tell a True War Story" (1987), Tim O'Brien insists that true war stories must be grounded in immediate, concrete details that feel right at a gut level. "True war stories do not generalize. They do not indulge in abstraction or analysis," he writes. "It comes down to gut instinct. A true war story, if truly told, makes the stomach believe."[10] O'Brien's words echo Ernest Hemingway's from sixty years earlier, when Hemingway wrote that "abstract words such as glory,

honor, courage, or hallow were obscene beside the concrete names of vil-
lages, the number of roads, the names of rivers, the number of regiments
and the dates."[11] A true war story, O'Brien and Hemingway agree, should
not make grand claims about war but communicate how it looks and feels
on the ground through the eyes of the combat soldier. It should not tell
the story of the war but the story of the individual in the war. Even as the
fighting continues, the true war story ends. The soldier dies, or the soldier
comes home. The national security state has faced a different challenge in
struggling to translate permanent war into a story of national defense. That
story indulges in abstraction. It generalizes. It strains under the weight of
its own contradictions and undergoes constant revision. Some writers, including radical journalist I. F. Stone and antiracist activist William Patterson, met the Cold War state on its own terms by drawing out these contradictions in official accounts of the Korean War, demonstrating how to tell a
permanent war story through the contradictions and failures of the idea of
defense. Narrative structures the meaning and making of war. It also structures resistance to it. "Emphasis, omission, and distortion," Stone wrote in
1952, "rather than outright lying are the tools of the war propagandists."[12]
The story of permanent war gets told, but it gets told in pieces at the limits
of narrative form. The cultural politics of war are not only shaped by remembering and forgetting but also by the gray areas of the war story.

The National Security Council's Blueprint for Empire

National Security Council Report 68 remained classified until 1975, and,
at sixty-six pages, it is hard to imagine Truman's successors reading it
cover to cover. But, as Robert Blackwill, a career diplomat, reflects, "What
really counts is not whether presidents had read or knew about NSC 68,
but instead if the ideas contained in the document were specifically familiar to the occupants of the Oval Office and, more important, if those
ideas had held up over the years. The answer to both these tests is an em-
phatic yes."[13] Blackwill, who later served on the National Security Council under President George W. Bush, is referring to the document's recommendation that the United States build and maintain a vast military
infrastructure, including a nuclear arsenal, that could dissuade adversaries and cultivate allies. What he and others don't acknowledge is that the
authors of NSC 68 did more than define a course of action for the Cold
War state; they also modeled a story that made sense of war as the nation's

new normal. The paper imagined the United States as a "protagonist" acting on the world stage to save humanity from itself.[14] It read like a political thriller. Nitze, the director of Policy Planning at the State Department, insisted in a Policy Review Group meeting on March 10, 1950, that the government needed "a gospel which lends itself to preaching."[15] The following week, Robert Lovett, acting as a consultant to the writing team, advised that the document be written in a "telegraphic style" with lean "Hemingway sentences." If American businesses "can sell every useless article known to man in large quantities," he concluded, then "we should be able to sell our very fine story in large quantities."[16] Acheson later wrote in his memoir, *Present at the Creation* (1969), that the intention behind NSC 68 was not to achieve nuance but to "bludgeon the mass mind."[17] The National Security Council needed to tell a good story, and it needed to tell that story with force.

The drafting of the document was animated by the tension between Acheson's two closest advisers, George Kennan and Paul Nitze. Kennan had created and directed the Policy Planning Staff before Nitze, who replaced him in the first weeks of 1950, and had been instrumental in devising and implementing the Marshall Plan that distributed some twelve billion dollars in aid to anemic Western economies. His 1946 "Long Telegram" to Washington and his 1947 *Foreign Affairs* article "The Sources of Soviet Conduct" laid out what became known as the containment doctrine and established Kennan as one of the Cold War state's "wise men." In the article, which Kennan published under the name "X," he argued that the Soviet Union, motivated by "Marxian-Leninist teachings," sought to overthrow all liberal capitalist governments and that its efforts must be "contained" by strengthening Western institutions "at a series of constantly shifting geographical and political points."[18] Kennan recognized the need for rearmament but did not see the military as the most effective vehicle for containing Soviet communism. He petitioned Truman and Acheson to call off the government's hydrogen-bomb program, even writing a never-delivered speech for the president announcing the program's cancelation. But Kennan's influence with the Truman administration had waned, while Nitze's had grown. The new director of Policy Planning pushed for the militarization of containment and wrote a memo to Acheson arguing that the administration could not risk giving Soviet nuclear scientists a head start. Nitze's argument won out. Years later, Kennan told a historian, "With the preparation of NSC 68 I had nothing to do. I was disgusted about the assumptions concerning Soviet intentions."[19]

But Nitze would never concede that he had disagreed with Kennan's articulation of containment. When, near the end of his life, a student sent Nitze his master's thesis, in which he made the argument that NSC 68 had "militarized containment," Nitze crossed out the student's words and wrote, "This paper *more realistically set forth the requirements necessary to assure success of* George Kennan's idea of containment."[20] He believed that NSC 68 had actualized Kennan's vision by deterring all-out war through defense-minded rearmament. This was his position in 1950 as well. He and the Policy Review Group recommended that the president build the world's largest armed forces while describing military state-building as an "attempt to change the world situation by means short of war." Nitze and his writing team used that line five separate times. "We have no choice but to demonstrate the superiority of the idea of freedom by its constructive application, and to attempt to change the world situation by means short of war in such a way as to frustrate the Kremlin," they wrote.[21] Whereas Soviets used force without hesitation to advance their own interests, Americans turned to violence as a last resort to safeguard human freedom. Preventive war was, they believed, antithetical to liberal democratic governance. The United States could be drawn into a war by a belligerent Soviet Union, but it could not instigate that war without forfeiting the high road; it must maintain a defensive rather than offensive posture toward the Stalin government. But the council concluded its assessment by reframing national defense as a "real war," writing that "the whole success of the proposed program hangs ultimately on recognition by this Government, the American people, and all free peoples, that the Cold War is in fact a real war in which the survival of the free world is at stake."[22] The government must deter war, and yet it was already waging one. The Cold War was being fought by means short of war, and yet it was a real war that, if not pursued, could hasten the demise of the free world.

Was the United States at war? Nitze answered no and then yes. His recommendation did not constitute a call to arms, he suggested, because it ensured against an even larger conflict; containment could not be construed as war, because it deterred more violence than it incited. Postcolonial scholar Rey Chow argues that the atomic bombing of Hiroshima and Nagasaki ushered in an era in which war would be ended through its continuation. "The pursuit of war—with its use of violence—and the pursuit of peace—with its cultivation of knowledge—are the obverse and reverse of the same coin," she writes. The United States cultivated knowledge that cast its militarism in "the form of enlightenment and altruism, in the form of an aspiration simultaneously toward technological perfection and the pursuit of peace."[23] Nitze and his colleagues on the Policy Planning Staff and the National Security Council forged a blueprint for waging permanent war by framing its violence as liberal defense—a blueprint for an empire against imperialism.

But Nitze was careful to describe his Cold War agenda as a mere continuation of the nation's founding ideals. He cited the Constitution, the Bill of Rights, the Declaration of Independence, and the Federalist Papers in making his case to Truman. NSC 68 began with two sections titled "Fundamental Purpose of the United States" and "Fundamental Design of the Kremlin." The former stated, "The fundamental purpose of the United States is laid down in the Preamble to the Constitution: '. . . to form a more perfect Union, establish Justice, insure domestic Tranquility, provide for the common defence, promote the general Welfare, and secure the Blessings of Liberty to ourselves and our Posterity.' In essence, the fundamental purpose is to assure the integrity and vitality of our free society, which is founded upon the dignity and worth of the individual."[24] Nitze and his team described the Cold War between the United States and the Soviet Union as the event that would define the future, resulting in either the "fulfillment or destruction not only of this Republic but of civilization itself." But they also suggested that their plan for saving the free world was nothing more than a recitation of the Constitution, rearticulating the Preamble as if it had, a hundred and sixty years earlier, announced the Republic's commitment to "the common defence" of "free society" the world over. Nitze, Acheson, and the rest of the Policy Review Group treated the Constitution as a framework for international governance while suggesting that this was, "in essence," the framers' intention. The Soviet Union served as their antithesis. It had a "design" rather than a "purpose" and acted on the will of its government ("the Kremlin") rather than its citizens. Nitze introduced the United States and the Soviet Union as "two protagonists" locked in an existential struggle as if he were outlining a novel for the president.[25] It was good versus evil. The American individual versus the Soviet "apparatus." Nitze advised Truman on how he should confront the Soviet Union, but he also sketched a story that the president could tell the American people about that confrontation.

Nitze and his writing team argued that communism had consigned Soviets to the outer limits of human life. The Stalin regime worked through coercion and consent. It bent individuals to its will and then conditioned them to embrace and even defend their unfreedom. Where a communist dictator reigns, they wrote, "all other wills must be subjugated in an act of willing submission, a degradation willed by the individual upon himself under the compulsion of a perverted faith."[26] Nitze's diagnosis of communist life reflected an emergent form of race-making that, while drawing on color-line racialization, also detached color from race by ascribing Soviets' lack of liberal humanness to internal beliefs rather than external attributes. He assumed the relative valuelessness of Soviet life because a "perverted faith" had distanced them from a liberal human norm embodied by white Western man. Communists must, he concluded, either be converted to liberal principles by force—"conferred" liberal consciousness—or contained or eliminated in the interest of defending those principles.[27]

Nitze's writing as the director of Policy Planning institutionalized the racial regime of defense that isolated communists as deserving objects of national defense who may be assimilable (deferred human) or unassimilable (nonhuman), but all of whom lack the free will to commit legitimate violence (war). He showed how the government could continually exercise "means short of war" by dictating who could conduct acts of legitimate violence and which illiberal societies needed to be converted or contained by such violence. NSC 68 modeled how the empire of defense would see the non-Western world for decades to come. It divided Asia, Africa, and Latin America into two unequal parts, a part to be targeted for integration into liberal capitalism and a part to be targeted for destruction. Neither would be "conferred" equal status to white Western liberalism, but the promise to integrate some—to enlighten dark worlds—allowed officials to maintain the fictions of state antiracism and liberal universalism. All people were equal, almost, if they embraced the right ideas. The Policy Review Group articulated a racial regime of defense that would form and govern the categories of the human, the deferred human, and the nonhuman by distinguishing those authorized to police societies, near and far, from those who allied with them and those who didn't. This regime installed hierarchies of human value that it attributed not to skin color but to belief. The "dark continents" were dark not because they were black, racial liberals argued, but because they leaned communist. The racial discourse of whiteness and blackness bled into the ideological discourse of liberalism and illiberalism, obscuring the white administration of racial hierarchies in the defense era. So while Truman had the Soviet Union's detonation of an atomic device and the "loss" of China on his mind when he asked his secretaries of state and defense to review the government's readiness for a nuclear conflict, Nitze, Acheson, and their colleagues at the National Security Council set a more ambitious course on which the state could (and would) conduct unending war across the second half of the twentieth century and into the twenty-first, beginning with a "police action" on the Korean Peninsula.

The authors of NSC 68 racialized communism, but they also reassigned their country's own histories of racial violence, exclusion, and domination to the Soviet Union. Nitze described the USSR as a "slave state" that could not tolerate racial, ideological, and religious difference, an anachronistic government that felt threatened by the existence of human freedom in the West and sought to undermine it where it flourished most, in the United States. "The antipathy of slavery to freedom explains the iron curtain, the isolation, and autarchy of the society whose end is absolute power," he wrote. "The existence and persistence of the idea of freedom is a permanent and continuous threat to the foundation of the slave society; and it therefore regards as intolerable the long continued existence of freedom in the world." The forward march of history, Nitze believed, would lead to the eventual demise of communism and other forms of illiberalism, and it fell to the United States to accelerate that demise. Of course, declaring the Soviet Union a slave state elided his own country's origin as a slaveholding republic and distracted from the ongoing racial disenfranchisement and extralegal (and legal) violence under Jim Crow. Liberal internationalists like Truman recognized their nation's own existing racial order—visible segregation and extralegal violence, most of all—as a significant obstacle as it vied with the Soviet Union for access to the markets of the decolonizing world. This led some cold warriors to embrace limited civil rights reform as an anticommunist cause, but it also necessitated that the defense establishment be understood as an instrument of antiracism.[28] The Soviet Union needed to be an unfree slave state so that the United States could be the solution to that unfreedom across Asia, Africa, and Latin America.

The launch of the national security state under Truman destabilized the meaning of war for Americans, who, until then, knew it as an event, a discrete crisis that could be communicated in story form. Officials now had to make sense of war as a norm rather than an event; they had to tell a war story without an ending. The National Security Council outlined how that story could be told through the idea of defense. Its recommendation to Truman wielded national defense as a mechanism of racialization through which it devalued non-Western societies and delegitimized their use of force as criminal. Soviets could not wage war because they had surrendered their free will to an illiberal belief, communism. His government was not at war with the Soviet Union, Nitze concluded, but defending humanity against the belief that had "enslaved" it. NSC 68 designated the United States an arbiter of legitimate violence by advancing liberalism as the only form of rational thought. The Cold War state asserted the right to deem any act of violence committed by an illiberal state or non-state actor as illegitimate and criminal, while assuming its own violence against such actors to have a humanizing effect by drawing them into its own liberal sphere.[29] That violent conversion then allowed officials to rewrite an act of defense as a "small war" in which the United States liberated a vulnerable nation from an irrational antagonist. But the Truman administration did not have occasion to tell that story until the escalation of the Korean War, a war that began as a police action against Sino-Soviet communism (defense) and that officials later reframed as the liberation of South Korea (a small war), even as the war dragged on.

Proof of a Thesis at the Thirty-Eighth Parallel

On January 31, 1950, Truman directed Acheson and Secretary of Defense Louis Johnson to "undertake a reexamination of our objectives in peace and war and of the effect of these objectives on our strategic plans."[30] The Soviet Union had detonated a fission bomb in August, three years earlier than his advisers had anticipated, and the president wanted advice on how to confront a nuclear-capable Kremlin. Two months later, the State–Defense Policy Review Group delivered NSC 68 to Truman with signatures from Acheson, Johnson, the Joint Chiefs of Staff, and the secretaries of the services. The president demurred. He had made promises to cut defense spending and wanted to see an itemized budget before considering their recommendations further. Nitze, Acheson, and their team had not yet undertaken the requested revisions when, at dawn on June 25, fighting broke out across the thirty-eighth parallel with the Korean People's Army pushing south down the peninsula. Later that day, the United States introduced a resolution to the UN Security Council demanding the immediate retreat of KPA forces. On June 27, it introduced a second resolution calling for member nations to intervene on South Korea's behalf. Truman signed NSC 68, without revision, later that year.

The absence of a budget from the first draft was not an accident. Nitze calculated that including a dollar figure would doom his agenda before

it could get off the ground. The government, he wrote, "should first decide the policy it ought to follow and then deal separately with imple-
mentation."[31] Acheson agreed, believing that "to have attempted [a cost
estimate] would have made impossible all those concurrences [between
departments and committees] and prevented any recommendation to the
President."[32] But Nitze and Acheson's plan was more underhanded than
they let on. The "concurrences" that Acheson celebrated between different wings of the National Security Council were almost nonexistent
at the drafting stage. The Policy Planning Staff did the lion's share of the
work and had to because Nitze classified all of the associated materials
as "top secret—restricted data," limiting access to the small number of
officials with "Q clearance."[33] This meant that drafts of NSC 68 were out
of the reach of the Treasury Department and the Bureau of the Budget,
which would have been alarmed by the scale of the federal growth being
recommended without any reference to its cost or potential effect on the
national debt. Truman had earlier announced that he would bring defense
spending down to 13 billion dollars in 1951, a reduction of 1.5 billion dollars from 1950. Instead, after the Korean War escalated and led him to
authorize NSC 68, Truman raised the defense budget to more than 58 billion dollars in 1951 and almost 70 billion in 1952. The national security
state that his administration had installed with the National Security Act
of 1947 and the amendments of 1949 found itself flooded with resources.
NSC 68 was, as Paul Hammond, author of the first detailed examination
of its writing, remarks, "distinctive for what it did not say as much as for
what it did say." He points out that, while Nitze's blunt prose and exclusion of a dollar amount eased his agenda through committee review, it
also "had the effect of leaving the administration free to proceed as it
wished," granting the executive branch even wider latitude to administer
large-scale violence in the future.[34]

The breach of the thirty-eighth parallel was the event that, Acheson
suggested, validated the National Security Council's "thesis."[35] The Korean War turned that thesis, NSC 68, into doctrine and modeled a new
liberal internationalism that would dominate the next half century. The
Policy Review Group described the threat of world communism in broad
strokes. It was long on ideas about the Soviet Union and Marxist thought
and short on evidence. The intensified fighting on the Korean Peninsula,
the group believed, gave it that evidence. Nitze wasted no time in connecting the conflict in East Asia to his account of the Cold War as a clash
of civilizations between freedom and bondage, the endurance of free will

and its ruin. "A failure to act prudently, and in time," he declared that fall, "might involve our nation in the greatest ordeal of its history."[36] Before the Senate Appropriations Committee, General Omar Bradley, the first chairman of the Joint Chiefs of Staff, urged Congress to authorize an additional ten billion dollars in defense spending to aid the war effort in Korea and increase the government's presence in other vulnerable parts of the world. "It is now evident that we must have an even greater flexibility of military power in the United States itself not only for our protection, but also to give us a ready, highly mobile standing force which we can bring to bear at any threatened point in the minimum time," he told the committee.[37] Like other hawks making the case for rearmament, Bradley led with the crisis on the Korean Peninsula and ended with a more general call for the United States to police illiberal states and nonstate actors. If NSC 68 articulated a form through which Americans and their government could account for the normalization of war, then the Korean War delivered the content that Nitze, Acheson, and others had been searching for.

That summer and fall, although it wouldn't be declassified for another twenty-five years, NSC 68 could be heard in all of Truman's addresses to the nation on the Korean War. On July 19, 1950, the president delivered a fireside chat to a combined radio and television audience of some 130 million Americans. He described how "communist forces" had attacked the "free and independent" Republic of Korea (South Korea) three weeks earlier. That "sneak attack" was "an act of raw aggression, without a shadow of justification," he stated. "I repeat it was an act of raw aggression. It had no justification whatever." Since then, he continued, the United Nations had formed an international consensus that the rule of law must be restored by force on the Korean Peninsula, that it must "put down lawless aggression" and defend against "communist slavery."[38] Like Nitze and his Policy Review Group, Truman did not refer to North Korea, China, and the Soviet Union as nations but as slave states that could not claim legitimate status because, under communism, they lacked free will. There violence was raw, unjustified, and lawless, and therefore the "situation" in Korea was not a war but an act of defense carried out by free societies united against criminal behavior.

Truman outlined a three-part response that echoed the recommendations made to him that spring by his National Security Council. The United States needed to send more men and guns to the peninsula; it needed to build its "Army, Navy, and Air Force over and above what is needed in Korea"; and it needed to accelerate its "work with other countries in strengthening our common defenses."[39] The president cast the Korean War within an international drama in which the United States was leading a unified front of free nations acting of their own volition in a struggle with communists who, subverted by a corrosive belief, were acting against their own best interests. The Korean War gave him and his advisers an event through which they could tell a story of war that was humane, humanitarian, and not war at all. It gave them an event through which they could represent this new kind of war as good for all and forgotten long before it ends.

The war was more than an excuse for rearmament, though. While the National Security Council had focused most of its attention on the Soviet Union in making its recommendation to Truman, it recognized Asia as the venue in which the Cold War would be waged. Nitze informed the president that Soviets had found "a particularly receptive audience in Asia, especially as the Asiatics have been impressed by what has been plausibly portrayed to them as the rapid advance of the U.S.S.R. from a backward society to a position of great world power." He suggested that the Soviet Union sought to lead an "international crusade" that would grow from the Asian continent, where "backward" societies identified with the USSR and admired its swift rise. China gave communists a base from which to build their influence in South and Southeast Asia. The Cold War state would need to undertake extensive institution-building across the continent, Nitze added, so that "the peoples of Asia can make more effective use of their great human and material resources."[40] The outbreak of violence on the Korean Peninsula transformed the Cold War into the Asian war that the National Security Council had seen it as all along.

The Korean War became the testing ground for a new kind of belief-based racialization that extended and exceeded color-line racialization. Some cold warriors like Nitze treated communism as an "Asiatic" form of government that attracted "backward" cultures to its cause. White Western men were, they suggested, less vulnerable to communism's allure. But the anticolonial and antiracist movements that accelerated in the wake of World War II forced the United States to subordinate race-based arguments about which societies were and weren't eligible for self-government. Officials recognized that they could rearticulate existing racial ideas and hierarchies in the deracinated language of beliefs and behaviors. Critical race theorist Jodi Melamed contends that the racialization of communism and other ideologies and religions can be attributed to the emergence of a "formally antiracist, liberal-capitalist modernity" in which the state forms new differential relations of value and valuelessness while acting as if it is merely sorting human beings into stable categories of difference. "Racialization beyond color lines," she writes, has allowed the modern state to exercise "legitimate violence through proliferating norms that render some forms of humanity and their social imaginaries rational and others irrational, some legal and others illegal, some criminal and others law-abiding."[41] The defense establishment racialized communism as irrational, illegal, and criminal, but it also grounded that "new" racial knowledge in existing anti-Asian racist discourse. It orientalized communism and assumed Asians to be communism's most "receptive audience."

Even as the United States waged war along racial lines in Korea, some government officials and writers celebrated the war as a civil rights achievement. In his 1954 book *Breakthrough on the Color Front*, Lee Nichols, a journalist with United Press International, described the integration of the armed forces on the Korean Peninsula as "a racial about-face unparalleled by any similar development in modern history." The Korean War was the first fought by integrated units, after Truman issued Executive Order 9981 in 1948, and Nichols argued that the successful enactment of that order was one of the most overlooked stories of the decade. "For the nation as a whole, the military was spearheading an accelerated shift away from the long-standing pattern of racial segregation throughout the United States," he wrote. "Negroes and whites in the armed forces were not just training and fighting together; they were eating at the same tables, sleeping next to one another and drinking beer together at military post canteens."[42] Nichols recognized how domestic black-white integration fit into the global contexts of the Cold War and decolonization. He observed that Soviet media propagated the idea that Americans "sought literally to exterminate dark-skinned peoples." But with "negro and white [soldiers] visibly intermingled [and] stationed in nearly fifty countries on six continents," the United States, Nichols reasoned, had built an armed counter-narrative that stretched around the world.[43] (He later claimed that a draft of his book had been read by two Supreme Court justices as they argued *Brown v. Board of Education*.[44])

Nichols exaggerated the military's commitment to integration in Korea, or at least his sources (senior defense officials, for the most part) did. The divisions that fought in East Asia were almost as segregated as they had been at the end of World War II. Truman's executive order called for "equality of treatment and opportunity" rather than integration, allowing recruiters and draft boards to enlist and induct black soldiers in record numbers without abandoning the custom of assigning them to segregated combat and labor units.[45] But Nichols's book told a story that officials were eager to share. Senator Hubert Humphrey wrote a blurb for the book, calling the institutional change it chronicled "the first truly effective step that has been made in implementing the Emancipation Proclamation." S. L. A. Marshall, a retired army general and historian, reviewed it in the *New York Times Book Review*, writing that "it is a truly felicitous thing that a nation can change its ways because of the deathless courage of a few mixed rifle squads in the nameless ridges north of Parallel 38."[46] Nichols, Humphrey, and Marshall embraced the military as a model antiracist institution that could teach Americans from different racial backgrounds how to live together and demonstrate to the world that the United States could be trusted to dismantle rather than form racial hierarchies.[47] Nichols's writing reflected the Washington consensus formalized in NSC 68 that state violence could be a force for good, that it could disseminate liberal ideas and inhibit illiberal ones. That narrative gained traction among officials and most Americans, but it also, as journalist I. F. Stone identified in his own account of the Korean War, contained enough holes and incongruities to make the careful reader scratch her head and wonder if there wasn't another story to be told.

I. F. Stone's Hidden History

In 1983, looking back at his years in the Truman administration, Paul Nitze defended the shrill language he used in authoring NSC 68. "The world has changed in preferences, and tastes have changed somewhat. Particularly in the political field. So you wouldn't express things in the same way today if you're writing that document," he acknowledged. "But it wasn't too black-and-white for those days."[48] Nitze admitted that, were he to deliver the same recommendation three decades later, he would not use the language of good and evil to describe the Cold War with the Soviet Union. Tastes had changed. But national politics had, too. The story told by Nitze and other Truman administration officials in 1950 benefited from the second red scare that marginalized some of the nation's leading leftist thinkers and artists, who, like Stone, had cut their teeth in the antifascist, fellow-traveling Popular Front. Stone refused to be silenced by the ascendant coalition of conservatives and anticommunist liberals and wrote a critical account of his government's war on the Korean Peninsula,

The Hidden History of the Korean War (1952), that tugged at the loose ends of the official version of events offered by politicians and "access journalists." He recognized that some of the government's darkest secrets were not secrets at all but rather minimized by officials and forgotten by most Americans. State documents need to be read against the grain, he believed, as a constructed narrative rather than as a string of facts. His hidden history of the Korean War was not even hidden. It could be read in the margins of the official record.

Stone's career suffered as the Cold War escalated and an anticommunist consensus formed in Washington. Having written for the leftist dailies *PM* and the New York *Daily Compass*, he struggled to find a venue for his work as they shut down amid the McCarthy freeze. (*PM* ended its run in 1947; the *Daily Compass*, in 1952.) He moved to Paris in 1950 as General Douglas MacArthur led the coalition forces north toward the Manchurian border, drawing China into the war and guaranteeing that it would not, as the general claimed that fall, end by Christmas. Noticing some "contradictions and discrepancies" between how his French and American colleagues covered the war, Stone decided to take a closer look at the origin of the US-led war on the Korean Peninsula.[49] He waded through US and UN documents and searched American and British news for clues. He consulted the "North Korean Blue Book" and statements made by Andrey Vyshinsky, the Soviet minister of foreign affairs, to the United Nations. Stone found little evidence to suggest that Stalin had masterminded the war from Moscow, as the White House claimed, and some evidence to suggest that hawkish members of the Truman administration had foreseen, welcomed, and even invited North Korea's attack on South Korea because it lifted the ceiling on defense spending and accelerated rearmament. Some two dozen publishers rejected his manuscript before Leo Huberman and Paul Sweezy of the new, socialist-leaning *Monthly Review* took it. The book was met by harsh criticism from anticommunist liberals, who declared Stone's account "fictive," "tendentious," and verging on "the official Soviet line."[50] Richard Rovere, the Washington correspondent for the *New Yorker*, went so far as to call Stone a once-promising journalist who had devolved into a "man who thinks up good arguments for poor Communist positions."[51] The out-of-work journalist had hit a nerve.

Stone's book bothered cold warriors like Rovere in part because his findings were difficult to refute. His research was, after all, grounded in the government's own conflicting record of events. Stone knew that he would be accused of exaggeration and guesswork by conservative and liberal hawks and labored to head them off. "I realized from the beginning that I could be persuasive only if I utilized material which could not be challenged by those who accept the official American government point of view," he wrote. "This book is what it purports to be, not 'inside stuff' or keyhole revelations but the hidden history of the Korean War, the facts to be found in the official accounts themselves if texts are carefully examined and reports collated."[52] Stone's method of investigative journalism could be described as a form of close reading. He scrutinized the story that the Truman administration told about the Korean War and zeroed in on the aspects of that story that didn't hang together. He identified narrative as one of the basic technologies of state violence and sought to tell an alternative story that addressed rather than masked the limits of narrative form. He wrote his nonfiction book, he said, like a novel, "with suspense and with three-dimensionality," while being mindful that "much about the Korean War is still hidden, and much will long remain hidden."[53] Some of what Stone investigated could not be answered and still can't be answered, but it was crucial, he suggested, that Americans ask not just "who" and "how" of their government but also "why." The official record of the war stresses which side won which battle and by what means, while it buries motive in vagaries about freedom and unfreedom, legitimate and illegitimate violence. A year later, in 1953, Stone asked, "Should peace begin to break out in Korea, so run the familiar speculations, how keep up the pressure on France for German rearmament? And what happens to the drive for bigger air force and air defense appropriations?"[54] He couldn't offer an answer but insisted that he and other journalists must ask.

The most divisive of Stone's theories was his suggestion that the North Korean invasion on June 25 was not, as Truman declared it, "an act of raw aggression" that had caught the United States and their allies off guard but a welcomed stimulus for rearmament.[55] On June 27, two days after the fighting began, the United Nations Commission on Korea reported that South Korea had been "taken completely by surprise as they had no reason to believe from intelligence sources that invasion was imminent." Days later, the United States and its allies were at war. But, as Stone points out, the commission had received intelligence reports from South Korean officials on three separate occasions that winter and spring indicating that North Korean forces were preparing to invade the south. He noted that Roscoe Hillenkoetter, the first director of the CIA, had told reporters on the day of the attack that "conditions existed in Korea that could have meant an invasion this week or next." Hillenkoetter would have been well informed, considering that the United States had some twelve hundred officers and technicians in South Korea on the day of the invasion. "Strange," Stone wrote, that hundreds of intelligence agents could have missed "a military buildup as impressive as that which went into action on the 38th parallel that Sunday morning."[56]

Why, he wondered, would the Truman administration announce an intelligence failure on the Korean Peninsula? And why, knowing that an attack was imminent, had it not acted sooner? Stone used the words of Tom Connally, the chairman of the Senate Foreign Relations Committee, to float an answer. A *U.S. News and World Report* interviewer had asked Connally on May 2 whether his colleagues in the Senate were concerned that an event somewhere in the world could set off a new world war. "Well," he began, "a lot of them believe like this: They believe that events will transpire which will maneuver around and present an incident which will make us fight. That's what a lot of them are saying: 'We've got to battle some time, why not now?'" Perhaps, Stone mused, the attack had been cheered rather than mourned by some officials in Washington, who saw the intelligence failure in Korea as a calculated error that compelled the president to rearm the nation for a long Cold War.[57]

In challenging Truman's claim that the Korean War had begun out of nowhere on June 25, 1950, Stone destabilized the idea of war as a discrete event that begins with a named battle and ends with signed treaties. *The Hidden History of the Korean War* arrived as the US-led United Nations Command, South Korea, North Korea, and China fought to a stalemate in the trenches along the thirty-eighth parallel. Negotiations had failed. The war had, *U.S. News* remarked, begun "receding in the minds" of most Americans, who could see "no end in sight" on the Korean Peninsula.[58] Officials addressed the war's irresolution by defining it as a nonwar—a police action, the defense of human freedom—and also as a small war that would end, they insisted, with the liberation of anticommunist Korea. Ethnic studies scholar Christine Hong argues that historians of the Korean War must reckon with state intelligence as a vehicle not for facts but for "an epistemology of war that paradoxically militates against knowledge." Stories of North Korean aggression and South Korean victimization, she writes, "have been marshaled to perpetuate an unyielding state of hostilities on the Korean peninsula" and have "destabilized the category of truth as an end unto itself." Intelligence, including that which established that the Korean People's Army invaded North Korea without warning or reason, "is justified by its ends and has little to do with the pursuit of verifiable truth."[59] Stone's assertion that the Korean War did not originate with an act of one-sided belligerence on June 25 but involved a tangled set of motives that stretched back years and even decades undermined Truman's nonwar/small war account of events on the Korean Peninsula and called attention to the normalization of military state-building under his administration. It challenged the president's effort to make the war forgettable as either a police action or a necessary but minor war.

Nitze, Acheson, and their colleagues on the National Security Council argued that all societies took one of three forms. Either they were free; they wanted to be free; or they had been coerced into a state of willed unfreedom. The United States could therefore execute discrete small wars to liberate those desiring freedom (anticommunist Korea) and co-ordinate an international defense against those who had fallen victim to the forces of unfreedom and forfeited their right to commit legitimate violence (communist Korea), but it could not, the council argued, fight a real war against illiberal societies. Instead, it would wage a Cold War against Soviet communism "by means short of war."[60] The idea of defense rests on the maintenance of the categories of the human, the deferred human, and the nonhuman. When a writer like Stone reveals that sorting for what it is, a form of race-making and a cover for permanent war, the fiction of liberal defense cannot hold. Noting that a Truman administration official had acknowledged to the *New York Times* "the effect that the war ravages have had on the Oriental peoples, and the exploitation of it by Communist propaganda," Stone reflected, "If the war was a 'police action' against 'aggression,' a crusade to liberate Korea from Communist slavery, then one would expect the people of Korea to blame the damage on the Communist aggressors and accept its cost as necessary to their liberation. Perhaps some preferred slavery to the liberation."[61] Later, he wrote that "if a disregard for human life is supposed to be an Oriental characteristic," then "judging by the pace of negotiations in the Korean truce talks, all military men must be Oriental."[62] The Truman administration had described its war on the Korean Peninsula as a humanizing crusade to counter the inhuman violence of a communist regime. Taking another look at that official account, Stone asked whether violence could ever be, as his government claimed, rational and humane. He identified where the administration's deracinated anticommunism showed itself to be grounded in anti-Asian racism, wondering what other than color distinguished "Oriental" violence from that committed by white Western men. The national security state has, since the war for the Korean Peninsula, used the idea of defense to ease the tensions between war and nonwar, racism and antiracism, norm and event—tensions that, when drawn out, tell a story of permanent war.

Five years after Truman signed the National Security Act into law, Stone discovered that the goal of war had changed. The United States fought not to end the violence in Korea but to extend it. The mood in Washington, he wrote, reflected an "almost hysterical fear of peace," driven by government and business elites with elections and arms manu- facturing on their minds. "If peace came in Korea, there might be new Koreas in the making in Indo-China and Burma," Stone reasoned. "If not there, then with American troops in Korea, some new 'incident' might start up the war again. The dominant trend in American political, eco- nomic, and military thinking was fear of peace." He rested his case on the words of James Van Fleet, who succeeded MacArthur as the commander of the coalition forces in East Asia. "Korea has been a blessing," the gen- eral acknowledged in 1952. "There had to be a Korea either here or some place in the world."[63] Stone's book showed that the Korean War had not been concealed or forgotten in the United States but lost to Americans' uncritical reading habits. The same government archive from which the Truman administration had assembled a narrative of communist aggres- sion and American liberation could, he demonstrated, be turned back against the national security state. Of Stone, historian Bruce Cumings once wrote, he "reads a document the way Sherlock Holmes looks for fin- gerprints."[64] Americans should remember the wars that have been fought in their name, but they should also, like Stone, attend to how the generic conventions of the war story have been marshaled to make them forget that some of those wars have never ended, and some were never even acknowledged as wars.

A Charge of Genocide

The dogmatic anticommunism of the Korean War years decimated the old left and slowed government-driven reforms. That political culture led in- dependent journalists like Stone to adopt an anti-anticommunist attitude in their reporting, and it convinced black radicals like William Patterson to relocate their freedom struggles from the national to the international stage. Patterson, the chairman of the radical antiracist Civil Rights Con- gress, recognized that the intergovernmental bodies assembled at the end of World War II could be more effective venues for his organization's message than an administration allied with southern Democrats dead set against even the most limited civil rights legislation. In 1951, three years after the United Nations ratified the Universal Declaration of Human Rights, acknowledging "the equal and inalienable rights of all members of the human family," Patterson delivered a petition, titled *We Charge Genocide*, to the UN General Assembly in Paris alleging that the United States had carried out genocide against black Americans for more than three centuries.[65] The government had, he wrote, done nothing to counteract the "institutionalized oppression and persistent slaughter of the Negro people"; it had instead facilitated it.[66] Pointing to the findings of the president's own civil rights committee, Patterson concluded, as he later recalled in his memoir, that the government "admits the institutionalized Negro oppression, written into law and carried out by police and courts. It describes it, examines it, surveys it, talks about it, and does everything but change it. In fact, it both admits and protects it."[67] He brought his charge to the United Nations' Convention on the Prevention and Punishment of the Crime of Genocide because, he argued, domestic racial terror had fueled a race war on the Korean Peninsula. Genocide led to war, and war to genocide. The two could not be separated.

Patterson and the Civil Rights Congress hit the Truman administration where it hurt most by bringing their charge of genocide to the United Nations. A year earlier, the president and Acheson had broadcast the UN Security Council's condemnation of North Korea as evidence of an international consensus on the conflict. Although the United States furnished most of the Western divisions stationed in Korea, the UN resolutions demonstrated for Truman and Acheson that they had not acted alone on the peninsula but as part of a unified front of free societies allied against communist aggression. In his fireside chat that summer, Truman pointed out that fifty-two out of fifty-nine member nations had endorsed the actions taken by the US-led forces in Korea. "The free nations have now made it clear that lawless aggression will be met with force," he stated.[68] The United Nations gave his administration a formal avenue through which it could denounce the Soviet Union's human rights violations without drawing comparisons to its own blemished record.[69] But Patterson did not let officials' manipulation of international human rights instruments go unacknowledged, insisting that there were some in Washington who saw the UN Charter as little more than "a shield behind which American imperialism would seek to dominate the century."[70] He did not believe that the United Nations had to function as a shelter for militarism, but he also recognized racial liberalism as the unstable foundation of a new iteration of liberal empire and the six-year-old United Nations as its ideal vessel. In delivering *We Charge Genocide* to the UN General Assembly, he confronted Americans and their allies with the ambiguities of the Manichean world they envisioned and the illogic of a racist government waging war for freedom in Korea.

When Patterson submitted the petition to the General Assembly in Paris on December 17, 1951, he and his one hundred cosigners had few friends in the United States. The attorney general had declared the Civil Rights Congress, which published the petition, a "subversive organization controlled or dominated by the Communist Party," and Patterson had been twice charged with contempt of Congress for refusing to disclose its donors.[71] Patterson enlisted the entertainer and activist Paul Robeson to deliver the petition to the UN Secretariat in New York while he was in Paris. Soon after, the two men had their passports confiscated by government officials. Patterson was even denounced by the leaders of the National Association for the Advancement of Colored People, who, toeing the anticommunist line, disassociated themselves from Patterson, Robeson, and another of the petition's cosigners, W. E. B. Du Bois, who had cofounded the NAACP forty years earlier and prepared the association's own petition to the United Nations, *An Appeal to the World*, a precursor to Patterson's, in 1947. Walter White, the association's executive secretary, addressed the charges made by the black left in a "Progress Report" published in the *Saturday Review of Literature*, accusing radicals like Patterson of abetting communism in Asia, Africa, and Latin America. "Cruelty and hatred of human beings manufactured screaming headlines around the globe," he wrote, while the country's budding "decency and brotherhood made none."[72] Patterson's petition unnerved the American delegation to the United Nations and led the Truman administration to tell White that "it would be most desirable for some outstanding Negro leaders to be present in Paris."[73] White obliged, recruiting Ralph Bunche, Rayford Logan, and Channing Tobias to attend the General Assembly meeting. The Civil Rights Congress had been blacklisted by the attorney general, derided by liberal news media as a Soviet front, and marginalized within the emerging black civil rights movement. It had limited funds and few allies. Yet the Cold War state dedicated enormous resources to refuting its self-published petition.

At least one person had an explanation for why the Truman administration felt so threatened by the petition. On December 20, three days after Patterson visited the UN General Assembly in Paris, Stone wrote in the *Daily Compass* that the petition's charges were "not to be lightly dismissed" because Patterson had marshaled the state's own evidence against it by compiling a record of legal and extralegal racial violence that had been documented by federal agencies and defended in public by government agents. The Civil Rights Congress had taken a page right out of Stone's book. "Under the circumstances I see no reason why a Negro group should not utilize the Genocide Convention as a means of call-ing world attention more forcibly to the condition of the Negro in this country," Stone wrote. "The strongest legal argument in the document is that so many of those in this country who opposed the Genocide Conven-tion did so on the ground that it might permit lynchings and race riots to be brought before international tribunals."[74] Southern senators, includ-ing Tom Connally of Texas and Walter George of Georgia, had acknowl-edged years earlier that the antiblack violence executed in their home states could fall under the United Nation's definition of genocide. All Pat-terson had to do was remind his readers of the senators' words. Officials could not tolerate *We Charge Genocide* because it traced the limits of the liberal antiracist, humanitarian idea of defense with which the United States carried out empire-building after the decline of colonialism. It re-connected racism to the nation's "anticommunist" wars.

The petition argued that modern war could not be waged without the construction of racial divisions—divisions that, it suggested, were formed at home and then disseminated to the world through war. The Jewish le-gal scholar Raphael Lemkin had devised the Genocide Convention as a safeguard against a second Holocaust, and Patterson contended that one of the lessons of Nazi Germany was that intranational genocidal violence could lead to and model a wider genocide of "predatory war." The United Nations couldn't afford to ignore the destruction of black life in America because it organized hierarchies of human value that could and would be inflicted on Korea and other countries. "White supremacy at home makes for colored massacres abroad. Both reveal contempt for human life in a colored skin," the petition warned. "Jellied gasoline in Korea and the lynchers' faggot at home are connected in more ways than that both result in death by fire. The lyncher and the atom bomb are related. The first cannot murder unpunished and unrebuked without so encouraging the latter that the peace of the world and the lives of millions are endan-gered."[75] Condoning domestic racial violence meant consenting to a world war waged along racial lines. Robert Jackson, the US chief of counsel at the Nuremberg Trials, had made a similar argument years earlier when he declared that domestic "terrorism was the chief instrument for securing the cohesion of the German people in war purposes."[76] Jackson's claim, Patterson added, held true for his country's own wars, from the Mexican–American War and the Civil War to the "period of American imperialist adventure" at the turn of the century. But the Truman administration had charted a new course by submerging the continued racial structure of war in "tributes to the sacredness of the individual" and "talk of liberty" so that American elites could "transform their guilt into high moral purpose."[77] To maintain that fiction, the United States needed to sever the connection between the lyncher and the atom bomb, between its devaluation of black bodies across the Jim Crow South and its policing of Asian bodies along the thirty-eighth parallel.[78]

We Charge Genocide showed how the Cold War state had not mitigated antiblack racism but rearticulated it in the deracinated language of anticommunism. Patterson noted the conflation of blackness and communism in his own encounters with the state. In August 1950, two months after conventional combat began on the Korean Peninsula, Henderson Lanham, a Democratic congressman from Georgia, interrogated Patterson before the House Select Committee on Lobbying Activities on the undisclosed patrons of the Civil Rights Congress. When Patterson suggested that the state of Georgia had encouraged lynch law, the congressman called the civil rights leader a "god-damned black son-of-a-bitch" and tried to engage him in a fistfight.[79] Later, at Patterson's first trial, Lanham addressed the dispute by subordinating the civil rights leader's blackness to his communism. "I should have used the word Communist instead of black," he said of his language at the earlier hearing, "but it just rolled out."[80] The congressman's words signaled a broader shift in racial discourse as cold warriors constructed an anticommunist consensus grounded in antiblack racism while laboring to obscure that connection, even suggesting that one could not be an antiracist *without* being an anticommunist. Whereas an earlier generation of black leaders had advocated military service as an engine for civil rights demands—calling for a two-front war against Nazi and American fascism during World War II, for example—Patterson, Robeson, and others saw the Korean War as a form of genocidal violence against "colored peoples" like themselves. "As they observed anticolonial and democratic struggles in Asia and Africa," historian Kimberley Phillips writes, "black antiwar activists strengthened their arguments that the Cold War not only fueled and justified the terror blacks experienced at home, but that the wars it engendered were inimical to their pursuit of racial justice."[81] Civil rights advocates could not, they argued, back the war effort in Korea and also combat Jim Crow. One drove the other. Patterson and the Civil Rights Congress showed that legal and extralegal violence against black Americans escalated "in direct ratio to the surge towards war."[82]

Patterson contended that resistance to war should not just incorporate but begin with black freedom struggles. Genocide and war were motivated by wealth accumulation, he stated, which led a small number of elites to use their influence to institutionalize genocidal violence. He suggested that modern war could not be sustained without race as an ordering framework and that ending war must therefore begin with the abolishment of that framework. While the goal of genocide had once been "the subjection of American Negroes for the profits of chattel slavery," Patterson wrote, "now its aim is the splitting and emasculation of mass movements for peace and democracy, so that reaction may perpetuate its control and continue receiving the highest profits."[83] The violent division of social worlds into human, deferred human, and nonhuman categories created and justified the uneven distribution of wealth and well-being. Profits could not be enhanced without war, and war could not be waged without a regime of racialization. Ending war meant confronting that regime. If the United Nations wanted to end genocide and war, Patterson asserted, it would first need to eradicate the racial system on which they depend.[84]

Marginalized in the red scare years, Patterson and Stone found new audiences for their writing as the war in Southeast Asia intensified and the antiwar movement gained a mainstream foothold. In 1970, the Marxist press International Publishers put out a new edition of *We Charge Genocide* with a foreword by Patterson. Introducing a new generation of readers to his petition, Patterson asserted that, while much had changed since he first published it, world events had validated his argument that combating American racism must be treated as an international cause. "It is now historically necessary and also incredibly easy to submit that racism U.S.A. is an export commodity breeding aggressive wars and threatening the peace of the world," he wrote. "The wantonly murderous and predatory racist attacks on Korea, Vietnam and Cambodia are proof. These criminal wars are inseparably related to the equally criminal murders of rebellious black youth in Chicago, Illinois, New Haven, Connecticut, Augusta, Georgia, and Jackson, Mississippi."[85] While officials like Paul

Nitze and liberal journalists like Lee Nichols extolled the military as a messenger for the liberal racial ideal of integration, Patterson identified it as a conduit for domestic racial hierarchies. The policing of "criminal" black bodies in Chicago, New Haven, and Jackson modeled the policing of "communist" Asian bodies in Korea, Vietnam, and Cambodia. Two decades after delivering his petition to the UN General Assembly, Patterson no longer believed that the Genocide Convention could be counted on to combat American racism. Instead, he argued that by advancing an alternative narrative—by not letting the state separate the lyncher from the atom bomb—"such an appeal can mobilize worldwide action against genocide" and the international wars it fosters.[86] In the first years of the Korean War, Patterson and Stone recognized that the greatest weakness of the national security state was the uneven story it sought to tell about race and defense. That story remained uncertain and unresolved throughout the twentieth century, even as the post–Cold War state set it in stone on the Washington Mall.

A Memorial to the Number Thirty-Eight

With the erosion of the anticommunist consensus in the Vietnam War years, the official account of the Korean War shifted. A police action to contain communism became a war waged to defend and liberate South Korea. A nonwar against Sino–Soviet communism became a small war for the South. Americans know the Korean War as forgotten in part because the state has sheared it of the anticommunism that motivated the fighting. That historical negation hangs over the Korean War Veterans Memorial on the Washington Mall, a memorial that looks back on a war that has never ended. Located at the foot of the Lincoln Memorial and across the Reflecting Pool from the Vietnam Veterans Memorial, the Korean Memorial grew out of a decade-long struggle between committees, designers, architects, and veterans organizations. That struggle, which culminated in its 1995 dedication by President Bill Clinton and South Korean President Kim Young-sam, unfolded as the United States asserted itself as a force for good in the post-Soviet world, waging wars in the name of human rights in Iraq, Somalia, and Bosnia. Clinton declared the memorial a belated acknowledgment of a war fought "to defend [South Korean] independence" and "safeguard other Asian nations from attack." But even as the president sought to resolve the war, setting it "in steel

and granite" beside Lincoln and Jefferson, the memorial's chaotic design
signals how the state has strained to contain permanent war within the
generic conventions of what Tim O'Brien calls a true war story—to hide
the Korean War's unendingness behind concrete details of the soldier's
service, sacrifice, and return.[87]

Three years after Congress authorized the construction of a Korean
War memorial, in 1988, the American Battle Monuments Commission
issued guidelines for a design contest that, alluding to Maya Lin's Vietnam Memorial, stressed that the design should not stand in contrast to
or "detract from the other great memorials on the Mall," because in
Korea, "unlike Vietnam, there was a victory in a geopolitical sense."[88]
The commission wanted a design unlike Lin's minimal, modernist wall,
and it got what it wanted. The Korean Memorial features a mix of design elements that include a black-granite mural wall etched with more
than twenty-four thousand images from the National Archives, a "pool of
remembrance," and its most recognizable element: nineteen seven-foot-
tall, stainless-steel statues of American soldiers, marines, sailors, and airmen cloaked and marching, their rifles held out at their sides or slung
over their shoulders. The memorial heroizes the Americans who served
in Korea while distracting visitors from the war itself. An extension of the
mural wall declares in large white letters that "freedom is not free." And
at the corner of the triangular field in which the soldiers stand, the memorial announces, "Our nation honors her uniformed sons and daughters
who answered their country's call to defend a country they did not know
and a people they had never met." Nowhere does it mention communism,
the Cold War, or the country in which the war was fought. The memorial
instead stresses that these men—they are all men, despite the dedication's
allusion to "daughters"—sacrificed their lives to defend freedom in an unnamed country from an unnamed antagonist. Like most veteran novels,
the memorial manages to find a sense of closure by conflating the commemoration of the American soldier with the remembrance of the war.
But the noise surrounding the nineteen statues and the heated debates
that formed the memorial's muddled design point to the limits of that
veteran-centered remembrance.[89]

If the Korean Memorial has an organizing motif, it is the number
thirty-eight. The winning design, submitted by a team of architects from
Pennsylvania State University, called for thirty-eight statues because combat had lasted thirty-eight months and ended with the Korean Peninsula
divided along the thirty-eighth parallel. When the Commission of Fine

FIGURE 1.1. Korean War Veterans Memorial. Library of Congress, Prints and Photographs Division (photograph by Carol M. Highsmith [LC-DIG-highsm-13268]).

Arts raised concerns about cost, scale, and the crowdedness of the de-sign, the American Battle Monuments Commission offered a "last com-promise." It agreed to reduce the number of statues to nineteen so that, when reflected in the mural wall, they could still be seen as thirty-eight men marching.[90] Why insist on nineteen statues and nineteen reflections? Why the commitment to the number thirty-eight? That number suggests a desire among the architects, commissions, and veterans organizations to treat the thirty-eight months of combat that stretched from the sum-mer of 1950 to the summer of 1953 as a well-defined event rather than as one phase of an unending war. And it naturalizes the division along the thirty-eighth parallel that the United States and the USSR created in 1945 and that became a demilitarized zone with the signing of the armistice agreement eight years later. The memorial acknowledges that what the Truman administration had called a police action was, as one vet put it at the dedication, finally "being recognized as a war."[91] But it also contains the conflict within a small-war narrative by isolating thirty-eight months of combat as the beginning and end of the Korean War.

The Korean Memorial commemorates American fighting men who, it imagines, led the world toward freedom and their own nation toward racial integration. The nineteen stainless-steel statues include twelve white and three black servicemen, two Latinos, one Asian American, and one American Indian.[92] That distribution turns actual racial and ethnic statistics into an image of cross-racial and cross-ethnic martial bondedness.

FIGURE 1.2. Korean War Veterans Memorial. Library of Congress, Prints and Photographs Division (photograph by Carol M. Highsmith [LC-DIG-highsm-16419]).

It reminds visitors that the Korean War had been the first waged by de-segregated units, and it alludes to the first Bush and Clinton administrations' post–Cold War use of diversity in the armed forces to present the United States as representative of and containing the world.[93] Like Lee Nicholas's book thirty years earlier, it locates the military in the vanguard of American racial liberalism but refracted through post–civil rights multiculturalism. Standing beside the "United Nations' Curb" that honors all twenty-two nations that fought on the UN side, the multiracial statues send the message that the United States had led a liberal coalition in Korea as a model of racial tolerance. Of course, the nineteen men shown marching on the Washington Mall never would have served together, with de facto segregation having outlasted Truman's executive order barring racial discrimination in the armed forces. But it was a useful fiction. Clinton made much of the statues' diverse faces at the dedication, noting that "the memorial brought to life the courage and sacrifice of those who served in all branches of the Armed Forces from every racial and ethnic group and background in America." Together, he added, "they represent, once more, the enduring American truth: From many we are one."[94]

But the number thirty-eight and declarations of racial liberal ideals could not offset the absence of an ending on the Korean Peninsula. The day after the dedication, journalist Todd Purdum recounted the event on the front page of the *New York Times*. An image of Clinton and Kim admiring one of the statues ran above the fold, and Purdum led with a sentence that contrasted the last decade of the century with the early years of the Cold War: "Under a sweltering sun worlds away from the Cold War combat being commemorated, President Clinton and President Kim Young-sam of South Korea dedicated a new national memorial today intended to assure that the long-gone Korean War does not remain forgotten." The chill of the Korean War had, he suggested, given way to a new era of recognition and reconciliation. But a reader who had turned to page eighteen and read the last sentences of the article would have found a conflicting account of Kim's visit. The morning of the dedication, Clinton and Kim had met at the White House, where, Purdum wrote, "Mr. Clinton assured the South Korean leader that American troops would remain on the Korean peninsula as long as they are wanted."[95] Clinton gave Kim his word that the United States would maintain its force level of some thirty-six thousand military advisers in South Korea. He promised that his government would continue to back Kim's in the Korean War. Then, a few hours later, the two men memorialized that war. Clinton found himself imagining the war's end as he arranged for its continuation. The Korean War gave ideological structure to an empire against imperialism, but that structure could not reconcile the twinned crises of race and war that have haunted the meaning and making of empire ever since. It was remembered as forgotten but wasn't. It couldn't be. It never ended.

CHAPTER TWO

Antiwar Liberalism against Liberal War

A decade after returning from Vietnam, journalist Michael Herr, in his 1977 book *Dispatches*, described the war as mediated by movies about earlier wars. Through a combination of frontline vignettes and abstract musings, he recalled how Americans arrived in Southeast Asia with Hollywood movies on their minds. They began their tours, Herr wrote, "fantasizing privately about other, older wars, Wars I and II, air wars and desert wars and island wars, [and] obscure colonial actions."[1] The soldiers entertained their own big-screen fantasies, because they knew that Hollywood would never make a film about their war. "Vietnam is awkward, everybody knows how awkward, and if people don't even want to hear about it, you know they're not going to pay money to sit in the dark and have it brought up," Herr concluded.[2] Without commercial films to distill the war, he took it as his charge to "make [his] own movies," and he introduced his book as the closest thing to a Vietnam War film. But, of course, moviegoers would later show a willingness, even a desire, to sit in the dark and consume the war as entertainment, and Herr himself would contribute to the box-office successes of Francis Ford Coppola's *Apocalypse Now* (1979) and Stanley Kubrick's *Full Metal Jacket* (1987).[3]

While Herr regarded his writing as a kind of filmmaking, his book, which the *New York Times* declared the best written about the war, shows the distinct influence of Joseph Heller's World War II novel *Catch-22* (1961).[4] Heller's novel about a mismanaged Army Air Forces base on a remote Mediterranean island became a sensation during the Vietnam War when antiwar activists, college students, and draftees embraced it as a model for challenging their government's conduct in Southeast Asia. Herr wrote that Vietnam was "just like" *Catch-22*, which became "a Nam standard because it said that in a war everybody thinks that everybody else is crazy."[5] Like the *MASH* film (1970) and television franchise (1972–83)—a fictional treatment of the Korean War received as "about" the war in Southeast Asia—Americans read *Catch-22* not as analogous to the Vietnam War but *as Vietnam*, transforming it into what the *Washington Post* called "the darkly comic bible of the anti-war generation."[6]

Herr borrowed much from Heller's absurdist novel in treating modern war as a fool's errand in which the state's effort to order the world clashes with the world's inherent disorder. Like Heller before him, Herr admired the soldier's ironic awareness of the tension, within and outside the military, between institutional organization and real-world chaos. After learning of a friend's suicide back in New York and feeling numb to the news, he reflected on the disorienting effect of combat, describing it as an elevated state of consciousness. "Life-as-movie, war-as-(war) movie, war-as-life," he wrote, "a complete process if you got to complete it, a distinct path to travel, but dark and hard, not any easier if you knew that you'd put your own foot on it yourself, deliberately and—most roughly speaking—consciously."[7] Through combat, Herr came to see, and could no longer ignore, the broader absurdities of life and death. Asking why his friend's suicide had not affected him, he concluded that his time in Vietnam had endowed him with a new kind of self-knowledge. He had arrived in Southeast Asia believing that life conformed to a narrative order (life-as-movie) and assuming that war shared that order (war-as-war movie). But he had come to recognize that war stories were nothing more than state-sanctioned inventions and that the struggle to survive (war-as-life) was the one true thing. After two years in Vietnam, he understood war not as a break from normal life but as normal life in its clearest form. His acknowledgment of "war-as-life" draws attention to war as the new normal in his lifetime—the Truman administration having formed the national security state during his generation's childhood—while celebrating it as a "dark and hard" road to enlightenment. Although he wrote *Dispatches* as nonfiction and more than a decade after first reading a World War II novel about a malingering soldier named John Yossarian, Herr set his book in the imagined cultural world of Heller's Vietnam.

No author had a greater influence on the antiwar movement than Heller. Admired by the new left and read out loud at college rallies, his novel found an audience with young Americans who had become disillusioned with their government and its death-dealing in Southeast Asia.

Antiwar slogans referencing the novel's hero—"Yossarian Lives" and "Better Yossarian than Rotarian"—could be found on leaflets, buttons, and graffitied walls from San Francisco to Manhattan. The transformation of *Catch-22* from a World War II novel into a fable about the Vietnam War made Heller an icon of the antiwar movement. At the height of the war in Southeast Asia, he led demonstrations against it, addressing crowds of activists and reading from his satirical novel. News media sought him out as a voice of the movement, based on his newfound fame as the nation's most recognized antiwar writer. A first-time novelist with middling book sales, Heller became a household name as resistance to the war grew.

His absurdist vision of war reached a wide audience of college-age readers during the 1960s and 1970s and served as a model for a future generation of self-identified antiwar novelists and filmmakers, including veterans Tim O'Brien, Oliver Stone, and Gustav Hasford (whose first novel, *The Short-Timers* [1979], formed the basis of *Full Metal Jacket*). As veteran and English professor John Clark Pratt remembered, Heller's novel established "a paradigm" by which soldiers came to know the war in which they were fighting. "*Catch-22* as a novel had influenced our thinking, but Vietnam as Catch-22 itself affected our immediate existence," he recalled.[8] Heller's novel had an outsize influence on how Americans encountered the war. Even those who served in Vietnam couldn't distinguish it from the author's absurdist fiction. While scholars have shown how cultural work surrounding the Vietnam War—from rock music to the Vietnam Veterans Memorial and refugee memoirs—has remade the nation's memory of the war, Heller's World War II novel began forming that memory *before* it escalated.[9]

How does Heller's novel, as the bible of the antiwar movement, challenge the state at war? What makes it an antiwar novel? And what do we mean when we describe a book or movie as antiwar? Scholars and students have for generations noted how *Catch-22* refracts war through the lens of absurdism, observing how it glorifies Yossarian's struggle against the human desire to rationalize an irrational world—an erring desire embodied by the bureaucratic defense establishment he serves. But they haven't considered the rise of absurdism in relation to the Cold War or interrogated how it works, or doesn't work, as a vehicle for denouncing the national security state. When traced to its origins in the anticommunist 1950s, antiwar absurdism may affirm rather than challenge the ideological basis of Cold War militarism in its celebration of liberal freedoms, its condemnation of communism and other illiberal ideologies, and its belief that the free individual can transcend ideological bounds. Heller and the antiwar writers who followed him imbue war with intellectual value as a means of confronting the absurd. While assuming liberal democratic governance to be a universal good, they differentiate the enlightened white American soldier—who achieves a heightened liberal consciousness through the execution of state violence—from the unenlightened decolonizing world in which he finds himself. This kind of antiwar writing stages not the state's violent conversion of illiberal societies to liberal capitalism but the white soldier's intellectual liberation as the model individual of the modern state.

The antiwar story, from Heller's *Catch-22* to Stone's *Platoon* (1986), combats wars fought in the name of liberal freedom with tales of men realizing their own freedom through war. The genre reviles the Cold War state but contributes to the racial regime of defense with which the state has policed the boundaries of legitimate being—defending, above all else, the white soldier's liberal consciousness. It condemns the state but endorses the idea of defense through which it has waged permanent war. This began with Heller's World War II novel, which forms a bridge from the anticommunist intellectual culture of the 1950s, when absurdist thought first achieved wide recognition in the United States, to the antiwar movement of the 1960s. The first English translation of French philosopher Albert Camus's *The Myth of Sisyphus* arrived in American bookstores in 1955, and theater critic Martin Esslin coined the term "theatre of the absurd" in 1960 to describe a new form of dark, comedic drama that he saw as era-defining.[10] Written between 1953 and 1960, Heller's novel internalizes Camus's and Esslin's ideas in its ahistorical focus on the individual soldier's struggle for liberal self-knowledge and its erasure of race and colonialism as driving forces behind modern war.

This absurdist understanding of the Vietnam War endured into the 1980s, when Americans crowded into theaters to see a slew of liberal antiwar movies that included *Platoon, Full Metal Jacket, Hamburger Hill* (1987), *Gardens of Stone* (1987), and *Casualties of War* (1989). Following the white liberal soldier into battle, the antiwar films of the Reagan era reveal the white enlisted man as the defender and defended of the Cold War. He seeks nothing more than to survive his tour—to defend himself—and embodies the values of liberal democratic governance and individual freedoms in his rebellion against the state for which he fights. Independent filmmaker Trinh T. Minh-ha, herself a refugee of the war, noted the contradiction at the heart of liberal antiwar culture, writing in 1991, "Common reactions presented as oppositions to the government's stance often involuntarily met the latter's ultimate objective in its foreign interventions, which was that of defending and promoting a specific life-style."[11] Released amid a wave of Vietnam War movies, her *Surname Viet Given Name Nam* (1989) considers the lives of Vietnamese and Vietnamese American women rather than American men and, by showing how filmmaking is mediated and selectively framed, draws attention to the overwhelming whiteness and fictive endings of Hollywood's liberal return to Vietnam. The antiwar story—showered year after year with acclaim, book awards, and Oscars—has not slowed the march to war. It is an alibi for that march.

The Cold War Rise of the Absurd

Heller may have based his novel on his tour as a bombardier on the Italian front in 1944 and 1945 and embedded himself in the antiwar movement of the 1960s, but his writing reflects the intellectual culture of the 1950s. That decade brought Camus's theories to the attention of American scholars and artists. Although Camus wrote his clearest articulation of the absurd, *The Myth of Sisyphus*, in 1942, his nonfiction writing didn't find an audience in the United States until 1955, when that book made its English-language debut. Two years later, Camus won the Nobel Prize in Literature, and the *New York Times* declared him "the conscience of our era."[12] The liberal West's admiration for Camus stemmed in part from his denunciation of communism in *The Rebel* (1951; translated into English in 1956), which announced his break with Jean-Paul Sartre and the French Marxist left. Camus argued in *The Rebel* that communism validates a form of "State terrorism" and would instigate "the totalitarian revolution of the twentieth century."[13] Seeing communism as a futile struggle to order an unordered world and an excuse for large-scale state violence, he instead urged the individual's unending rebellion against the "inhuman excesses" of "the age of ideologies" through a commitment to moderation.[14] It is no coincidence that Camus became an intellectual star in Cold War America, which was then imagining itself as a nation founded by revolutionaries that had since matured into a moderate world leader acting in the interest of the individual rather than out of an allegiance to doctrine. The Cold War state sought to characterize itself as the most suitable adviser to decolonizing nations; it alone, cold warriors suggested, could defend Asia, Africa, and Latin America from the "inhuman excesses" of communism by integrating them into its own liberal capitalist sphere. This anticommunist agenda explains why the *New York Times* described Camus's writing in 1957 as if it were a tribute to the Constitution of the United States, "consistently proclaim[ing] the dignity of the individual, the necessity of justice and the primacy of freedom."[15]

But Camus offered his most thorough account of the absurd in *The Myth of Sisyphus*, where he defined it as the confrontation between the human need for reason and the world's refusal to conform to reason. He lamented that Western thinkers had negated the absurd by either finding order in consciousness itself (Husserl) or assuming the irrational to have a divine basis that the human mind cannot know (Kierkegaard). Instead, Camus argued that to achieve freedom, a person must embrace the absurd and live "without appeal" to a scale of values.[16] Americans first encountered his absurdist idea of freedom—a freedom realized when individuals liberate themselves from the confines of ideological thought—as the Cold War state set about naturalizing liberalism as non-ideological in contrast to the arch-ideological governments of the Soviet Union and China. The cultural figure of the rebel emerged at this time, cultural historian Leerom Medovoi writes, as the embodiment of "a great American tradition of 'critical non-conformity'" and "the innate resistance of American identity to regimented mass mentalities," including, most of all, communism.[17] Camus's meditations on individual rebellion, liberal freedoms, and the dehumanizing effect of fascism and communism aligned with the Cold War state's belief that liberalism transcended the ideologies that contained human life under illiberal forms of government.

Camus reached the conclusion that modern man must struggle against "the bureaucrats of the mind" (fascists, communists, totalitarianists) who insisted on ordering an unordered world.[18] The individual carries out that struggle, he suggested, by maintaining a constant awareness of the absurd, or what he called "lucidity." Having reached this heightened state of consciousness, enlightened individuals recognize the value of their own survival above all else. "If I convince myself that this life has no other aspect than that of the absurd, if I feel that its whole equilibrium depends on that perpetual opposition between my conscious revolt and the darkness in which it struggles," Camus wrote, "then I must say that what counts is not the best living but the most living."[19] Without a governing scale of values, lucid individuals must struggle to defend themselves from death,

to achieve "the most living." It is not difficult to see how an intellectual
culture that celebrated Camus's ideas would also produce Heller's novel
about a soldier who rebels against the bureaucratic armed forces and,
abandoning the nationalist ideal of self-sacrifice, seeks nothing more than
to survive his tour.[20]

Camus's articulation of absurdist freedom, though written in France
during World War II, lent itself to the racial regime of defense that the
United States wielded in Korea, Southeast Asia, and elsewhere. The
state had, by the time Camus's nonfiction reached American shores, announced liberal humanness as the universal it had militarized the world
to defend, while situating the white soldier as the normative inheritor of
liberal consciousness. The eagerness with which cold warriors took to Camus's ideas reveals how the state's anticommunist wars functioned less to
free former colonies from illiberalism than to enhance white American
soldiers' sense of their own liberal freedoms in relation to the unfreedom of non-Western, non-Christian, communist life. Antiwar writers and
filmmakers imagined the American soldier in Asia as the embodiment
of Camus's absurd man. While they did so to condemn the state's wars
and their effects on the men who carried them out, absurdism, as itself a
liberal idea, may have had the unintended effect of authorizing a liberal
empire.

Camus was also a novelist, of course, and touted fiction as the most effective medium through which to communicate the absurd. Writers heard
him and agreed. In 1960, as Heller revised his World War II novel, the
drama critic Esslin introduced the term "theatre of the absurd" in a *Tulane Drama Review* article in which he described a genre defined by its
recognition of "the irremediable character of the human condition."[21] He
followed that article with a book-length investigation of the genre, *The
Theatre of the Absurd* (1961), that the *Guardian* later hailed as "the most
influential theatrical text of the 1960s" and the *New York Times* called
a book that "certified [Esslin's] position as one of the most influential
critics of the second half of the 20th century."[22] Esslin's model absurdists
were Arthur Adamov, Samuel Beckett, and Eugène Ionesco, all of whom
Heller read and borrowed from in writing for the theater himself in the
late 1960s.[23] Drawing on Camus, Esslin showed how absurdist drama denies its audience the anchor of "accepted values and a rational view of
life" through which it might foresee, and take comfort in, an assumed
resolution.[24] Adamov's, Beckett's, and Ionesco's audiences must reckon
with irresolution, Esslin argued. Without an anchoring scale of values,

they have no choice but to consider what *is* occurring rather than what *will* occur. The characters they encounter conform to Camus's ideal of the lucid individual who liberates herself from social norms; they endure on stage without a belief in the rational or the good to direct their behavior.

While the *New York Times* regarded Camus as "the conscience of [the] era," Esslin saw the art his theories influenced as the truest reflection of modern life. Adamov, Beckett, and Ionesco confront their audiences, he wrote, "with a grotesquely heightened picture of their own world: a world without faith, meaning, and genuine freedom of will," concluding, "In this sense, the Theatre of the Absurd is the true theatre of our time."[25] When American writers seized on the absurd as an instrument for making sense of and challenging the state's growing defense establishment, they substituted the combat zone for the theater as the venue from which a man might achieve an elevated understanding of an irrational world. The absurd had emerged as "the conscience of [the] era" and "the true theatre of [the] time." Then it offered "a paradigm for the Vietnam War."[26]

How *Catch-22* Became a "Nam Standard"

When Simon and Schuster published *Catch-22* in November 1961, the war in Southeast Asia had not yet escalated. Critics and readers received Heller's debut as a new kind of World War II novel. It drew mixed reviews. Some condemned Heller's writing as an "emotional hodgepodge" of disconnected anecdotes—"the book is no novel," one reviewer declared[27]—while others admired its irreverent humor and original, antiheroic take on men at war. But most critics, regardless of their judgment of Heller's writing, measured the book against the two established classics of World War II fiction: Norman Mailer's *The Naked and the Dead* (1948) and James Jones's *From Here to Eternity* (1951). Nelson Algren wrote in the *Nation*, for example, that "*Catch-22* is the strongest repudiation of our civilization, in fiction, to come out of World War II. *The Naked and the Dead* and *From Here to Eternity* are lost within it."[28] So while Heller's readers may have distinguished his novel from Mailer's and Jones's realist fiction, they read it, at first, as the World War II novel that it was.

Heller himself worried about how his writing might be weighed against that of Mailer and Jones, whose big war novels he envied and resented when they came out.[29] The cover art for the 1962 mass-market Dell edition reinforced the novel's association with realist veteran writing, featuring a

stoic airman gazing into the distance with a B-25 bomber readied for take-
off behind him. Neither the Simon and Schuster nor the Dell edition sold
well. Most of the book's readers were concentrated in New York, where
it achieved an aura of cool for its absurdist sketches and unconventional,
fragmented structure. Embracing the novel's cult following as a market-
ing device, Simon and Schuster ran a "happy birthday *Catch-22*" ad in
the *New York Times* in 1962 that hailed its readers as "in *Catch*-lovers."[30]
Heller's novel had found an audience but only among literary-minded
New Yorkers, who read it as an eccentric account of a war that still belonged to Mailer and Jones.

The first-time novelist's fortunes changed as the Vietnam War intensified. As it and the movement against it grew throughout the mid-1960s, so
did sales of *Catch-22*. Once a commercial failure, Heller's novel reached
a new audience with liberal collegians who saw it as a biting criticism of
their government's mass bombing of North Vietnam. Although Heller,
then in his mid-forties, belonged to Mailer's and Jones's generation—they
too had served overseas in World War II and mined their tours for material in their debut novels—critics and readers began associating him less
with his own than with his children's generation. He owed his success to
college-age readers' inclination toward his dark, Camusian sense of humor, a form of comic writing that they could laugh at but that also felt
substantial, serious in its satire. Richard Brickner, a critic for the *New
York Times Book Review*, observed of collegians' reading habits in 1966,
"Much of the college rebellion against what threatens outside (and within)
the campus, takes the form of an interest in plunging satirical humor, as
revealed by the sustained and marked popularity of the anti-military
Catch-22."[31] When columnist Jack Newfield diagnosed the counterculture
in 1967, he located Heller among new left artists like Bob Dylan, Stanley
Kubrick, and Phil Ochs. These "absurd artists," he wrote, "have given the
under-30 generation its . . . prophetic vision—that of comic-apocalyptic
absurdity and chaos."[32] Heller's novel had emerged as the defining book
of the antiwar movement through which "the under-30 generation" imagined and resisted the Vietnam War. That Yossarian serves not in Southeast Asia but on an Italian island during World War II did not discourage
college activists from reading it aloud at antiwar demonstrations.

Heller's writing contributed to an antiwar culture that would later
deliver the television series *MASH* and O'Brien's *Going after Cacciato*
(1978). After having itself been reviewed in relation to earlier World War II
fiction, *Catch-22* became the standard against which book critics assessed

veteran novels about the war in Southeast Asia, most of which, lamented *New York Times* reviewer Christopher Lehmann-Haupt, were stale imitations of Heller's novel, with an "absurdity . . . considerably less than profound" when considered alongside the writer they had tried to emulate.[33] *Catch-22* had become a model for Vietnam War fiction, and that fiction would forge the enduring national memory of the war in the following decades.

Heller's novel attracted more than college readers, though. It was a "Nam standard" among American soldiers, as Herr wrote, who saw themselves in Yossarian's struggle to endure the senselessness of his commander's orders. When assigned to Southeast Asia in 1969, Pratt, a lieutenant colonel in the Air Force, brought one book with him—*Catch-22*—rereading it throughout his tour and taking solace in its absurdist account of military life. He was not alone. Heller's novel allowed him and his comrades, he recalled, to reckon with "the unreal reality" of the Vietnam War by revealing and interrogating its absurdities. "When looking at the 'facts' as well as at the fiction written about the war," Pratt wrote, "to ignore what Heller has written is to obfuscate, misunderstand, and more dangerously, I think, distort what the Vietnam experience really was."[34] He argued that Heller's novel influenced not only Vietnam War fiction—Pratt himself authored a novel, *The Laotian Fragments* (1974), about the air war in Laos—but also the American soldier's understanding of his own tour ("the Vietnam experience") and the historical record of the war itself ("the 'facts'"). The soldier's struggle with the irrationalities of war constituted, he believed, "what the Vietnam experience really was" and how it should be remembered. Pratt's memory of reading Heller in Southeast Asia—and the effect it had on him—offers insight into why vets like Hasford, O'Brien, and Stone later reimagined the war as a white soldier's internal struggle to come to terms with the absurd and then survive his tour. Pratt didn't overstate the degree to which Heller influenced the cultural narrative of the Vietnam War. But the World War II novel introduced its own obfuscations, misunderstandings, and distortions by focusing the younger generation's attention on the soldier's achievement of an elevated liberal consciousness while eliding the racial violence he carries out in policing the boundaries between the human (himself), the deferred human (Asian "friendlies"), and the nonhuman (communists).

Heller, for his part, encouraged the transformation of his book into a "Vietnam War novel." He read his World War II novel to crowds of anti–Vietnam War demonstrators throughout the mid- to late 1960s and backed

antiwar presidential candidate Senator Eugene McCarthy's run for the
White House in 1968, serving on a slate of New York state antiwar del-
egates.[35] He gave countless interviews during this time that focused more
on the war in Southeast Asia than on fiction writing. (Heller wasn't writing
much at the time and didn't publish his second novel until 1974.) In a 1968
New York Times interview, Heller urged American men to resist the draft
so as not to "die for something in which you don't believe."[36] His account
of the historical basis for *Catch-22* also changed as he got more involved
in the antiwar movement. Having once agonized that he could not match
Mailer's and Jones's writing about their shared war, he no longer viewed
himself as an author of World War II fiction at all. "*Catch-22* wasn't really
about World War Two," he later stated. "It was about American society
during the Cold War, during the Korean War, and about the possibility of a
Vietnam."[37] Heller discouraged readings of his novel that assumed he had
based it on his own tour as a bombardier during World War II. He asked
instead that readers recognize it as a Cold War novel that had foreseen
"a Vietnam." In relocating his novel in the Cold War, Heller validated an
ahistorical understanding of Vietnam that fails to account for French colonialism and the anti-Asian racism that informed his own government's
war there. When reframed as a Vietnam War novel, *Catch-22* encouraged
American readers to see the war as a battle between a deracinated American soldier (read white) and the bureaucratic government he serves in a
foreign land defined by its foreignness, a mere venue for America's own
internal crisis. Heller went so far as to declare in 1968 that "the American government is making war on the American people—not on Ho [Chi
Minh]."[38] He imagined a war in which the United States struggled against
itself for national self-knowledge, the enlightened individual versus his
own rigid, unthinking government that was, as Yossarian concludes, "trying to kill [him]" by sending him into combat in the first place.[39]

    The remaking of *Catch-22* as a Vietnam War novel draws attention
to the continuous growth of the defense establishment since Heller returned from World War II in 1945. His refusal to assign *Catch-22* to a
discrete wartime—that it could be "about" World War II, the Korean
War, the Cold War, and the Vietnam War—signals the unsettled cultural
politics of war since the Truman administration dissolved the Department
of War and replaced it with a Department of Defense. But his antiwar
novel, informed by Camus's absurdism, also offers a subtle defense of war
by presenting it as a trial through which the absurd man achieves a new
form of liberal being. In Heller's Vietnam, the white soldier fights not to

defend Southeast Asians from illiberalism but himself from any form of government that might interfere with his liberal freedoms as the defender and defended of liberal humanity. He attains liberal antiwar knowledge through the execution of liberal war. He denounces war as illiberal while elevating it as the path to liberal enlightenment.

Joseph Heller's Grim Secret

The national security state has faced continuous criticism from leftist and liberal writers as it has extended its reach around the world. But when critics and scholars declare a novel or film to be antiwar, they tend not to interrogate why or how it constitutes an indictment of state violence. This term found new life in the 1960s, as resistance to the war in Southeast Asia swelled and entered the national mainstream. As writers from Herr to O'Brien have acknowledged, no book had a greater role in guiding antiwar culture at this time than Heller's World War II novel. Since the antiwar movement emerged in the mid-1960s, readers have celebrated *Catch-22* as a "comic anti-war masterpiece" for its absurdist rendering of bureaucratic disorder in the armed forces and Yossarian's decision to desert rather than conform to the self-interested demands of his commanding officer.[40] But, despite its scathing denunciation of self-interested and bureaucratic decision-making, Heller's absurdist novel aligns on a basic level with the state's liberal agenda for waging war in Southeast Asia. Like the Camusian absurd that informs it, the novel stresses individualism and the virtues of rebelling against ideological thought and rigid forms of government—ideas it shares with the Cold War state, which had declared itself to be defending Vietnam against communism on the same grounds. This alignment of antiwar liberalism with liberal war has been obscured by antiwar writers' narrow focus on the white soldier's rebellion against his own commanders, a focus that allowed Heller's novel—set on the Italian front of World War II—to be read as Vietnam War fiction. The novel introduced a model for future liberal antiwar writing in its account of one soldier's traumatization, enlightenment, and survival in a decontextualized war for national self-knowledge rather than a war that originated in colonialism, in which millions of Southeast Asians lost their lives.

Though fragmented and nonlinear, the novel builds toward a climactic revelation that clarifies Yossarian's disillusionment with war. Stationed on the Italian island of Pianosa, Yossarian, an Army Air Forces bombardier,

resists the orders of the novel's antagonist, Colonel Cathcart, who volun-
teers his men for dangerous missions with the ambition of advancing his
own career. The colonel aims to be a general by war's end. The reader
first meets Yossarian in a sick ward, where he has been feigning illness
for weeks, suffering from what he describes as a "a pain in his liver that
fell just short of jaundice."[41] He hasn't been the same since witnessing the
gruesome death of his crew's teenage tail gunner, Snowden. But Heller
withholds the details of Snowden's death until the novel's conclusion, and
it is in watching the young man die, we learn, that Yossarian achieves a
kind of combat-zone enlightenment.

When German antiaircraft gunners hit their B-25 bomber, wounding
the "childlike" Snowden, Yossarian is the first to reach him. He removes
Snowden's flak suit and watches the man's intestines fall from his stomach
to the floor:

> [Yossarian] felt goose pimples clacking all over him as he gazed down despon-
> dently at the grim secret Snowden had spilled all over the messy floor. It was
> easy to read the message in his entrails. Man was matter, that was Snowden's
> secret. Drop him out a window and he'll fall. Set fire to him and he'll burn. Bury
> him and he'll rot, like other kinds of garbage. The spirit gone, man is garbage.
> That was Snowden's secret. Ripeness was all.[42]

Yossarian's recognition of Snowden's "grim secret" acts as the novel's big
reveal. He sees in the tail gunner's fatal wound the irrational desire to give
life meaning (the nationalist ideologies that motivate modern war) coming into conflict with its inherent meaningless (man as mere matter). The
reader learns that Yossarian's comic schemes to survive his tour all stem
from Snowden's death, after which he commits himself to resisting the
deindividuating conditions of the soldier's life. He doesn't blame the German anti-aircraft gunners for Snowden's death—they are not characters at
all in Heller's intranational war—rather, he blames Colonel Cathcart for
having issued the orders that led to their aerial confrontation with them.
Heller takes the war out of the war novel, transforming it into one man's
struggle against the government he himself serves. While Heller satirizes
a defense establishment governed by double binds and led by self-serving
careerists, drawing attention to some of the institutional arrangements
that have sustained the world's largest military, his fiction also stages combat as an environment of elevated liberal consciousness in which the white
Western soldier (Yossarian) might achieve new insight into the human

condition (Snowden's "grim secret"). Heller's novel reflects—in the act of denouncing—the stated agenda of national defense since the late 1940s: to model and defend liberal humanity from the unfree societies the state has deemed communist, totalitarian, criminal, terrorist, and insurgent.

This confusion between criticism and consent emerges from the contradictions inherent in the idea of defense. Throughout the war in Southeast Asia, officials sought to define their investment in the region as an effort to deliver freedom to Vietnamese. But the liberal stories told in Heller's novel and Herr's nonfiction reveal the white soldier to be both the giver and receiver of that freedom. The idea of Western militaries as agents of freedom in Asia, critical refugee studies scholar Mimi Nguyen argues, founds a debt relation between refugees and the liberal state that disallows them from inhabiting liberal consciousness in full, from settling the debt of a "conferred" freedom. "In the carving out and delimiting of areas of social existence and belonging, the gift of freedom is normative, as a means of making other ways of being in the world into spaces commensurate or incommensurate, comparable and incomparable, with the rule of liberalism," Nguyen writes.[43] The gift of freedom offers cover for the racial regime of defense through which the state distances the deferred human (the refugee "given" freedom) and the nonhuman (the "unsaved") from full liberal being (the white solider). The antiwar writing of Heller, Herr, and others shows the white American man to be the giver and receiver of the gift of freedom who accrues no debt as its lender and borrower. The contradictions of liberal antiwar writing—that it absolves what it alleges to indict—brings to light the race-making function of liberal war in its valuation of whiteness as the normative embodiment of liberal consciousness and as a condition for the execution of legitimate violence.

But Heller's novel imagines the white soldier as the model individual of the liberal state *because of his outsiderness*. It is his individual rebellion against the regimented order of the armed forces—his decision to refuse Colonel Cathcart's directives and then desert to Sweden—that locates him within the liberal idea of national defense. Heller stressed in interviews that he didn't conceive of Yossarian as, like himself, Jewish but rather as "somebody who would seem to be *out*side the culture in every way—ethnically as well as others." He chose the name Yossarian because he believed it to be an Assyrian name (it is not) and understood Assyrians to be "extinct" (they are not). "Now, because America is a melting pot, there are huge concentrations of just about every other kind of nationality," he told an interviewer in 1962, when asked about his hero's ethnic background. "I didn't want to give him a Jewish name, I didn't want to give him an Irish name, I didn't want to symbolize the white Protestant—but somebody who was almost a *new* man. . . . my purpose in doing so was to get an outsider, a man who was *intrinsically* an outsider."[44] He wanted Yossarian to be the image of the American "melting pot," while also casting him as an outsider to national culture.[45] Heller suggested in this and other interviews that American culture is defined by an outsider ethos as a multiracial nation of revolutionaries and nonconformists. But the idea of the United States as "*intrinsically* an outsider" in the world was also mobilized by government officials to represent the United States as a model for decolonizing nations like Vietnam and to distance its conduct in Asia from that of earlier colonial actors. Yossarian, if against Heller's intentions, embodies the liberal antiracism that the Cold War state used to wage defense in Korea, Southeast Asia, and elsewhere.[46]

Yossarian's outsiderness acts as both a form of racial identification and a claim to deracination. He is an intrinsic ethnic outsider without an ethnic background. While Heller stated that he did not intend for his hero "to symbolize the white Protestant," his remarks overlook the fact that, in the United States, to be undifferentiated by race is to be assumed white. That deracinated whiteness, when read in the context of the Vietnam War, has the effect of concealing the service of black, Latino, and American Indian soldiers—who were drafted at higher rates and into more dangerous combat roles than their white comrades—and the far greater losses suffered by Southeast Asians in a war that killed and refugeed millions. This simultaneous racialization and deracination makes Yossarian an outsider to the empire of defense while all the while serving as its agent. If defense functions as an instrument of racialization by which the liberal state reinforces and creates hierarchies of human value, then Yossarian manages to straddle the divide between racial valuation and devaluation. He doles out state violence as an Air Force bombardier while also situating himself and other white men as the foremost victims of their own violence. Heller's antiwar novel distracts from the broader race-making idea of defense by reframing it as an internal conflict in which the white soldier acts as aggressor and victim, defender and defended, redeemer and redeemed. Snowden's death and Yossarian's trauma make them the sufferers of wartime loss—loss blamed on their commanding officer, Colonel Cathcart, and the larger defense establishment they serve. This internalization of war as a struggle for self-knowledge (to discover Snowden's "grim secret") and against institutional deindividuation (to refuse Colonel Cathcart's self-interested orders) reemerges in Vietnam War fiction, from Herr's nonfiction to O'Brien's novels and short fiction and Stone's movies. Heller's World War II novel gave the next generation of liberal antiwar writers a model for imagining the white soldier in Southeast Asia as a knowing insider and rebellious outsider waging a war with himself and his government in an otherwise uninhabited land.

Although Heller wished to write his hero as unraced, Yossarian stages his rebellion through an enactment of blackness. Having achieved lucid knowledge in witnessing Snowden's death, Yossarian finds his foil in "the soldier in white"—a wounded, voiceless man encased in a head-to-toe cast and consigned to the sick ward with Yossarian and his fellow malingerers. Nurse Cramer checks the man's vital signs on her morning and afternoon rounds. One afternoon, she discovers that the soldier in white has died. The other men conclude that "the Texan"—a good-natured but disliked resident of the ward—had "killed him because he was a nigger." The Texan defends himself by reminding them that the Air Force, segregated during World War II, "don't allow niggers in here." He adds, "They got a special place for niggers."[47] This dialog is one of the rare instances in which Heller's novel addresses race in the armed forces. The soldier in white, who frightens the other men, signifies the mandated whiteness of their segregated base, a whiteness that Heller associates with a kind of unfree conformism against which his enlightened hero must rebel. Yossarian models the ethic of liberal antiracism as a white man who has internalized a rebelliousness he correlates with an abstracted blackness—in the total absence of black characters. Through a disembodied blackness, Yossarian sheds his whiteness. He assumes the status of raced outsider, a status that allows him to disacknowledge his role in conducting bombing runs on his government's behalf. Unlike the soldier in white, he refuses to conform to the rigid order of the Air Force and survives to act as its critic. Yossarian's desire to distance himself from state violence by associating himself with blackness suggests how whiteness has continued to function as a condition of legitimate violence since World War II. But Heller's novel also obscures the whiteness of war in its deracinated abstraction of blackness as something enacted rather than lived.[48]

The soldier in white demonstrates how the absurdist antiwar novel imagines war as an internal struggle among Americans. After first accusing the Texan of killing the soldier in white, Yossarian later concludes that it was Nurse Cramer who, in recording the man's death, had "murdered" him. While unfounded, of course, Yossarian's allegation draws attention to the novel's focus on intranational violence. All deaths are suffered by Americans and caused by, or blamed on, Americans. The most dramatic instance of American-on-American violence unfolds after mess officer Milo Minderbinder, who founds an international black-market "syndicate" in which "everybody has a share," strikes a deal with the German air force to bomb his own base. His commanding officers are horrified until Milo shows them his sizeable returns, after which they allow him to continue growing his business. "Frankly," Milo tells them, "I'd like to see the government get out of war altogether and leave the whole field to private industry."[49]

Milo's business deal with the Germans may be Heller's shrewdest challenge to the defense establishment, revealing how it had, since its formation in the late 1940s, facilitated war industries that demanded war rather than war that necessitated war industries. But it also highlights the limits of Heller's absurdist novel as a model for criticizing the war in Southeast Asia. When writers dramatize war as an internal struggle, they contribute to Americans' willful forgetting of the non-American lives lost and refugeed in its wars in Asia, Africa, and the Americas. When they imagine combat as a means for the white soldier to achieve a heightened sense of liberal being and renounce illiberal societies—from communists and drug traffickers to human rights abusers and terrorists—their writing's antiwar edge dulls. Yossarian, the model "antihero," plays the same role as the war hero once did: he gives Americans a vehicle for imagining their relation to the state and its ideological orientation to the rest of the world. Forming "a paradigm for the Vietnam War," Heller's novel affected how American soldiers understood their own tours of Southeast Asia. When those soldiers emerged as the war's foremost chroniclers in the 1980s, they continued to see it through the absurdities of Heller's Vietnam.

Not Coming to Terms in Hollywood's Return to Vietnam

Michael Herr assumed in 1977 that Hollywood would never make a movie about the "awkward" war in Southeast Asia. But a decade later it became a box-office draw. After years of lukewarm interest from studios, Oliver Stone made his first Vietnam War film, *Platoon*, in 1986. To the amazement of studio executives, it brought in more than a hundred million dollars in ticket sales and went on to win the Academy Award for Best Picture. The commercial success of Stone's mid-budget film fueled a boom in Vietnam War movies that included *Full Metal Jacket* (1987), *Hamburger Hill* (1987), *Gardens of Stone* (1987), *Good Morning, Vietnam* (1987), *Off Limits* (1988), *Bat*21* (1988), *84 Charlie MoPic* (1989), *In Country* (1989), and *Casualties of War* (1989). Stone himself directed two more Vietnam War films, *Born on the Fourth of July* (1989) and *Heaven and Earth* (1993). "Vietnam chic"—that was what Philip Caputo, author of the memoir *A Rumor of War* (1977), called the surge of movies and books about the war in 1987. How, he asked, had something so "unfashionable in 1977" become so "wildly fashionable" ten years later?[50] In that time, President Ronald Reagan had re-escalated the Cold War, invading Grenada and sending armed forces to El Salvador, Lebanon, and Libya, keeping the promise he made in his 1980 campaign to "restore the margin of safety" through rearmament.[51] Reagan associated himself with the conservative action-adventure films of Chuck Norris and Sylvester Stallone. In 1985, a live mic caught the president praising Stallone's *Rambo: First Blood Part II* and suggesting that he had learned a thing or two about how to handle a hostage crisis from the action hero. "Boy, after seeing *Rambo* last night, I know what to do the next time this happens," he said, minutes before addressing the nation from the White House.[52] The president was later photographed on Air Force One holding a bumper sticker reading "Rambo is a Republican." But, for all of Reagan's promotion of the conservative Rambo franchise, his hawkish policies also benefited from the liberal Vietnam War films of Stone and others, which treat the war as an unfortunate but, for the young white solider, elucidating encounter with an otherworld called Vietnam.

The new liberal Vietnam War movies were among the first written and directed by veterans, including James Carabatsos, Patrick Sheane Duncan, David Rabe, and Stone, men who, like John Clark Pratt, had gone to war with Heller's absurdist novel on their minds and sometimes in their rucksacks. Their films are less satirical and more melodramatic than *Catch-22*. But they retain the Camusian self-reckoning of Heller's novel, with the soldier confronting the absurd in combat and then committing himself to surviving his tour, to defending his own life. Their movies, all critical darlings, embrace Heller's antiwar liberalism in their focus on the ontological struggle of a white American man who identifies the confines of ideological thought, gains new insight into his own liberal being, and models a limited antiracism organized around a white norm. Critics celebrated the films as signaling the nation's coming-to-terms with its war in Southeast Asia. Hal Hinson, the *Washington Post* film critic, wrote in

1987, "What the current emergence of the war on film signifies, perhaps, is the beginning of a new phase in the Vietnam experience—the end of a period of mourning and the beginning of a real rehabilitation."[53] The new veteran-filmmakers may have allowed audiences to come to terms with the war, but they achieved that resolution not through an interrogation of the nation's war culture but through the erasure of Southeast Asian lives and American soldiers of color.

Black, Latino, and American Indian soldiers served and died at higher rates than white servicemen in Southeast Asia. But most Vietnam War movies star a middle-class white enlistee, an alien among his working-class comrades. *Platoon*, based on Stone's own tour in Vietnam—after he, a stockbroker's son, left Yale University short of graduation—follows well-heeled recruit Chris Taylor (Charlie Sheen) as he struggles to find his footing in a working-class military culture as foreign to him as Vietnam. Chris arrives "somewhere near the Cambodian border" in late 1967 and, over the course of two hours, matures from naive recruit to enlightened veteran.[54] Chris documents his own growth through a series of self-narrated letters to his grandmother. He tells her that he had enlisted to "do my share for my country" but now sees the error in his uncritical nationalism. "Someone once wrote hell is the impossibility of reason," he reflects. "That's what this place feels like, hell." While lacking Heller's dark humor, Stone's movie reflects the absurdism of his antiwar satire. Through combat, Chris comes to recognize the senselessness of his government's effort to order an unordered world ("the impossibility of reason") and discards the scale of values to which he had once subscribed (to "do my share for my country"). The war's origins, stakes, and destruction of Southeast Asian life fade to the background as the white American recruit cultivates new self-knowledge as an agent of liberal defense. Subordinating the role of Vietnamese, American soldiers of color, and women—the voiceless addressees of Chris's letters—Stone's antiwar film condemns the effects of combat on the white American man while also revering the wisdom it grants him.

But it is hard to miss the movie's diverse cast, which includes black and Latino characters who afford Chris's wartime education in liberal antiracism. Stone's hero had enlisted to rebel against the bourgeois social world of his mother and father. His parents had wanted him, he tells his grandmother, "to be just like them: respectable, hard-working, a little house, a family." Instead, he left college and enlisted in the army at the height of the war. As the antithesis to his own middle-class background, Chris fetishizes his working-class, black, and Latino comrades, describing them as "the unwanted" and admiring their genuineness. "Maybe I've finally found it way down here in the mud," he writes. "Maybe from down here I can start up again, be something I can be proud of without having to fake it, be a fake human being. Maybe I can see something I don't yet see or learn something I don't yet know." The film suggests that war has an educational value for the sheltered white middle-class teenager, who, as a soldier, gets to know men from different racial and class backgrounds.

The Vietnam War movies of the 1980s reimagined the armed forces as a substitute for a multicultural college education. Chris reflects the anti-redistributive white racial liberalism of post–civil rights higher education.[55] He sees his serving alongside soldiers of color as a lesson in antiracism. But he doesn't consider the material conditions that made black and Latino men more vulnerable to the draft than he, a white volunteer, was. Rather, he sees war as a chance to "learn something [he doesn't] yet know" from the multicultural institution. Stone's film acknowledges the inordinate burden shouldered by working-class soldiers of color during the Vietnam War while containing that burden within a white hero's liberal enlightenment. Stone's movie and the movies that followed it situate the white soldier as a student of multicultural racial knowledge as well as a victim of his own racial violence. The liberal war film restages acts of American violence against Southeast Asian civilians, including the My Lai massacre (*Platoon*) and the rape and murder of Phan Thi Mao (*Casualties of War*), but treats the American soldier rather than the Vietnamese civilian as the victim of his own brutal acts.

Stone's movie includes just one scene, based on the My Lai massacre, in which Southeast Asian characters are more than shadows on the other end of a firefight, but they serve as a mere externalization of the white soldier's internal struggle. Chris, as he settles into army life, finds himself caught between two charismatic father figures, the liberal, meditative sergeant Elias (Willem Dafoe) and the brutal, war-hardened staff sergeant Barnes (Tom Berenger). On a scouting assignment, a concealed bomb kills two men, and a third is found tied to a tree, his throat slit. With Elias absent, Barnes leads the men into a neighboring village where they discover a cache of guns and food, suggesting that the village may be under the control of the National Liberation Front (Viet Cong). Distraught, the men begin murdering the unarmed civilian villagers. Under Barnes's influence, Chris himself tortures a one-legged man (Romy Sevilla) by shooting at his foot and telling him to "dance, motherfucker." The camera focuses on Chris's face as he torments the villager, and he cries as he registers his

FIGURE 2.1. *Platoon* (1986).

own ruthlessness. Looking on, Bunny (Kevin Dillon) calls Chris a "fucking pussy" and then beats the one-legged man to death with the butt of his
rifle. Chris recoils as the man's blood strikes his face. The audience must
visualize the man's death—a murder that unfolds off-screen—through
the blood on Chris's cheek and helmet. The white American's trauma at
witnessing his own wickedness subsumes the Vietnamese's trauma of suffering it. Considering the English-language audience and lack of subtitles,
the film marginalizes the Vietnamese villagers' words as extraneous to
the white soldier's coming-to-terms with his own acts of violence in a war
in which he is aggressor and victim, fighting for his own liberal being in
Southeast Asia.

    Critics commended Stone's film as a sign of the nation's readiness to, at
last, acknowledge its moral failures in the war. Journalist David Halberstam declared in a 1987 review that *Platoon* had struck "an enormous blow
for reality" by showing the foreignness of Americans in Vietnam. "It is
we, not those whom we would track, who are the aliens," he wrote of the
film. "It is the Americans, despite their immense firepower, who are always surrounded, either by the terrain, or by the enemy, or by the enemy
using the terrain."[56] Halberstam, a self-identified antiwar writer, wanted
to underscore that the United States didn't belong in Vietnam, that American soldiers were "aliens" there. But his review reinforced the film's narrow focus on the alienation of the white soldier and the containment of

Southeast Asian life within his struggle. He described Vietnamese as an ethereal extension of the land, conflating "the enemy" with "the terrain." Americans waged war in Vietnam, it seems, with a brutal environment and themselves, not with Vietnamese.

The coming-to-terms that Halberstam identified necessitated that the suffering of Southeast Asian bodies be transferred to American bodies, from the unarmed Vietnamese civilian to Chris. It assumed the liberal soldier's absurd reckoning to be the central drama of the Vietnam War. Chris's recognition of his transgression in torturing the Vietnamese villager illustrates what ethnic studies scholar Cathy Schlund-Vials terms the "Cold War apologetics" of white liberal culture, which she describes as "an expression of remorse and an excuse for problematic action" couched in "an ostensibly universal humanism and humanitarianism."[57] In restaging the My Lai massacre, Stone's film communicates, through Chris's grimacing face, remorse for his sins and foregrounds his identification with the Vietnamese civilian. But it also stresses the degree to which Chris's actions were determined by a combat environment of inhumane violence and redeems its hero as he matures into liberal consciousness, a maturation achieved through the execution of state violence against, rather than in defense of, Vietnamese. Chris has no higher calling than defending himself and his hard-won liberal knowledge, and that belief reflects the idea of defense with which his government authorized itself to wage war in Southeast Asia. Chris, the antiwar warrior, a seeming critic of the state, may be its most valuable ideological agent.

Stone's film translates war into an internal struggle for individual (Chris) and national (Chris as the nation) self-knowledge, a struggle it externalizes in the conflict between Elias and Barnes. As Barnes threatens to kill a village girl, Elias arrives, averting a massacre, and brawls with the ruthless staff sergeant in front of their men. Stone envisioned their fight as a clash of giants. His original stage directions read, "They struggle in the dust, two titans, their faces equally consumed with rage, clawing, spitting, punching, kicking, pounding each other's skulls in the dirt. . . . Most of the men seem to be pulling for Barnes—Chris just watching, neutral."[58] Chris witnesses his own crisis of self embodied in his two warring father figures, the liberal Elias versus the authoritarian Barnes. An admission of American guilt in murdering civilians at My Lai turns into a struggle *between* Americans. The Vietnamese villagers vanish from sight as the two American "titans" wrestle in the dirt.

After Barnes kills Elias and Chris kills Barnes—like Heller, Stone transforms war into an intranational struggle—Chris, having realized the

absurd wisdom of combat, leaves Vietnam on a didactic note. Wounded in
the New Year's Day Battle of 1968, he is airlifted out of Vietnam. Looking
down at the dense forest below, he reflects in a voiceover,

> I think now, looking back, we did not fight the enemy. We fought ourselves, and
> the enemy was in us. The war is over for me now, but it will always be there, the
> rest of my days. As I am sure Elias will be, fighting with Barnes for . . . posses-
> sion of my soul. There are times since I have felt like the child born of those two
> fathers. But be that as it may, those of us who did make it have an obligation to
> build again, to teach to others what we know.

This concluding voiceover is directed to the audience rather than his grandmother and assumes the wisdom of hindsight, as if a middle-aged Chris is
looking back on his tour from 1986. He remembers the war as a conflict
among Americans ("we fought ourselves") and within himself (Elias and
Barnes fighting for "possession of my soul"). Chris concludes that the war
was never about Vietnam and Vietnamese but rather a struggle to define
America's role in the world and the setting for his own self-searching as
a young man. Wearing a red bandana as Elias had and advocating a national moral education, Chris has embraced the humane sergeant's liberal
ethic. The film begins with Chris deboarding in Southeast Asia and struggling to see through the wind on the tarmac, and it ends with him looking out across Vietnam, with sunlight in all directions, suggesting that he
has matured from a sightless recruit to a sighted veteran. But Chris has
learned nothing about the country below him and shows no awareness of
why or how the United States had waged a decades-long war in Southeast
Asia. This lack of historical knowledge makes it difficult to see what Chris
intends "to teach to others" as a veteran. But, with the erasure of Southeast Asians and American soldiers of color, the white soldier's account
of the war figures as universal. The lesson Chris (and Stone's film) has to
teach is that war is hard, uncontrollable, unknowable, and, for the white
liberal man, transformative.

Citing their firsthand knowledge of Vietnam, the veteran-filmmakers of
the 1980s stressed the realism of their antiwar movies. Stone gave a series
of interviews in 1986 and 1987 in which he conflated his own tour with
that of his hero, Chris. His ambition in writing the film, he told the *New
York Times* in 1986, was to "make a document of a time and place" so that
Americans who didn't serve could know "what it was like to be there."[59]
News media took him at his word. *Time* featured Berenger, Dafoe, and

Sheen on the cover of a 1987 issue with the headline "*Platoon*: Vietnam as It Really Was." Stone encouraged moviegoers to see his film not as a credible fiction about the Vietnam War but *as Vietnam*. He wanted them to believe that they could know "what it was like to be there" for the cost of admission.

Michael Herr also regarded the film he wrote with Stanley Kubrick and Gustav Hasford, *Full Metal Jacket*, as a window onto the "real" Vietnam War. He and Kubrick decided, Herr recalled in 1987, that "the audience would not be told how to watch this movie." Instead, they set out to make a film "non-explicit in its meaning" and "minimal in expression."[60] Like Stone, they envisioned themselves as documentarians and believed that such "non-explicit" realism was in itself an antiwar statement. But, while moviegoers might "not be told how to watch" it, the movie does tell them through whom to encounter it. It follows white marine recruit James "Joker" Davis (Matthew Modine) as he endures basic training at Parris Island, South Carolina, in 1967 and then serves in Vietnam during the Battle of Hue in 1968. Kubrick's film, though more irreverent than Stone's melodrama, also tells of a white, middle-class soldier's maturation from innocence to alienation to absurd enlightenment.

The first hour of the film, set at basic training, establishes the marines as the social microcosm through which the audience will encounter Southeast Asia in the second hour. At Parris Island, drill instructor Hartman (R. Lee Ermey) introduces himself to the new recruits. With the men standing at attention in front of their bunks, he strides across the barracks. Glancing at a black recruit, Hartman informs the men that in the marines they will not be differentiated by race. "There is no racial bigotry here," he tells them. "I do not look down on niggers, kikes, wops, or greasers. Here you are all equally worthless." Hartman then addresses a second black recruit whom he nicknames "Snowball" and informs him, "There's one thing that you won't like, Private Snowball. They don't serve fried chicken and watermelon on a daily basis in my mess hall."[61] Hartman's deracinated racism is meant to suggest that, as marines, the recruits will not be discriminated against based on their race due to a culture of universal discrimination in which all men are "niggers, kikes, wops, [and] greasers." He insists that their status as marines will now subsume all other identities through which they may have understood themselves and others in their civilian lives. The men are all, as marine recruits, "equally worthless." The racial slurs Hartman hurls at Snowball are not, as he sees it, directed at a black man but rather at a deracinated marine. The drill instructor's account of race in the military clarifies how the Vietnam War movies of the late 1980s could situate their white middle-class heroes as deracinated universals and racialized outsiders. They act as "unraced" agents of the state, broken down and then rebuilt as soldiers, marines, sailors, and airmen. But they also assume a sense of outsiderness, alienated from a nation divided over the war in which they are serving—and in which they fight alongside working-class black, Latino, and American Indian recruits without the resources to obtain draft deferments. Although soldiers of color have limited roles on-screen, they reinforce the sense of raced outsiderness that these films assign to their white characters. Hartman directs his racist diatribe at two black recruits, but he also addresses it to the "equally worthless" white hero whose alienation masks how the film centers whiteness as the norm around which basic training is organized.

Before the recruits ever set foot in Southeast Asia, the film casts them as the aggressors and victims of the war. Throughout basic training, Hartman abuses an overweight recruit named Leonard "Pyle" Lawrence (Vincent D'Onofrio), who lags behind the other recruits in conditioning exercises and fails to follow the drill instructor's orders. Leonard shows talent as a marksman, but he becomes withdrawn as the other recruits, following Hartman's lead, abuse him. His bunkmate, Joker, worries about Leonard's mental well-being after witnessing him talk to his rifle in the barracks. On their last night at Parris Island, Joker, having drawn "fire watch," finds Leonard in the latrine loading his M14 with live ammunition. When Hartman hears them and enters, Leonard shoots the drill instructor and himself. The film then cuts to Vietnam. So before the action ever moves to Southeast Asia, the white marine has been identified as the agent and receiver of state violence, making Vietnamese characters— and the war itself—all but redundant. The Vietnam War is an American suicide. Through Hartman's character, Kubrick's film satirizes the racism, sexism, and authoritarianism of the marines at its worst. It seems to ask, Do we want men trained by Hartman armed and stationed around the world? But it also obscures the racial regime governing the war by focusing inward on the struggles of an individual marine rather than outward on the state's role in dividing humanity in the act of defending it. Like Stone's film, it stages the conflict among and within American men as a war-in-miniature through which the nation might come to terms with the Vietnam War without having to reckon with the millions of Southeast Asians killed so that the white soldier could find himself.

Kubrick's film includes almost no Vietnamese characters. Other than two sex workers who solicit the marines in Saigon and Hue, the one non-American character is a Vietnamese markswoman (Ngoc Le) who, in the aftermath of the Battle of Hue, takes out half of Joker's unit from the roof of a burned-out building. Infuriated, the marines enter the building and shoot the Vietnamese woman. As she bleeds to death on the floor, she urges the men to kill her rather than leave her to die a slow death. But the unit's commander, Animal Mother (Adam Baldwin), tells the men to move out. When Joker insists that they "can't just leave her here," Animal Mother agrees, on the condition that Joker be the one to "waste her." Joker stares at the woman for a long time before firing his handgun. Her death isn't shown; instead, the camera focuses for more than a minute on Joker's face as his comrades congratulate him: "Hardcore, man. Fucking hardcore." Herr cited Carl Jung's idea of the shadow—that a person's mind contains an irrational subconscious that informs his or her behavior and can be recognized through self-individuation—as an influence on his and Kubrick's writing, calling war "the ultimate field of Shadow-activity, where all of [the shadow's] other activities lead you."[62] Herr saw war as a manifestation of the irrational subconscious and distinguishes it as a singular encounter with the shadow. When he shoots the Vietnamese woman, Joker confronts the shadow—or what Camus calls the absurd, what Heller terms Snowden's "grim secret," and what Stone describes as "the impossibility of reason." After killing her, he bears what his comrades revere as "the thousand-yard stare" of a man who has seen combat. Like the one-legged villager's murder in Stone's film, the markswoman's death functions as an enlightening event for the white soldier. He sees, in the act of killing, how the Cold War state has endangered his liberal freedoms by forcing him to conform to its scale of values. The movie reassigns the blame for the Vietnamese woman's death to the government that trained him to kill and sent him to war. It made him do it. Critics received *Full Metal Jacket* as an antiwar film because it shows American marines committing acts of monstrous violence against Southeast Asian civilians. Kubrick's film is "not an attempt to work through the experience [of the war] and come to some peace with it," Hinson wrote, but rather "an honest description of it," calling it the director's "the-white-race-is-the-cancer-of-the-world movie."[63] But Kubrick's film does "work through" the war by chronicling the white soldier's recognition of his basest instincts—a recognition reached through the absurdities of combat—and the wisdom attained through it.

The release of Stone's and Kubrick's antiwar films coincided with an alleged crisis of white masculine values as the Reagan administration

FIGURE 2.2. *Full Metal Jacket* (1987).

nurtured a sense of alienation among white working-class men who faced
new economic vulnerabilities due to the stagnation of real wages, the
decline of American manufacturing, challenges to organized labor, and
cuts in social welfare benefits.[64] But the president and his allies blamed
the worsening conditions of the white working class not on his administration's policies, of course, but on the civil rights, feminist, and antiwar movements that had challenged the nation's structural investment in
whiteness. He and conservative intellectuals attacked the modest redis-
tributive racial reforms of the civil rights era as a form of "reverse racism" against white men. This articulation of white grievance was imagined
through the cultural figure of the alienated white Vietnam vet, who had
risked his life, Reagan asserted, "in a war our government [was] afraid
to let [him] win."[65] Made to serve in a mismanaged, losing war effort and
abused by Hartman and their commanding officers in Vietnam, Kubrick's
white characters have been abandoned by their government in Southeast
Asia. But, in assuming the raced outsiderness of their comrades of color,
they suggest an anti-redistributive liberal antiracist knowledge of black,
Latino, American Indian, and Vietnamese life. Moviegoers are invited to
come to terms with the Vietnam War through a recognition of white innocence, grievance, and liberal antiracism that recenters and rehabilitates
the nation's aggrieved white men.[66]

   White soldiers and veterans have suffered and died by the thousands
in America's modern wars, and writers and filmmakers should document

that loss—as Heller, Herr, Kubrick, and Stone have. But the absurdist antiwar narrative that Heller introduced in 1961 has focused on the alienation, traumatization, and enlightenment of the white soldier to the exclusion of stories of American soldiers of color, Vietnamese, Cambodians, Laotians, and those living in other countries that the United States has invaded in the name of defense. This has allowed Americans to set aside the larger histories, human costs, and racial structure of liberal war. For more than five decades, Heller biographer Tracy Daugherty acknowledges, it has been the "'next war' that *Catch-22* was about, which is why it came to be read, in the sixties, as a Vietnam book and why it seems to readers today prescient about the war on terror."[67] The novel's continued relevance indicates how routine war has been since a young Joseph Heller returned from the Italian front in 1945. But its evolution from a World War II novel to a "Vietnam book" to a fiction "prescient about the war on terror" also draws attention to its ahistorical account of war as one man's struggle for survival and the achievement of liberal consciousness. This is a narrow kind of war story that has resurfaced throughout the late-twentieth and twenty-first centuries—from *Platoon* and *Full Metal Jacket* to Kathryn Bigelow's Best Picture–winning *The Hurt Locker* (2008) and Phil Klay's National Book Award–winning *Redeployment* (2014)—and has been treated as an indictment of war by audiences. How does a writer resist liberal war through an antiwar discourse founded on liberalism? What other forms might antiwar culture take?

Whiteness by Other Means

The new veteran-filmmakers of the 1980s invited moviegoers to come to terms with the Vietnam War through stories of alienated white men. Their films treat Vietnamese women as embodiments of their nation and its suffering and then reassign that suffering to the white soldier who caused it. Visual culture scholar Sylvia Chong argues that the news media of the 1960s and 1970s, because of the informal censoring of their visual content, used images of Southeast Asian death and disfigurement as stand-ins for American casualties. But over the course of the late 1970s and 1980s, the wounded white vet emerged as the new visual icon of the war, subsuming Southeast Asian suffering, Chong writes, "just as the racial formation of Asian Americans gains political traction."[68] While Stone's and Kubrick's films made millions in ticket sales and garnered Academy

Awards, Southeast Asian American writers and filmmakers were also revisiting the war.

Trinh T. Minh-ha made her third film, *Surname Viet Given Name Nam*
(1989), about Southeast Asian women in Vietnam and America with
an ironic nod to Hollywood's Vietnam War boom. Whereas Stone's and
Kubrick's movies allege to offer unmediated knowledge of the war—
communicating "what it was like to be there," in Stone's words—Trinh's
film denaturalizes the truth claims of the medium by unsettling acts of linguistic and culture translation. The first half of the film features Vietnamese American women recreating interviews first conducted in Vietnam by
Mai Thu Van for her French-language book *Vietnam: Un peuple, des voix*
(1983). The women are amateur actors Trinh met in California. Delivered
in accented English, the restaged interviews are twice translated, from
Vietnamese into French and then from French into English. The second half of the film then turns to "real" interviews with the Vietnamese
American actors. The film is intercut with stock footage of Vietnam and
home videos of social gatherings in California, scored with folk songs, and
overlaid with irregular English subtitles. *Surname Viet Given Name Nam*
challenges both Vietnam's and America's representation of Vietnamese
women as heroes and victims by negating filmic claims to direct knowledge and decentering stories of white vets.

Trinh's film reveals how the idea of defense creates racial and gender
hierarchies of human value through the women's translated words and the
staged reenactment of those words. Delivering an English translation of
a 1982 interview given by Vietnamese health technician Thu Van, actor
Khien Lai describes how, in casting women as heroic and virtuous, Vietnam has transformed them into "ghost women, with no humanity." Why,
she asks, "don't we want to admit that these women are tired of seeing
their children exposed to war, deprivations, epidemics, and diseases? The
very idea of heroism is monstrous!" She insists instead that we acknowledge the difference between "the image of the woman" and "her reality."[69]
While Thu Van's translated words address the condition of women in 1982
Vietnam, they also, when delivered by Vietnamese American Khien Lai,
call attention to American media's one-dimensional image of Vietnamese
women as embodiments of suffering and as a human background to the
white soldier's reckoning with his own acts of callousness. Trinh accentu-
ates the communist and liberal states' negation of the Vietnamese woman's
humanness by shifting the camera angle and distance throughout the re-
enacted interviews, forcing her audience to acknowledge the documentar-

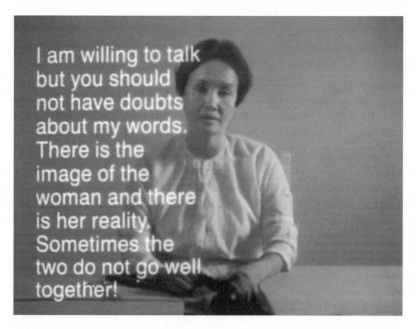

FIGURE 2.3. *Surname Viet Given Name Nam* (1989).

ian's role in framing the interviewee and rendering her knowable. Instead of using a conventional "talking heads" interview format, Trinh moves the shot back and forth between Thu Van's face, hands, and feet. She includes large, misaligned subtitles that sometimes crowd out Thu Van and force the audience to choose between listening and reading. The intentional staginess of the interview unsettles how the medium has conditioned viewers to assume unmediated knowledge of women of color's lives.[70]

In the second half of the film, Trinh reflects on her own filmmaking method while locating it in and against American cultural knowledge about the Vietnam War. Following an interview with actor Tran Thi Bich Yen, who notes in Vietnamese how Americans "look at Vietnam with their own eyes" in a "black-and-white, clear-cut manner," Trinh reflects on the form's contribution to modern war. In an extended voiceover, she states,

> War as a succession of special effects; the war became film well before it was shot. Cinema has remained a vast machine of special effects. If the war is the continuation of politics by other means, then media images are the continuation of war by other means. Immersed in the machinery, part of the special

effect, no critical distance. Nothing separates the Vietnam war and the super-
films that were made and continue to be made about it. It is said that if Americans lost the other [war], they have certainly won this one.[71]

As Trinh addresses the militarization of her medium, the audience sees
a series of black-and-white images of Vietnamese civilians and American
soldiers. Rather than showing each image in full, the camera moves across
them, reminding the audience of the selective framing of visual media.
With a reference to Carl von Clausewitz's dictum ("War is the continuation of politics by other means"), Trinh identifies filmmaking's role as an
instrument of state violence through which the nation imagines its future
wars ("the war became film well before it was shot") and renews its earlier
wars ("the continuation of war by other means"). She sees the revisionism
of Hollywood movies not as a benign form of entertainment but as itself
an act of violence that presents Vietnamese as lacking full human status
and imagines the Vietnam War as a bloodless self-reckoning for the white
soldier. As Trinh herself wrote in 1991 of the nation's new fascination with
the war, "Vietnam as spectacle remains passionately an owned territory,"
regardless of a person's stated resistance to the war.[72] The United States
has "won" the filmic afterwar, she suggests, by viewing Vietnam through
an antiwar liberalism that disacknowledges the consciousness of those it
declared itself to be defending in its war with communism.

In decentering the white hero who has dominated the national memory of the Vietnam War and centering the stories of Vietnamese and Vietnamese refugees, Trinh's film draws out the contradictions of the empire
of defense. As black-and-white footage of Vietnamese women runs in
slow motion, Trinh states, "There is always a tendency to identify historical breaks and say 'This begins there,' 'This ends here,' while the scene
keeps on recurring, as unchangeable as change itself."[73] War has long
served as a means of dividing historical time into manageable intervals to
be recorded and measured against earlier and later stages in the life of the
nation. Trinh's use of black-and-white stock footage communicates how
American writers and filmmakers have resigned the Vietnam War to an
earlier time from which the United States has long ago moved on. Trinh
interrogates the tidiness of that ending in situating antiwar fiction and
film within rather than against the Cold War state. Her film shows how
the liberal antiwar stories told by Heller, Herr, Kubrick, and Stone create
the conditions for the continuation of war by centering the white soldier's
search for meaning in Southeast Asia. But for Vietnamese and Vietnam-

ese American women, the war neither began in 1955 nor ended in 1975; rather, it "keeps on recurring" in their lives as well as in classrooms, bookstores, and movie theaters—a war lost and then won. The war story is the continuation of war by other means. The antiwar story is the continuation of whiteness by other means. War may be hell, but it is also the path to white enlightenment.

CHAPTER THREE

Dispatches from the Drug Wars

Weeks before North Vietnam launched the Tet Offensive, setting the United States and its South Vietnamese allies back on their heels, John Steinbeck IV asserted in a *Washingtonian* article that some 75 percent of American soldiers were getting stoned on a regular basis.[1] The feature article, "The Importance of Being Stoned in Vietnam," caused a stir when it arrived on newsstands in late 1967. It was the first most Americans had heard of an alleged drug crisis in the armed forces, and it wouldn't be the last. The son of the Nobel Prize–winning novelist, Steinbeck had volunteered for the army in 1966 and served one tour in Vietnam, where he wrote for Armed Forces Radio and Television. The war had, Steinbeck admitted, transformed him from a hawkish conservative into "a veritable Turtle Dove."[2] He became a vocal critic of the war, converted to Buddhism, and, aided by his famous name, received invitations from news media to comment on Southeast Asia and the armed forces stationed there. He described Vietnam as "that huge garden [the American teenager] has always dreamed of," where cannabis is easier to find than "a package of Lucky Strikes." The drug was not regulated by the local government, he added, or distributed through a central market. "It is simply a way of life." It didn't take long for the naive American to realize that "for all intents and purposes the entire country is stoned."[3]

Steinbeck's account of the Vietnamese drug trade was, he later acknowledged, overstated. He thought he could accelerate his government's withdrawal from Southeast Asia by exaggerating drug use among its soldiers. But it fueled domestic concerns about narcotics, their effect on the counterculture generation, and their role in the looming defeat in Vietnam. The image of stoned Americans in uniform raised fears of national decline. In the next four years, narcotics would be blamed for everything from a lack of morale among soldiers to the antiwar movement and the My Lai massacre.

Steinbeck's article suggests why. He described how fighting while stoned alters a person's senses so that war becomes beautiful, granting the soldier "a detached and esthetic vantage point" from which to observe the fighting. Steinbeck recalled how he and twenty of his comrades had gotten high on "Papa-san's grass" during a nighttime firefight. On a mountain overlooking the South China Sea, the men watched flares and machine-gun fire light the darkness around them, causing them to break into a chorus of "ohs and ahs." "A sigh of 'did you dig that?' whispered past the shuffling of grenades and ammunition," Steinbeck wrote. "The clatter of the machine guns was like a Stravinsky percussion interlude from 'La Sacre Du Printemps.' There isn't a psychedelic discotheque that can match the beauty of flares and bombs at night."[4] This sensationalized account of soldiers oohing and aahing at the destruction surrounding them contributed to the emerging figure of the debauched Vietnam veteran and motivated a crackdown on illicit drug use in the military, Southeast Asia, and across the United States. Steinbeck's own story demonstrated for some how narcotics had derailed the war effort. Once a clean-cut army volunteer fresh from basic training who, thanks to his famous father—himself hawkish on the war—had shaken hands with Lyndon Johnson in the Oval Office, he had returned from Vietnam a dovish druggie.

Not every American soldier had been so transformed by his tour, though. Steinbeck wrote of the "average soldier" who, like himself, matured from sober newcomer to streetwise stoner. He used "average" to mean white. Whereas the white soldier returned from war a changed man, the black soldier, he suggested, needed no acclimation to Vietnamese drug culture. His black comrades "brought [with them] the implements, effects, and customs of what, for the most part, might have been a predominantly shabby environment . . . by the white soldier's standards," he wrote. "As any narcotics agent or *Time-Life* staff writer will tell you when not asked, the original marijuana traffic in America came out of the same parts of town that the colored boys have been caught in all their lives."[5] After describing Vietnam as alien to white bourgeois culture, he cast it as familiar—even homelike—for the working-class black soldier raised in a "shabby environment" with all of the "implements, effects, and customs" associated with drug trafficking. While Steinbeck distanced himself from the narcotics agent who assumes that illicit drugs originate from black communities, he also tied blackness to crime, albeit with a liberal nod to "root causes."

He reflected that "the Negro soldier's predilection for 'boo' is far more a matter of metropolitan geography than it is of color," while noting that "African *dagga* [cannabis] came over with slavery."[6] Steinbeck acknowledged the structural forces that had barred black Americans from wealth accumulation—redlining, restrictive covenants, legal and extralegal violence—while assuming that these structural forces had conditioned black communities for criminal behavior. He mentioned that cannabis first arrived in North America from Africa through the transatlantic slave trade, reinforcing the idea that narcotics were foreign to white American culture. Marijuana had been introduced to and subverted good boys like Steinbeck by their black comrades and Vietnamese allies.

Steinbeck was motivated to write "The Importance of Being Stoned in Vietnam" by his own run-in with the law. After returning from his tour, he was arrested in California on possession charges. The *Washingtonian* article was his way of calling attention to what he saw as the "ridiculous contradiction" that the United States condoned drugs in Southeast Asia that it criminalized at home—arresting veterans who had taken on the habit to manage the stress of combat.[7] Steinbeck drew out the contradictions inherent in how the state distinguishes legal from illegal, safe from dangerous, and healthful from harmful substances. He remarked that all American soldiers carried a "survival kit" containing dextroamphetamines and wondered what a People's Army of Vietnam (North Vietnam) soldier might think if he discovered these "dexies" and "peps" on a dead American. "Who looks worse, and whose government is supplying whom, with what?"[8] This selective criminalization of drugs—dextroamphetamine versus marijuana—suggests how the state has marshaled narcotics control as a mechanism for valuing some ways of being in the world and devaluing others, of assuming the innocence of some and the criminality of others. The irony of Steinbeck's article is that he wrote it out of frustration with the government's harsh antidrug laws, but the image he advanced of the stoned soldier encouraged a series of new, draconian drug-control measures that would culminate in 1971 with President Richard Nixon's declaration of a war on drugs.

The addicted soldier is a central character in the story of how the empire of defense—a state formation that has, since the late 1940s, defined and policed the boundaries of liberal humanity through the idea of defense— endured the crisis of the defeat in Vietnam. The empire of defense emerged from the anticommunist consensus assembled in the wake of World War II. When that consensus came apart in Southeast Asia, it survived by transi-

tioning to an anticrime crusade that necessitated covert wars in Asia and
Latin America and against criminalized communities of color in the United
States. Nixon's war on drugs may seem to be of a different kind than the
wars in Korea and Vietnam. It may seem metaphorical, not a real war at
all. But it was a continuation of the same idea of defense that had, since the
formation of the Department of Defense, blurred the thin line between policing and war. If the wars in Korea and Vietnam turned war into a form of
policing—both were first defined as police actions—then the war on drugs
turned policing into a form of war. Defense, whether called policing or war,
does not conform to national borders. It governs what counts as a legitimate form of life in and outside the United States, through police actions
in Asia and wars in American cities.[9] Nixon's war on drugs did not end one
war and begin another but reorganized the racial regime of defense around
the figures of the criminal and the drug trafficker. The addicted white Vietnam vet served as the imagined victim of the narcotics trade and offered
Nixon a means by which he could tie the failures of the Vietnam War to a
softness on crime and drugs, solving one war with another and ushering in
a new stage of permanent war. The first commissioner of the Federal Bureau of Narcotics, a forerunner to the Drug Enforcement Agency, Harry
Anslinger, had long connected communism to narcotics, suggesting in 1952
that "Red Chinese" had been bankrolling North Korean forces through
the sale of drugs to the West and sabotaging American and UN soldiers by
"making them narcotics addicts."[10] But as the United States and its allies
lost ground in Vietnam, and resistance to the war grew, the Cold War state
shifted its focus from communists who might be drug traffickers to drug
traffickers who might be communists.

The regulation of controlled substances allowed officials to continue
defining some bodies, territories, and societies as liberal and legitimate
and others as illiberal and illegitimate. The determination of which drugs
harmed and which drugs healed, historian Suzanna Reiss writes, "extended
into the social and cultural life of the community and often provided the
evidentiary basis for discrediting (or glorifying) people, states, cultural
practices, political systems, and alternative systems of value."[11] The state
vilified Southeast Asians, Mexicans, black Americans, and Latinas/os
through medical-scientific and legal language that hid the race-making
work of its selective criminalization of substances and their means of
distribution.

The modern drug wars may have formed under Anslinger in the first
years of the Cold War, but the federal government did not take the lead on

crime and drug control until 1965, when Johnson signed the Law Enforcement Assistance Act into law, and 1968, when he authorized the Omnibus
Crime Control and Safe Streets Act.[12] The wave of legislation that followed under Nixon built the modern carceral state. This federalization of
crime and narcotics control was achieved through its militarization. Nixon
mobilized the discourse of war (and the authority it confers on the president) to transfer the regulation of crime and drugs from state and local
governments to the federal domain. His administration did so by telling
a story in which the nation—embodied by the addicted white soldier—
was endangered by a "rising sickness in our land" that originated from
both Southeast Asia and American communities of color.[13] But black,
Latina/o, and white radical writers told a different story about the antidrug crackdown, uncovering the state's collaboration with anticommunist
drug traffickers and showing how it had not racialized crime but *criminalized race*—barring Southeast Asians and Americans of color from being
law-abiding.

Bringing the War Home

Nixon's war on drugs grew out of a broader law-and-order agenda that had
won him the White House in 1968. That year, he and Alabama Governor
George Wallace, who ran on the right-wing American Independent Party
ticket, collected a combined 57 percent of the general-election vote and
won thirty-seven states by vowing to restore order to American streets.
Eighty-one percent of Americans, a Harris poll showed, agreed with the
statement that "law and order had broken down," with most blaming
"Negroes who start riots" and "Communists."[14] Nixon had found a winning issue. Political scientists have identified how law-and-order legislation allowed conservatives, who had been on the losing side of civil rights
reform, to change the terms of the debate, seeking to reduce rising crime
rates that they associated with black freedom struggles.[15] But Nixon's success also stemmed from how he catered his message to a liberal audience
through the language of rights and reform. In a May 1968 position paper
titled "Toward Freedom from Fear," Nixon declared that "the first civil
right of every American [is] the right to be protected in his home, business, and person from domestic violence," a right that was, he added, "being traduced with accelerating frequency in every community in America."[16] With reference to Franklin Roosevelt's four freedoms ("Toward

Freedom from Fear") and the mainstream civil rights movement ("the right to be protected . . . from violence"), he insisted that enforcing law and order was the way to safeguard civil liberties. Unlike Wallace and Arizona Senator Barry Goldwater, he sought to bring liberals on board and form a new consensus around crime control.

This consensus was slow in forming. It was not until Steinbeck's article stirred fears of drug addiction in Vietnam that the federal government began to get tough on crime—and turn its attention to a new war at home. "The myth of the addicted army," historian Jeremy Kuzmarov writes, was a story conservatives and liberals could agree on. "It helped divert public attention from the policies that had produced and perpetuated the war in Vietnam, intensified public fears of the growth of the 1960s drug culture, and thus created an opportune political climate for an expansion of the federal drug war."[17] Although the rate of drug use among American soldiers in Southeast Asia was identical to the rate among men of the same age at home, it gave Nixon and other antidrug crusaders a focusing event through which to redefine the state's war on what they saw as nonhuman, illiberal social worlds. The communist shaded into the drug trafficker.

Steinbeck's "The Importance of Being Stoned in Vietnam" ran weeks ahead of the Tet Offensive, a devastating setback for the United States and its allies. It didn't take long for lawmakers to begin blaming drugs for a disaster of their own making in Southeast Asia. In March 1970, Senator Thomas Dodd, a Democrat from Connecticut, convened a congressional subcommittee hearing on drug use in the armed forces to which he invited veterans, National Liberation Front (NLF) defectors, medical officers, and journalists, most of whom agreed with his assessment that drugs had undermined the war effort in Southeast Asia. (Steinbeck was among his selected witnesses.) Sergeant Charles West, who had served in the company that had carried out the My Lai massacre—in which American soldiers killed five hundred unarmed Vietnamese civilians in Quang Ngai—told the subcommittee that he had witnessed five of his comrades smoking marijuana the night before the mass killing. When Dodd asked him if this could have affected their behavior the following day, West said he didn't know. So the senator answered for him, stating, "I think it did [influence their behavior]," adding, "Our soldiers aren't murderers."[18]

Dodd had good reason to blame My Lai on drug use among enlisted men rather than command decisions. As a member of the Senate Foreign Relations Committee, he had been an advocate for the escalation of the war in Southeast Asia. Narcotics allowed him to minimize his own role in creating the conditions for American war crimes. Dodd suggested that four out of every five American soldiers were smoking marijuana in Vietnam, with drugs "almost as available as candy bars."[19] He bolstered his claim that My Lai could be attributed to drugs by calling on medical authorities. A doctor who had treated drug addiction in Vietnam testified to the violent effects of cannabis, telling the committee, "Contrary to many popular opinions held here in the States, the drug could cause people to become fearful, paranoid, extremely angry, and led, in a number of cases, to acts of murder, rape, and aggravated assault."[20] The conclusion of the subcommittee hearing was that Vietnamese drug culture, and not American men, was at fault for the My Lai massacre. Dodd suggested that Vietnamese had contaminated American soldiers with its "marijuana plague" and instigated violence against their own people.[21] But Dodd's account of marijuana use in Vietnam was inconsistent. On one day of the hearing, he cast Vietnam as a nation of drug addicts. On another, he indicated that no NLF soldiers smoked marijuana due to a strict ban; they used it instead to sabotage the health of American soldiers and undercut their efforts, one addict at a time.[22] Dodd's conflicting tale of Vietnamese drug culture—sometimes meant to illustrate Southeast Asians' lack of self-control, sometimes their achievement of absolute control—reflects the incoherence of Asian racialization during the Vietnam War. Even as officials like Dodd described Vietnamese as drug addicts, as they earlier had Americans of Chinese descent, the emerging idea of Asian Americans as model minorities took hold, the term having been coined in the *New York Times* in 1966, a year after Lyndon Johnson signed the Immigration and Nationality Act into law. Malleable racist ideas about Asian behavior allowed Dodd to reconcile one idea with the other, the criminal with the model minority.[23]

The story of the addicted soldier grew more sensational as state officials and news media turned their attention from marijuana to heroin. A year after Dodd organized the first hearing on marijuana use in the armed forces, in May 1971, Congressmen Michael Murphy, a Democrat from Connecticut, and Robert Steele, a Republican from Illinois, released a coauthored investigation of the narcotics trade in Southeast Asia, "The World Heroin Problem." On the basis of anecdotal evidence, the congressmen alleged that 10–15 percent of American forces were hooked on low-cost, high-grade heroin that had been refined in Burmese and Laotian laboratories and marketed to American soldiers in South Vietnam.[24] Looking to make their names (and win reelection), the first-term congressmen wrote editorials and did the rounds on television news. Steele contributed an account of their investigation to *Nation's Business*, in which he asserted that "a once-magnificent fighting machine" had "suffered heavy losses in discipline, morale, and effectiveness—not because of the enemy, but because of an insidious white powder."[25] He faulted South Vietnamese officials for condoning and even facilitating the sale of heroin to Americans and recommended that the United States pull out of Southeast Asia if the local government did not curb drug trafficking.[26] News media detailed the congressmen's findings with excitement and alarm. *Newsweek* columnist Stewart Alsop made the outrageous claim that their "horrifying new estimate" made heroin addiction among American soldiers "the worst horror to emerge out of the war—worse even than My Lai."[27] The congressmen's agreement on the issue, one being a conservative and one a liberal, also signaled the establishment of common ground on the war. Defining hard drug use as a Southeast Asian custom enabled by crooked government officials, they agreed that Vietnam might be unsaveable and that its drug trade was an affliction on the United States.

Coverage of the congressmen's investigation tended to focus on the connection that they drew between heroin use in Vietnam and rising crime rates in the United States. Steele warned that, given the higher cost and lower grade of heroin available in North America, addicted veterans would turn to crime to sustain the high to which they had become accustomed while serving abroad. He imagined narcotics as an "epidemic" emerging from Asia and infecting America through soldier-carriers. But he also suggested that drug addiction had been "spawned in the [American] ghetto" and had "hedgehopped to middle-class suburbs, colleges and high schools."[28] The two congressmen had visited nine nations in Southeast and Western Asia as part of their investigation for the House Foreign Affairs Committee. They did not visit American cities or research the domestic drug trade. But in their interviews with news media they stressed the continuities between the drug cultures of Asia and of urban American communities from which narcotics "spawned."

News reporters reinforced this association between drugs, Southeast Asia, and American communities of color. Tom Buckley, citing the Murphy-Steele investigation, described how American soldiers bought heroin in Vietnam's "scag alleys" and then noted that "most of the big cities in [the United States] have their scag alleys, too—usually in the fetid tenements that line the garbage-strewn streets of the ghettos, but more and more frequently in recent years in the middle-class suburbs and on the fringes of college campuses as well."[29] A *New York Times* article featured an interview with a medical officer who stated, "Vietnam in many ways is a ghetto for the enlisted man. The soldiers don't want to be here, their living conditions are bad," so, he concluded, "They react the way they do in a ghetto. They take drugs and try to forget."[30] Like Steele's own editorial, these news articles eschewed the language of race, electing instead to talk about drugs in terms of regions of the world and "ghetto" neighborhoods. But their effect was to characterize decolonizing Asian nations and domestic black and Latina/o communities as harboring and disseminating a kind of cultural contagion—drug use—assumed to be foreign to white "middle-class suburbs." While liberal news media stressed the root causes of drug use (as an effort to "try to forget" difficult circumstances), they naturalized an association between crime, Southeast Asia, and black America— even if they suggested that Asian and black criminality was the result of colonialism and structural racism.

Through a story of narcotics arriving on the shores and in the suburbs of North America from Asia, Harlem, and East Los Angeles, conservative and liberal lawmakers, journalists, and medical scientists formed new racial categories—the drug trafficker and the criminal—that overlaid but hid their close association with existing racial identities. Conservatives and liberals shared in the criminalization of Southeast Asians and black and Latina/o communities by assuming that those living in Vietnamese "scag alleys" and urban American "ghettos" *must* be criminals or drug users, whether due to moral failings, as conservatives argued, or as a result of the conditions into which they were born, as liberals maintained. Their arguments set Vietnamese and Americans of color outside liberal law, ineligible for rights, leading something other than human lives. Criminalization obscures how liberalism founds rather than mends breaks in humanity. It renders nonhuman being understandable, if not deserved. This racial criminalization allowed one lieutenant general to argue before a congressional committee in 1971 that the "riff-raff" serving in Vietnam were more inclined toward narcotics than the military's more "careerist personnel" and that drug use in the armed forces would decline as fewer men entered through the draft.[31] He suggested that black, Latino, and poor white soldiers were bound to shoot heroin and steal; they were criminals.[32]

This was the environment in which Nixon declared his war on drugs on June 17. In a briefing at the White House, he called drug abuse "America's public enemy number one" and stated that, "in order to fight and defeat this enemy, it is necessary to wage a new, all-out offensive."[33] Nixon announced that he had, earlier that day, issued Executive Order 11599 to establish the new Special Action Office for Drug Abuse Prevention (SAODAP) that would be located within the executive branch and coordinate his antidrug agenda across the federal government. In the briefing room, he introduced its inaugural director, Jerome Jaffe, a University of Chicago researcher and a leading advocate for treating heroin addiction with methadone. Naming Jaffe, a medical doctor and distinguished academic, as the first executive "drug czar," Nixon counterbalanced his more belligerent declarations with a discussion of the new SAODAP director's initiatives on rehabilitation, research, and education.

The legislation that Nixon outlined built on the Law Enforcement Assistance Act of 1965, the Omnibus Crime Control and Safe Streets Act of 1968, and his own administration's Comprehensive Drug Abuse Prevention and Control Act of 1970, which established the five modern classifications, or "schedules," of controlled substances and authorized the use of no-knock search warrants. But the antidrug agenda Nixon laid out in 1971 was new in its scale, in its centralization within the federal government, and in its militarized methods for controlling the flow, sale, and use of narcotics in and outside the United States. To federalize the drug wars—a move that, he admitted, contradicted his commitment to states' rights— Nixon needed to tell a convincing and urgent story about the threat of narcotics to the nation. The woes of the addicted soldier, dramatized in congressional hearings and on television news that summer, gave him that story. Although Nixon's remarks are remembered for his vow to "wage a new, all-out offensive" on drugs, he devoted the longest segment of the briefing to drug use in the military. The Vietnam War "has brought to our attention the fact that a number of young Americans have become addicts as they serve abroad, whether in Vietnam, or Europe, or other places," he stated. "That is why this offensive deals with the problem there, in Europe, and will then go on to deal with the problem throughout America."[34] Nixon imagined illicit drugs as the most dangerous of the nation's *foreign* enemies, necessitating that his administration turn its attention (and vast military resources) from the Asian "communist" to the black and Latino "drug trafficker." And it was the figure of the addicted soldier through whom he connected one war to the next.

Crisis and the New Consensus

Nineteen sixty-eight, the year Nixon was elected to his first term, was a time of crisis and transition for the United States. The Tet Offensive had

revealed its weakness in Southeast Asia, and the growing antiwar movement at home signaled that the anticommunist consensus that had facilitated the state's massive military growth since World War II had cracked.
The country was also facing an economic slowdown that would culminate
in August 1971—the same summer as Nixon's declaration of a war on
drugs—with his administration's decision to terminate the Bretton Woods
agreement that had governed international financial relations since 1944.
The empire of defense endured these crises by reframing its war against
illiberalism as a struggle to control narcotics and crime rather than communism. Geographer Ruth Wilson Gilmore, in her account of how and
why the state of California turned to incarceration as a catchall solution
for addressing social turmoil, argues that change unfolds through the interaction between individuals and groups and the existing structures they
must navigate. "In a crisis, the old order does not simply blow away," she
writes, "and every struggle is carried out within, and against, already existing institutions."[35] This is not to suggest that the war on drugs—and
the resulting mass incarceration of black and Latino men—was an inevitable outcome of the breakdown of state anticommunism. But out of
the crisis of the Vietnam War, government officials revised the idea of
defense and redirected the resources of the national security state toward
the regulation of drugs that they associated with Southeast Asians, black
Americans, and Latinos. This association allowed them to blame criminals and drug traffickers for the defeat in Vietnam; the United States had
lost, they suggested, because its South Vietnamese allies had subverted
good American boys with heroin and because Americans of color had
done the same to white middle-class suburbs in the United States, foster-
ing a culture of decadence and lawlessness. Nixon's declaration of war on
drugs did not mark the end of the Cold War state but recalibrated it for
a new kind of defense. This transition necessitated not only institutional
changes but also changes to the story the government told about its role
in the world and within its own borders.

Nixon and his advisers created a new consensus out of the ideological
material of the old one. His administration formulated its law-and-order
crusade, like earlier articulations of anticommunism, in the language of
antiracism. As he endorsed harsh antidrug and anticrime legislation that
targeted working-class black and Latina/o neighborhoods, he insisted
that the legislation was the best defense against racial violence. Years earlier, in 1966, he wrote an editorial for *U.S. News and World Report*, "If
Mob Rule Takes Hold in U.S.," in which he bemoaned "the spread of the

corrosive doctrine that every citizen possesses an inherent right to decide for himself which laws to disobey and when to disobey them." Describing civil disobedience as a "contagious national disease"—and citing everyone from Geoffrey Chaucer to Abraham Lincoln—Nixon made the argument that the rule of law served the interests of racial minorities most of all and that resisting it invited the "majority's mob." "This is why it is so paradoxical today to see minority groups engaging in civil disobedience; their greatest defense is the rule of law," he wrote. "If the rule of law goes, the civil-rights laws of recent vintage will be the first casualties."[36] While it isn't difficult to see the racial coding in his statements, Nixon addressed his editorial to more than the resentful white conservatives with whom he is often identified. He also hailed racial liberals, making a case for himself as the candidate-to-be of rights and reform. When he took office three years later, his administration sought to form a new consensus around the rule of law that enlisted and revised the racial regime of defense, constructing new categories of the nonhuman (the criminal, the drug trafficker) through violence that it imagined as a solution to racial divisions.

But Nixon formulated his drug wars as the defense of the white Vietnam veteran and the rehabilitation of his innocent status. The American soldier, through no fault of his own, Nixon suggested, had been contaminated by Southeast Asian drug culture. The president's war on drugs mirrored his intended "Vietnamization" of the war in Southeast Asia. On November 3, 1969, addressing the nation from the White House, he outlined what he termed his own "Nixon doctrine." He announced that under his command the United States would continue to furnish its allies with military and economic assistance while leaving the fighting (and the casualties) to their allies. "The defense of freedom is everybody's business—not just America's business. And it is particularly the responsibility of the people whose freedom is threatened," he stated. "In the previous administration, we Americanized the war in Vietnam. In this administration, we are Vietnamizing the search for peace."[37] Vietnamization allowed Nixon to acknowledge the sovereign status of the South Vietnamese government while also representing South Vietnam as a nation of freeloaders who refused to take the lead in the defense of their own freedom. As he sought to *Vietnamize* the war by replacing American soldiers with American-trained Vietnamese soldiers, he imagined the drug wars as an effort to *Americanize* the United States by banning what he saw as a Southeast Asian custom from North America.[38] So while Nixon suggested that his Vietnamization of the war was a validation of Vietnamese self-government and that his crackdown on drug traffickers safeguarded minorities from extralegal violence, his administration marshaled its resources to defend the bodies and restore the innocence of white men.

It was this relation between the Vietnam War and the war on drugs that enabled the federalization of crime and drug control. Until the 1960s, the federal government had limited authority to enforce its drug laws, which remained the work of state and local agencies. Under the Harris Act of 1914, the government regulated narcotics through its right to tax the illegal trade. The Johnson and Nixon administrations changed this. Through the discourse of war and the wide latitude it affords the executive branch, they shifted drug enforcement from the state to the federal domain. (Johnson announced his own "war against crime" in 1965 with the formation of the Commission on Law Enforcement and Administration of Justice.) "Because," as Italian philosopher Giorgio Agamben writes, "the sovereign power of the president is essentially grounded in the emergency linked to a state of war, over the course of the twentieth century the metaphor of war becomes an integral part of the presidential vocabulary whenever decisions considered to be of vital importance are being imposed."[39] Nixon's declaration of a war on drugs was more than a rhetorical flourish; it was the means by which he brought narcotics under the control of his office and tied drug traffickers abroad—real and imagined—to those within the United States as constituting the most immediate threat to the country's liberal democratic order.

At a three-day conference on international narcotics control in 1972, for example, Nixon addressed sixty senior state officials in Washington on his "total war on drug abuse." The attendants were narcotics officers stationed at embassies in Asia and the Middle East and agents from the new Office of Drug Abuse Law Enforcement (ODALE), which Nixon had formed earlier that year and which would be reorganized as part of the DEA in 1973. From an auditorium at the Main State Building, he stressed the similarities between his administration's antidrug crusade and a conventional war. "I consider keeping dangerous drugs out of the United States just as important as keeping armed enemy forces from landing in the United States," he announced. "Dangerous drugs which come into the United States can endanger the lives of young Americans just as much as would an invading army landing in the United States." To his audience of foreign and domestic narcotics agents, Nixon insisted that the war on drugs was no different than, and "as important as," the war in Southeast Asia and that they must "fight this evil with every weapon at our command."[40]

While Nixon's words might be dismissed as mere bombast—a means of exciting a crowd of like-minded crusaders—it was the militarization of the drug wars that accelerated its federalization. In two years, the Nixon administration formed SAODAP, ODALE, and the DEA. When the Johnson administration formed the Office of Law Enforcement Assistance, the predecessor to the Law Enforcement Assistance Administration (LEAA), which funded, trained, and shared cutting-edge military technologies with local law-enforcement offices, in 1965, it allotted it an annual budget of $7.5 million. By 1973, that budget had grown to $850 million.[41]

But waging defense necessitates a right–left consensus. This was true of anticommunism in the 1950s and 1960s, and it was true of the war on drugs in the 1970s and 1980s. Racial liberals teamed with conservatives in stoking white fears of black lawlessness and seeking carceral solutions to racial violence. In the civil rights era, political scientist Naomi Murakawa writes, "There were 'competing' constructions of black criminality, one callous, another with a tenor of sympathy and cowering paternalism."[42] Although they stressed the "root causes" of black crime and drug use, liberals reinforced the idea that black and Latino men were conditioned for criminal behavior by a racist society. This understanding of "the black criminal" can be seen in Steinbeck's article "The Importance of Being Stoned in Vietnam," in which he attributes drug use among black soldiers to the fact that they had brought "their sorrows with them" from the "shabby environment" in which they were raised.[43] Conservatives and liberals united in conflating crime with black freedom struggles, the former attributing lawlessness to overgenerous civil rights reforms (Goldwater), and the latter attributing it to black disenfranchisement (Steinbeck). Conservatives may have racialized crime, but liberals criminalized race.

As the anticommunist consensus deteriorated, Nixon's message on drugs bridged the divide between conservatives and liberals to form a new consensus that sustained the empire of defense through its first crisis. His administration mobilized liberal rights ("the right to be protected in [one's] home, business, and person from domestic violence") to situate his law-and-order agenda as continuous with, rather than as a refutation of, the civil rights movement and earlier liberal racial reforms. It marshaled the concerns of the antiwar movement by bemoaning the effects of marijuana and heroin on American soldiers and veterans who, Nixon suggested, risked withdrawing into "the twilight world of crime, bad drugs, and all too often a premature death."[44] The crisis of one consensus became the foundation for the next.

The administration was most effective in recruiting liberals to its anti-drug cause through its endorsement (and distortion) of the liberal medical understanding of addiction as a disease. Naming Jaffe, a leader in addiction rehabilitation, as the director of SAODAP earned Nixon good will with liberal news media. Jaffe himself insisted that Nixon was a "secret liberal" who "walked the walk" when it came to instituting rehabilitative methods for treating heroin addiction.[45] But the funds his administration directed toward medical research and treatment were dwarfed by the billion-dollar budget of the LEAA. Most federal resources for the medical treatment of heroin addiction were earmarked for new Veterans Administration clinics, which attracted glowing coverage from news media but remained a small-scale initiative throughout the 1970s.

A month after Nixon declared his war on drugs, *Life* ran a feature-length article on a new veterans addiction clinic in Palo Alto, California, that combined methadone maintenance treatments with "encounter therapy" and family counseling. The article included more than a dozen images of the veterans interviewed, all of whom were white men. When asked about the "innovative program" in Palo Alto, Jaffe stressed that these veterans had a better chance of rehabilitating themselves than most "street addicts," because in Vietnam "you have people beginning to use drugs in an exotic situation—with a peer group that may never associate with each other again." He concluded, "It's not a part of the fabric of the lives of these men, any more than shooting people is a part of their lives. When they leave the service, hopefully they'll leave behind the identity of someone who has used heroin."[46] Given the overwhelming whiteness of the vets being treated at the Palo Alto clinic, Jaffe's words suggested that drug addiction was an "exotic" ailment for white men but normal for Southeast Asians and some of the less familiar members of their "peer group" in the armed services (read black). Rehabilitation has a high likelihood of success for these white vets, Jaffe argued, because heroin addiction is "not a part of the fabric of [their] lives" and not the basis of their "identity"—as it is for Vietnamese, black, and Latino men.

Nixon drew on this kind of language to paint drug addiction as a moral rather than medical disease. He called drug users "genuinely sick people" and insisted that Americans would be "physically, mentally, and morally destroyed" by narcotics without immediate, aggressive legislative action.[47] Like his drug czar, Nixon described drug use as an "exotic" custom, non-native to American culture. In a five-thousand-word message to Congress on the day he declared his war on drugs, he noted that the United States, although it neither grew opium poppies nor manufactured heroin, had the largest number of heroin addicts in the world. "This deadly poison in the American life stream is, in other words, a foreign import," he wrote.[48] This was the narrative that emerged from the accounts of addicted soldiers advanced by Steinbeck, Dodd, Murphy, Steele, and Jaffe: the country was under attack by foreign drug traffickers, who had undermined its men in Southeast Asia and now threatened to do the same within its borders. In all of their accounts, this illiberal actor, the drug trafficker, originated from Asia as well as from the black and Latina/o neighborhoods of American cities. The similarities between the criminalization of Vietnamese and Americans of color did not go unnoticed by black and Latina/o authors, whose writing reveals the racial work of the deracinated drug wars and connects them to longer histories of state violence in Harlem, Haiti, East Los Angeles, and Aztlán.

The Viet Cong of America

As news media delivered sensational accounts of heroin traffic in American cities and among American soldiers abroad, Nixon exercised his executive authority as commander in chief to federalize narcotics control. Drugs were, he argued, as grave a threat to the United States as an "invading army" landing on its shores and must be turned back with all of the country's military might. But he also distanced his antidrug crusade from "real" war by naming the state's antagonist as a thing—drugs—rather than a government or organization. His administration imagined the war on drugs as a new and urgent form of defense that, like anticommunism before it, necessitated continuous nonwar to secure the nation from illiberal, unfree beliefs and behaviors. Nixon and his team suggested that his declaration of war on narcotics was figurative—rhetoric meant to stress the seriousness with which he would take on the drug trade—while acting with the license of a wartime administration in combating and containing alleged drug traffickers. The state's governance of what does and doesn't constitute war has also defined the boundaries of war literature, a genre that has, for most Americans, continued to mean stories about combat soldiers engaged in discrete battles for land and resources with foreign foes. But other war stories have been told. We just haven't read them as war literature. Examining, for example, Ishmael Reed's *Mumbo Jumbo* (1972) and Oscar Zeta Acosta's *The Revolt of the Cockroach People*

(1973)—two novels that confront the criminalization of blackness and brownness in American cities—as war stories reveals the drug wars as a new stage in an old war.

Reed has long criticized the book, film, and television industries for selling images of black crime to white audiences. After the election of President George H. W. Bush in 1988, he slammed news networks for turning stories of black violence and drug addiction into big business and giving credence to the message of Lee Atwater's infamous Willie Horton ad. "The only difference between white pathology and black pathology," he concluded, "is that white pathology is underreported."[49] In a 2010 *Boston Globe* editorial, he condemned Harvard and other universities for teaching the television show *The Wire* (2002–08), which, he argued, exoticizes black Baltimore communities for the entertainment of white liberals.[50] But Reed first articulated his criticism of state and media accounts of black crime years earlier, amid Nixon's antidrug crusade. In his 1970 essay "Neo-HooDoo"—later collected as "Neo-HooDoo Manifesto"—he attributed war and antiblack racism to Western universalism, monotheism, and rationalism. The West, he suggested, believes in a "CopGod" that can "'subdue' the world" through acts of normative violence. This God, he added, "is why we are in Vietnam." Reed identified an alternative in the form of Neo-HooDoo, a "Lost American Church" of black cultural forms and religious beliefs derived from West African, Haitian, and South American voodoo traditions. Unlike Christianity, which he described as restrictive and static, Reed's Neo-HooDooism is diverse in its "styles and moods" and exists in a state of continuous formation.[51] In a 1973 interview, he stated that "the laws of so-called Western logic" had led to a limited awareness of the natural world. The methods of white scientists and detectives do "not apply to the world we are finding more and more," he argued. "All kinds of things don't do what Western logic [says phenomena are] supposed to do."[52]

Reed's third novel, *Mumbo Jumbo*, stages his Neo-HooDooist beliefs in the figure of a black scientist-detective, PaPa LaBas. As President Warren Harding takes office in 1921, an outbreak of "Jes Grew"—a virus that leaves its carriers with the uncontrollable urge to sing, dance, and "wiggle jiggle"—engulfs the nation, landing first in New Orleans and then moving north toward New York City. LaBas, a Harlem *houngan*, or voodoo priest, tracks the outbreak as it nears the city, seeking to locate the sacred Book of Thoth from which it is believed to originate. He is not alone. A secret organization known as the Atonist Path has instructed its military wing, the Wallflower Order, to find and burn the book. The Atonist Path is committed to Western rationalism, Christian monotheism, and white racial dominance and has carried out a centuries-long struggle to censor countervailing knowledge.[53] The historical novel, when situated in relation to the waning Vietnam War and rising drug wars, reveals the racial violence of liberal universalism. Likening the invasion of Haiti to the invasion of Vietnam decades later, Reed draws attention to how liberal knowledge has rationalized war as an act of freeing the universal human from the irrational nonhuman, whether the barbarian, the communist, or the drug trafficker.

The novel, though set during the brief Harding administration, acknowledges its Nixon-era origins. It ends in 1971 with a one-hundred-year-old (but somehow unaged) LaBas delivering a guest lecture on the Harlem Renaissance at a New York–area university. With a nod to Arna Bontemps's novel *Black Thunder* (1936), based on the 1800 Richmond slave rebellion, he concludes, "Time is a pendulum. Not a river. More akin to what goes around comes around." Telling the students of the Jes Grew outbreak and the war in Haiti, he suggests that the 1920s have come back around. The West has long sought to govern the meaning of the rational and the free, he argues. "This explains why Holy Wars have been launched against Haiti under the cover of 'bringing stability to the Caribbean.' [One] such war lasted longer than Vietnam. But you don't hear much about it because the action was against niggers."[54] LaBas asserts that wars fought against Haitians and Vietnamese have been dismissed as nonwars—efforts to stabilize unstable regions—through accounts of the Caribbean and Southeast Asia as illiberal, irrational social worlds. The Wilson administration's invasion of Haiti has been left out of official histories for categorical reasons; it was not a real war but an instrument for "bringing stability" to the country. It was not a real war because "the action was against niggers." LaBas's transhistorical account of the wars in Haiti and Vietnam suggests how war has, since before the launch of the national security state in the late 1940s, functioned as an instrument of racialization through which the liberal state defines the boundaries of the universal as the right to execute legitimate violence.

Reed represents the invasion of Haiti as part of a larger war against Jes Grew, a war reminiscent in rhetoric and racial meaning to Nixon's war on drugs. After Jes Grew arrives in the United States from Haiti (its "miasmatic source"), the Wallflower Order arranges for its eradication by installing Harding in the White House and then grooming a "Talking Android" who will embed himself in black communities to undermine the virus among its most active carriers. The Talking Android will infiltrate "the Negro, who seems to be its classical host; to drive it out, categorize it analyze it expell [*sic*] it slay it, blot Jes Grew," the Wallflower Order asserts. "In other words this Talking Android will be engaged to cut-it-up, break down this Germ, keep it from behind the counter."[55] Reed wrote *Mumbo Jumbo* in 1971, the year Nixon declared drug abuse "America's public enemy number one," and it is hard to miss the resonances between the order's anti–Jes Grew crusade and the Nixon administration's antidrug agenda. The order's account of Jes Grew assumes its foreignness—that it originates not from the United States but from Haiti—while also associating it with black American communities and culture. As in media accounts of the heroin trade, the secret organization is shocked to discover that middle-class, white Americans have also been "contaminated" with the virus. In substituting music and dance for narcotics, Reed satirizes how the war on drugs, with a color-blind rhetoric focused on behavior rather than skin color, functioned to criminalize blackness. Blackness became a condition for crime, drug use, and, in Reed's novel, infectious dancing. As one leader of the Wallflower Order suggests, in a nod to 1971, "Suppose we take [black] musicians out of circulation, arrest them on trumped-up drug charges and give them unusually long and severe prison sentences."[56]

The Wallflower Order organizes its crusade around controlling the boundaries between legitimate and illegitimate beliefs, licit and illicit behaviors. Its goal is to "keep [Jes Grew] from behind the counters," to ensure that it doesn't achieve legal status or recognition as harmless or beneficial in the commercial market. This racial criminalization in Reed's novel reflects the racial criminalization of the federal government's antidrug crackdown in the 1960s and 1970s in how it mobilizes the race-neutral language of legal/illegal to distract from its race-making function. Crime emerged during the Progressive era, as historian Khalil Gibran Muhammad documents, as the foremost mechanism for measuring black Americans' fitness for modern life. Liberal social scientists, he argues, contributed to "the condemnation of blackness" by replacing racial biological accounts of black crime with racial cultural accounts that, while couched in statistical methods framed as race-neutral, reinforced an assumed connection between race and crime. Whereas white ethnic crime was attributed to class disadvantage, leading to state interventions on behalf of white working-class communities, such as the New Deal reforms, black crime was attributed to black culture. "Liberalism," Muhammad concludes, "fueled [white] immigrant success even as racial liberalism foundered on the shoals of black criminality."[57] The result was a society in which white men "commit crimes" and black men "are criminals." This Progressive-era racial liberalism foreshadows Cold War–era racial defense in which the state would, after World War II, present itself as an arbiter of antiracism by defending universal humanity from illegitimate beliefs and behaviors—communism, crime, drug trafficking—that it associated with blackness. Reed's satire of the war on drugs allows us to see how these new racial categories revised and extended existing racist ideas for an age of state antiracism.

But Reed's novel also imagines alternatives to racial liberalism. The invasion of Haiti, which the narrator ascribes to the Wallflower Order's war on Jes Grew, leads black Americans to learn about, and align themselves with, the Caribbean nation. They read books about Haitian culture, learn Creole, and wear Haitian clothing: "As the war drags on it arrives upon American shores. The Wallflower Order launched the war against Haiti in hopes of allaying Jes Grew symptoms by attacking their miasmatic source. But little Haiti resists. It becomes a world-wide symbol for religious and aesthetic freedom. When an artist happens upon a new form he shouts 'I Have Found My Haiti!' "[58] So while the order seeks to stigmatize Haiti and black America through a military, intelligence, and media crusade against Jes Grew, its actions have the unintended effect of instigating new transnational coalitions against the narrow universalism and white racial rule for which it stands. American communities of color recognize Haitians to be undertaking an analogous struggle against state-sanctioned racial violence committed in the name of defense, order, and liberation. Reed does not dismiss the universal altogether but articulates an alternative universalism by adopting a different starting point that decenters whiteness and transcends and exceeds the nation.

The novel identifies a continuous undercurrent in black intellectual culture from the 1920s to the 1970s. As black Americans faced exclusion from the alleged universalism of national life, writers from W. E. B. Du Bois and C. L. R. James to Harold Cruse and Angela Davis sought to articulate alternative communal forms within and across state borders. These included Pan-African movements, like those dramatized in *Mumbo Jumbo*, as well as a sense of alliance with Southeast Asians during the war in Vietnam, when lawmakers were characterizing Southeast Asia and black American communities as the "miasmatic" sources of narcotics.[59] The narrator's account of black Americans' growing interest in Haiti's anticolonial struggles appears alongside a photograph of a Black Panther protest. Black men march in two rows, their arms swinging in unison at their sides. White helmeted law-enforcement officers look on.

A Panther sign is visible in the background. The image draws a line from the invasion of Haiti and the country's emergence as "a world-wide symbol for religious and aesthetic freedom" to the war in Southeast Asia and the black freedom struggles of the late 1960s and 1970s. At their height, the Panthers balanced a commitment to local autonomous black government with an identification with other victims of the American empire within and beyond the nation's borders.[60] The Panthers linked their fate to that of Southeast Asians in a shared struggle against Washington, seeing the liberal state as the source of, rather than the solution to, racial violence. Founder Huey Newton, in his 1970 essay "To the National Liberation Front of South Vietnam," wrote that, while the Panthers recognized Vietnam's "right to claim nationhood," they could not be nationalists themselves because "our country is not a nation, but an empire." His conclusion: "We have the historical obligation to take the concept of internationalism to its final conclusion—destruction of statehood itself."[61]

Reed doesn't mention the Panthers in the text of his novel, but their visual inclusion makes sense in the context of his satire. The Black Panther Party for Self-Defense had its satirical edge, too. The Panthers' commitment to "policing the police" and Newton's title as their Minister of Defense drew attention to how law-enforcement agencies did not defend them as black working-class men and women. Black people, they argued, must defend against defense. The Panthers enacted a satire of liberal governance that revealed defense as a race-making instrument through which the state differentiates the human (the defended) from the deferred human (the "liberated") and the nonhuman (the defended against). That defense, they recognized, did not conform to national borders but targeted them and NLF soldiers as criminal actors, external threats to liberal humanity. Written as the Nixon administration transitioned the national security state from anticommunism to drug control, Reed's novel replaces narcotics with black music and dance to suggest how the United States had criminalized blackness rather than substances through a new mode of violent defense that it called the war on drugs. But, like the Black Panthers, it also gestures to how the idea of defense might be turned back on itself—how resistance to the empire of defense can found new alliances and forms of belonging that transcend state and nation.

The Black Panthers weren't alone in seeing their struggles at home reflected in those of Vietnamese overseas. The Chicano movement, which emerged across the western states in the late 1960s, saw the invasion of Southeast Asia as continuous with the colonization of Aztlán—an imagined indigenous homeland stretching across the southwestern United States—in the nineteenth century. The movement marked a radical transformation in the long Mexican American civil rights movement that had earlier sought state-granted rights and advocated military service as a route for achieving government recognition and reform. This new generation of activists instead argued that Chicanas/os should fight at home for their *raza*, that their struggle was against, rather than for, the United States. In a 1969 letter to the Temescal, California, draft board, informing it of his refusal of induction into the armed forces, movement leader Manuel Gómez wrote, "It is well known that Mexicans were among the first victims of your empire. . . . The Vietnamese people are not my enemy, but brothers involved in the same struggle for justice against a common enemy."[62] Months earlier, he had declared in a coauthored statement at the Denver Youth Liberation Conference, "Because we know who we are, our nationalism becomes an internationalism."[63]

As Gómez and others were imagining a new transnationalism that united Chicanas/os and Vietnamese against imperial violence, the Nixon administration, with the assistance of alarmist news media, was advancing its own transnational narrative that represented Chicanas/os and Southeast Asians as analogous sources of illicit drugs and crime. These conflicting transnationalisms surface in Acosta's *The Revolt of the Cockroach People*, his fictional account of his legal work on behalf of Chicana/o activists in Los Angeles. Acosta's novelization of his life and law career through his alter ego, Buffalo Zeta Brown, refuses the static, subnational organization of racial difference into which the literary market has long sorted writers of color.[64] Like Gómez, Acosta imagines a Chicano movement engaged in the same fight as Vietnamese, a connection that he identifies through and against the emerging wars on drugs and crime. Like Reed, he reveals the racial work of antidrug surveillance by showing how it forms racial divisions abstracted from, but conforming to, the existing color line. In casting the drug wars within the long arc of white settler colonialism, Acosta's novel defines the antiracist Cold War state as a mere continuation of earlier racist state formations.

The novel, Acosta's second, articulates a Chicana/o alliance with Vietnam that traces the limits of rights-based freedom struggles. At an antiwar demonstration in Laguna Park, Brown stands on a bench and, before a crowd of fellow Chicana/o activists, describes the war as a threat to their own survival. "We may be the last generation of Chicanos if we don't stop the war," he declares.

If we don't stop the destruction of our culture, we may not be around for the next century. We are the Viet Cong of America. Tooner Flats [based on East Los Angeles neighborhood Lincoln Heights] is Mylai. Just because [Sheriff] Peaches and [Police Chief] Reddin haven't started throwing napalm doesn't mean they have stopped the war. The Poverty Program of Johnson, the Welfare of Roosevelt, Truman, Eisenhower and Kennedy, The New Deal and The Old Deal, the New Frontier as well as Nixon's American Revolution . . . these are further embellishments of the government's pacification program.[65]

While Brown's assertion that Chicanas/os are "the Viet Cong of America" effaces vast historical differences, it draws attention to the limits of liberal universalism. He focuses not on the Democratic Republic of Vietnam (North Vietnam) but on the National Liberation Front (Viet Cong). The NLF was an attractive model for Chicana/o radicals because, unlike the DRV and the Republic of Vietnam (South Vietnam), it was not a landed state government but a colonized insurgent organization. It did not and could not conform to a world of states and nations. Aligning Chicanas/os with the NLF, Brown identifies the unevenness of universal liberal rights. Reformist agendas from Franklin Roosevelt's New Deal to John Kennedy's New Frontier and Lyndon Johnson's Great Society were nothing more than "embellishments of the government's pacification program" for those denied the right to have rights. In an age of official antiracism, lawmakers had found new deracinated names—illegal immigrant, communist insurgent, drug trafficker—for those they distanced or excluded from liberal humanity.

While Brown's statement could be read as a testament to ethnic nationalism, it also, through his identification with Vietnamese, advances an alternative, extranational form of belonging. His and other movement radicals' connection to the NLF is not so much grounded in a shared national liberationist ethic as in their resistance to a government that seeks to either assimilate or eradicate them. Forced assimilation is, he suggests, its own kind of violence. Looking abroad to a country under attack by their own government, Chicana/o activists recognized the norms governing national belonging and the right to execute legitimate violence. The continuities between the policing of Tooner Flats and the killing of civilians at My Lai, Brown suggests, reveal liberalism not as an ever-widening universal but as a normative regime that seeks to transform or contain nonaligned societies and communities. His identification with the NLF highlights the fluid relation between the state's wars on communism, drugs, and crime and its use of violence to define and reinforce the boundaries between the liberal human, the unfree, and the illiberal nonhuman.[66]

Acosta's novel charts the transition from anticommunism to drug control as the foremost mechanism for regulating those boundaries from the Nixon administration on. As Brown readies his defense of the East LA Thirteen—demonstrators arrested for organizing walkouts at underfunded schools in Chicana/o neighborhoods—he and his friends travel to the desert to blow off some steam and take acid. Brown finds solace in the fact that in the desert he is "twenty-five miles and two mountain peaks from Edwards Air Force Base." But as he and his friends are relaxing beside a lake, a landowner flies overhead in a small plane and shakes his fist at them. Soon after, three more men arrive in a motorboat and begin shooting at Brown, calling him a "fucking greaser" and telling him to "get the hell off" their land. Hallucinating from the acid, Brown stumbles backward from the lake and imagines a "giant black bird floating above my head." It carries bombs and a thousand men. He throws rocks at the bird. He aims to strike it "before it can drop those bombs on downtown LA and East LA and downtown Mongolia or Saigon or Haiphong or Quang Tri or Tooner Flats and Lincoln Heights or wherever Cockroaches live."[67] Brown's hallucination connects the war against communism in Southeast Asia to the war against drugs in Los Angeles. His imagined black bird bombs the cities of East Asia and Southeast Asia and the Latina/o neighborhoods of California in one continuous run. Drug control is one more instrument with which the state can rationalize its policing of Asian, black, and Latina/o bodies without acknowledging it as a form of racial and class violence. Without their own land, Brown and his friends face continuous surveillance, whether by the state or white landowners acting with the license of state law. Later, Brown oversees a coroner's examination of a Chicano who had died in jail after being arrested "because he had heroin tracks on his arms."[68] Brown's black bird enacts the state's transformation of its anticommunist crusade into an antidrug one and indicates how a person's identification as an unredeemable communist or drug trafficker begins with being identified as Asian, black, or brown.

Associating black and Latina/o communities with drug use also served to turn acts of collective resistance into acts of individual irrational behavior. When Brown first joins the Chicano movement, after moving from Oakland to Los Angeles, an organizer asks him what kind of cases he has handled. "Criminal. . . . Dope busts and such," Brown answers. When the man asks why he hadn't taken on more "political cases," Brown insists that "every dope bust is a political event."[69] All drug trials are political, he argues, because they occur within a criminal justice system weighted against them as working-class Chicanos. Acosta's novel recognizes that, with liberal lawmakers and media representing drug addiction as a "disease," narcotics-related arrests had emerged as an effective mechanism for delegitimizing the actions of radical antiracist groups like the Black Panthers and the Brown Berets. Whereas the white landowners' innocence is assumed by the law—making their shooting at Brown and his friends a legitimate act of self-defense—Brown faces a criminal justice system that assumes his criminal status and dismisses his behavior as irrational, the result of a troubled mind rather than a valid statement of dissent. Like communism in the 1950s and 1960s, drug use emerged in the Nixon years as a form of unfreedom from which the state must free its hostages through violence in "Saigon or Haiphong or Quang Tri or Tooner Flats."

Acosta's novel interrogates the meaning of defense in an age defined by it. Echoing the Panthers, Brown runs for sheriff of Los Angeles County in 1970 and guarantees that, if elected, he would dissolve the office. (Acosta himself ran for sheriff, collecting half a million votes and finishing second to incumbent Peter Pitchess.) In a television interview with newsman Roland Zanzibar (based on famed journalist Ruben Salazar), Brown admits that he has little chance of winning. "My effort is an educational endeavor," he admits. "The law enforcement officers of this county, of this nation in general, are here for the protection of the few, the maintenance of the status quo. [Instead] I would have a People's Protection Department. I would enlist the aid of the community to find ways to protect ourselves from the violence of our society. Obviously, the answer is not more tanks, helicopters, and tear gas."[70] The LAPD had added the motto "to protect and to serve" to all of its vehicles in 1963. Brown's insistence that police officers are, for him and other Chicanos, a source of violence challenges the universalism of that motto. Who is being protected? And who is being served? He suggests that the state's defense of humanity at home and abroad doesn't extend to him. The LAPD sends "tanks, helicopters, and tear gas" into his neighborhood to secure the county's white bourgeois communities from him and other "cockroaches." Brown's intention to dissolve the sheriff's office and form a "People's Protection Department" forces the reader to ask who is being defended and who is being defended against by the military and the police.

In naming law enforcement as an instrument of racial violence, Brown argues that police violence should be understood as constitutive of, rather than a deviation from, state law. When lawmakers discuss the death of a black or Latino man at the hands of a law-enforcement officer, they tend to see it as an aberration or as the result of local human error, a violation of some institutional code. Instead, Acosta's novel locates racial violence at the center rather than the outer limits of the law. Ethnic studies scholar Dylan Rodríguez argues that the modern state functions through and because of its excesses and violations. "The state's contemporary modality of power and enunciation—its statecraft—works through the constant exceeding of its announced material boundaries and juridical limits," he writes. "Brutality, torture, and excess should be understood as essential elements of American statecraft, not its corruption."[71] The state's excesses aren't excesses at all; they form the basis of the liberal state and its means of governance. A person's or group's status as defended by the United States is made intelligible by bodies and societies that must be defended against. The existence of an institution undertaking "to protect and to serve" is founded on the idea that some deserve that service and others necessitate it. It must, Brown suggests, reinforce "the protection of the few, the maintenance of the status quo" because it has been forged through that uneven distribution of human value. His desire to dissolve the sheriff's office draws attention to the limits of reform-minded change. The trouble with the drug wars is not the misidentification of innocent black Americans and Latinas/os as criminals but the criminalization of blackness and brownness before the fact.

This criminalization was nothing new in the 1970s, as Reed and Acosta recognize, but built on centuries of colonial ideas about Haitians' and indigenous Americans' fitness for self-governance and a receding racial anticommunism. In his 1971 *Rolling Stone* article "Strange Rumblings in Aztlan," counterculture journalist Hunter S. Thompson identified the fluid relation between anticommunism and drug control as a rationale for the LAPD's crackdown on the Chicano movement. Thompson first met Acosta in 1967 and later immortalized him in *Fear and Loathing in Las Vegas* (1971) as the basis of the character Dr. Gonzo. On Acosta's urging, he traveled to Los Angeles to cover the fallout from a massive antiwar demonstration in which a white LAPD officer killed Salazar with a tear-gas bazooka. After conducting interviews with local lawmakers and police officers, including Sheriff Pitchess and Police Chief Edward Davis, Thompson summarized, "The Anglo power structure keeps telling itself that 'the Mexican problem' is really the work of a small organization of well-trained Communist agitators, working 25 hours a day to transform

East L.A. into a wasteland of constant violence." The white lawmakers, he wrote, imagined a combat zone with "mobs of drug-crazed Chicanos prowling the streets at all times, terrorizing the merchants, hurling fire-bombs into banks, looting stores, sacking offices and massing now and then, armed with Chinese Sten pistols, for all-out assaults on the local sheriff's fortress."[72] Thompson was not a radical himself, but his article, like Reed's and Acosta's fiction, distilled the incoherence of the idea of national defense in the Nixon years. Local law-enforcement agencies, militarized through LEAA-funded training and gear, blurred the line between communists and drug traffickers, anti-Asian racism and anti-Chicana/o racism, the war over there and the war over here.

When Nixon declared his war on drugs two months after Thompson wrote these words, he may have been seeking to distract Americans from the war in Southeast Asia—a week earlier, the Daniel Ellsberg revelations had brought to light his administration's secret bombing of Cambodia and Laos—but he also recalibrated it. The state refocused its war against illiberalism on alleged drug traffickers, while targeting some of the same bodies, territories, and societies it had earlier deemed communist. This war—this domestic police action—occasioned a new kind of war novel through which Reed and Acosta reveal racial anticommunism and racial criminalization to be two stages in one unending war.

The CIA as Book Critic

As the Nixon administration channeled federal resources and military technologies into the drug wars, it also faced challenges from radical academics and journalists who argued that the state's anticommunist agenda in Southeast Asia had run counter to its antidrug crusade. To recenter its war-making on the figure of the drug trafficker, the national security state needed its war on drugs to cohere with its containment of communism. This coherence hinged on the belief that communists were to blame for drug addiction among American soldiers and the influx of heroin into the United States. Nixon insisted that he had to Vietnamize the war in order to rescue American soldiers from combat casualties but also from communist-manufactured heroin. The imagined association between communism and narcotics was a difficult one to maintain, since some of the state's closest anticommunist allies in Southeast Asia were also high-volume drug traffickers. As a white Yale graduate student named Alfred

McCoy showed in his 1972 book *The Politics of Heroin in Southeast Asia*, the CIA knew that some of its Laotian and Vietnamese allies were involved in the heroin trade and in some cases even facilitated that trade. Breaking with institutional convention, the CIA tried to block McCoy's book and wrote letters to the editors of *Harper's* and the *Washington Star* in an effort to discredit his findings. The agency's willingness to launch an offensive against McCoy's academic book—a work that wouldn't have found more than a niche audience otherwise—suggests the significance of the antidrug iteration of the idea of defense to the endurance of the defense establishment at the end of the Vietnam War.

McCoy's book began with a visit to Paris in 1971. Having flown from New Haven to conduct research while on a mid-semester break, he interviewed a French intelligence officer who admitted that in the 1950s he had used narcotics trafficking in Southeast Asia to assemble and fund an anticommunist coalition that included high-ranking officials in Laos and Vietnam. When France left in 1954, he told McCoy, "'Your CIA' had taken over the whole thing, drugs included."[73] This interview led McCoy on a whirlwind research tour of Southeast Asia, during which he traced much of the region's heroin back to some of the Johnson and Nixon administrations' closest allies, including Laotian General Vang Pao, the commander of a CIA-trained "secret army," and associates of South Vietnamese Vice President Nguyen Cao Ky. In his book, he argued that the United States had contributed to the region's narcotics market by aligning itself with anticommunist drug traffickers, concealing their allies' involvement in the drug trade, and facilitating the movement of narcotics across borders by lending CIA-owned aircraft to known Laotian traffickers. "It is ironic," McCoy concluded, "that America's heroin plague is of its own making."[74]

Two months before the book's scheduled release, Senator William Proxmire, a Democrat from Wisconsin, invited McCoy to share his research in a congressional session on international narcotics control. In a twenty-minute statement, McCoy delivered a detailed account of how the CIA had, in the interest of subduing its communist enemies, created conditions that accelerated the manufacture and distribution of heroin in Southeast Asia. Citing rising rates of heroin addiction among American teenagers, he twisted the media narrative of the "heroin plague" that attributed drugs and crime to Asian, black, and Latina/o culture and instead laid the blame on anticommunist state agencies. Echoing sensational news media accounts of teenage drug use, he concluded his remarks by stating, "We now have to decide which is more important to our country—propping up corrupt governments in Southeast Asia or getting heroin out of our high schools."[75] McCoy's congressional statement identified the contradictions of the war on drugs. The United States was, he revealed, declaring itself to be at war with something that it had condoned and even abetted throughout its anticommunist crusade in Asia.

McCoy's book gave extensive attention to the alleged drug crisis in the armed forces. He argued that high-ranking officials in the Nguyen Van Thieu administration, including Generals Dang Van Quang and Ngo Du, had facilitated and enriched themselves through the sale of heroin to American soldiers in South Vietnam. American commanders had, he wrote, shielded their allies from criticism out of fear that revelations of the Thieu-Ky administration's involvement in the drug trade might further undermine the government's standing in the region. The United States had not concerned itself with halting the flow of heroin to its men in Vietnam, because that heroin was good business for some of Southeast Asia's most hardcore anticommunists. "World War II gave us a generation of collegians and suburbanites," McCoy wrote. "The Vietnam War seems to be fathering a generation of junkies."[76] McCoy's book did lean on inflated statistics about drug use in the armed forces and made more than a dozen references, echoing Nixon, to "America's heroin plague."[77] But it also reframed stories of addicted white American soldiers—around whom the state had organized its drug wars—in relation to the state's involvement in narcotics traffic rather than their immersion in an "exotic" cultural environment of illiberal beliefs and behaviors. The transition from anticommunism to drug control in the last years of the Vietnam War was an uneven one, and McCoy's book showed why.

The graduate student's statement before Congress that summer attracted the CIA's attention. A week later, agency official Cord Meyer visited the New York offices of McCoy's publisher, Harper and Row, and, claiming that McCoy's "distorted" research threatened national security, urged that it withdraw the book. Harper and Row refused but did allow the CIA to review the work ahead of its August release. A friend of McCoy's leaked this information to investigative journalist Seymour Hersh, who, in a *New York Times* article, detailed the CIA's "unusual public defense" against allegations made by a twenty-six-year-old graduate student that had, until the agency interfered, "failed to gain much national attention."[78] After Harper and Row dismissed the agency's criticisms of the book and announced that it would release it on schedule and unaltered, the CIA continued its effort to discredit McCoy and his research by writing letters to the editors of news media that had cited him, inter-viewed him, or served as a venue for his work. In a letter to the *Washington Star*, which had deferred to McCoy's account of the Southeast Asian drug trade in a recent article, CIA executive director William Colby wrote that "charges of this nature have been made previously and each time have been most carefully investigated and found to be unsubstantiated." After stressing that "the public record on this subject is clear," Colby went on to list statements made by the legal counsel for the Senate Foreign Relations Committee, Director of the Bureau of Narcotics and Dangerous Drugs John Ingersoll, and CIA Director Richard Helms.[79] Colby's defense of the national security state amounted to a series of denials made by its own officials. McCoy's book should not be believed, he contended, because it was not part of "the public record on this subject," and it could not be part of the public record because it was not issued or corroborated by the agencies incriminated in its findings. Colby's letters showed the state's struggle to control what counted as rational, fact-based information at the end of the Vietnam War. But as McCoy himself noted, "Given the rather incestuous nature of Mr. Colby's rebuttal, it is largely a question of whether his or any other Nixon Administration spokesman's optimistic, sanctimonious pronouncements . . . can be believed."[80]

Colby began all of his letters by acknowledging that "normally we do not respond publicly to allegations made against [the] CIA."[81] So why did the agency decide that it had to refute allegations made by an unknown, twenty-six-year-old graduate student writing his first book? Why did it break its own rule to contest his claims? McCoy delivered his statement before Congress as the Nixon administration was struggling to reorganize the racial regime of defense around the figure of the drug trafficker who had, it argued, undermined the nation's men in Southeast Asia and now threatened to do the same in cities across America. As the state wound down its war against communists in Southeast Asia, it began a new one against drugs there, throughout the Americas, and at home. Like the re-ceding anticommunism of the 1950s and 1960s, the war on drugs situated the state as an antiracist force in the world, defending free societies from agents of unfreedom who threatened to "enslave" the next generation with substance addiction. McCoy's book contradicted this account of the antidrug state by showing how its anticommunist wars had for decades run counter to its drug wars. His findings revealed the contradictions of world-ordering national defense. This is why the CIA felt that it had to delegitimize his research.

The defeat in Vietnam created an enduring crisis for the empire of defense, forcing it underground to conduct covert wars against alleged criminals and drug traffickers from Mexico to Colombia and from Washington to Chicago. That crisis did not mark the end of permanent war but a shift in how it would be waged. The United States turned its attention from the Viet Cong to the Viet Cong of America, from Vietnamese communists to drug traffickers the world over. It set out to defend humanity—to police the boundaries of human being—one drug bust at a time.

CHAPTER FOUR

Kicking the Vietnam Syndrome with Human Rights

On December 10, 1990, with four hundred thousand American soldiers and marines readied for war along the Saudi–Kuwaiti border, George H. W. Bush issued a presidential proclamation marking December 10 as Human Rights Day. First recognized by the Truman administration, Human Rights Day commemorates the UN General Assembly's signing of the Universal Declaration of Human Rights. Acknowledging Human Rights Day with a proclamation has, since Truman, been a routine event every December for the sitting president. With a war on the horizon, Bush used the occasion to address the looming Gulf War as a humanitarian cause. "In a world where human rights are routinely denied in too many lands, nowhere is that situation more tragic and more urgent today than in Kuwait," he said. Listing the atrocities reportedly committed by Iraqi soldiers in Kuwait, Bush concluded, "As long as such assaults occur, as long as inhumane regimes deny basic human rights, our work is not done."[1] The Iraqi invasion threatened the future of Kuwait, but it also, Bush alleged, threatened human rights the world over. Americans could not feel secure in their own liberal rights until those rights were restored to the citizens of this small, oil-rich state in the Persian Gulf. The war in the Middle East was not a war at all but, as Bush stressed that fall and winter, a unified "stand in defense of peace and freedom."[2]

Although humanitarianism is most identified with the Clinton administration's wars in Somalia, Bosnia, and Kosovo, it also informed the Gulf War—a conflict that, while remembered for its association with live television and oil, laid the groundwork for a decade of "one world" humanitarian wars. This new rationale for waging war necessitated rewriting the story of the Vietnam War for a post–Cold War world. The day after declaring Kuwait liberated, at a meeting of the conservative American Legislative Exchange Council, Bush clarified what he believed to be the broader significance of the US-led coalition's war. "By God, we've kicked the Vietnam syndrome once and for all," he told the room of state legislators, before leaning over to shake hands with his secretary of defense, Dick Cheney.[3] Ronald Reagan had introduced the idea of the "Vietnam syndrome" in his 1980 presidential campaign to describe the nation's unwillingness to intervene in overseas wars after Vietnam and the misguided belief, in Reagan's assessment, that American soldiers had been "aggressors bent on imperialistic conquests" in Southeast Asia. That story needed to be revised. Vietnam should instead be remembered, Reagan argued, as a "noble cause" in which "a small country newly free from colonial rule sought our help in establishing self-rule and the means of self-defense against a totalitarian neighbor bent on conquest."[4] Reagan believed that for the United States to reestablish itself as a moral leader in the world, it needed to reframe the Vietnam War as an act of defense, and his successor agreed. Bush knew that kicking the Vietnam syndrome meant kicking the idea of self-interested war. He recognized the need to revise the story the nation told about the Vietnam War if he were to restore his government's standing as the defender of liberal humanity, the leader of the free world. The president needed, he knew, to restore the idea of defense.

Bush owed his success in defining the Gulf War as the "noble cause" the Vietnam War never was to the emergence of post-Soviet human rights. Conservatives and liberals celebrated the end of the Cold War as evidence that liberal democratic values were, as they had long believed, universal values. With the Soviet Union on the verge of dissolution, they imagined an undivided world modeled on the ideals of liberal democratic governance and individual freedoms. After two decades in which the defense establishment had gone underground—waging a racial war against drugs and crime in the United States and by covert means in Colombia, Laos, Mexico, and elsewhere—the decline of the USSR and the rise of liberal humanitarianism offered the empire of defense new life as an aboveground force for good in the world. A year earlier, political scientist Francis Fukuyama had announced the end of history—declaring liberal democracy the highest achievement and final form of human government[5]—and Bush was listening. With the decline of Soviet communism, his administration envisioned a dawning future in which there would be universal consent to the values of the United States and its Western allies. After building a coalition of thirty-four states, including the Soviet Union, the architects of the war encouraged the idea that an international alliance had come to the rescue of the victims of human rights abuses, Kuwaitis, from a racist dictator, Iraqi President Saddam Hussein, who had not yet recognized the changing world order. The Bush administration's decision to station forces along the Saudi border was not figured as an act of war but as an insurance measure against further human rights abuses on the part of Hussein. It was codenamed "Operation Desert Shield." The president described it as an act of defense, a humanitarian stand against Hussein's racial and religious intolerance.

Bush considered the Gulf War a "rare opportunity" to achieve a post–Cold War consensus in which, as he told Congress that fall, "the rule of law supplants the rule of the jungle."[6] Though not naming Vietnam in his address—even, it seemed, going to lengths *not* to name it—Bush suggested that the United States, disoriented by an ideological struggle with communism, had lost its direction in the "jungle" of Southeast Asia. But the decline of Soviet communism offered the nation a renewed and clarified sense of who it was and what it stood for. A US-led internationalism could now form around the rule of law, a rule grounded in human rights. Bush articulated his new world order as a conclusive ending to the Vietnam War and the long Cold War, but he also suggested that it was the beginning of a new era in which war and human rights converged, masking the violence carried out by the humanitarian state. As earlier presidents had, he described war as antithetical to post–World War II liberal democratic governance rather than fundamental to it. The Gulf War could not, he maintained, be a real war because it was being fought to defend human rights against an illiberal actor who fell outside the new global order.

But most Americans remember the Gulf War for orchestrated, around-the-clock television coverage. CNN broadcast the conflict twenty-four hours a day. Viewers could watch recordings of bombing runs taken by cameras embedded in the missiles themselves, missiles that never seemed to miss their target. The footage contributed to the idea that Americans had access to uncensored knowledge of the war and that, with the introduction of GPS-guided bombs, coalition forces were waging a clean war against non-civilian, infrastructural targets.[7] That idea has come in for criticism. Anthony Swofford's memoir *Jarhead* (2003) and Jonathan Demme's remake of *The Manchurian Candidate* (2004), for example, address how state-regulated media constructed the conflict in the interest of subduing the kind of antiwar movement that, Bush and his advisers believed, had derailed the war in Southeast Asia.[8] But the architects of the war did more than overturn or erase the unsettling memory of the Vietnam War through the Weinberger–Powell doctrine's emphasis on the execution of overwhelming force and a swift, strategic exit; they also integrated it into a mandate for humanitarian war. The Bush administration created a right–left consensus behind a war in the Persian Gulf by channeling the kind of humanitarian affect associated with the antiwar movement of the 1960s, forming a martial bridge from the Vietnam War to the "interregnum" of the 1990s. The Gulf War, as the first humanitarian war, marked not the last shot of the Cold War but a continuation and reconfiguration of a liberal empire that had fought communism in Korea and Vietnam and narcotics in Southeast Asia, Latin America, and the United States, all in the name of defense.

The convergence of humanitarianism and militarism allowed the United States to reassert itself as a moral force in the world by reframing its wars—earlier defined as anticommunist and anticrime—as a defense against human rights abusers. Humanitarianism was nothing new in 1990, of course. But when President Harry Truman first recognized Human Rights Day in 1949, he had Soviet and Chinese communism on his mind. There was no separation for his administration between defending human rights and fighting communism. Four decades later, the fall of the Soviet Union threatened to undermine the idea of defense with which the United States had waged war since Truman's time. The defense establishment found itself a crusader without a cause. From Reagan, who re-escalated the Cold War, to Bush, the state underwent a transition from anticommunist humanitarianism to one-world humanitarianism, from asserting the dominance of liberalism to assuming it. It did not make that transition without some stumbles. With Bush at first struggling to tell a coherent story about his government's involvement in the Persian Gulf, a fifteen-year-old Kuwaiti girl named Nayirah showed him the high road to war. Her infamous statement before the Congressional Human Rights Caucus in October 1990 included the fictitious allegation that Iraqi soldiers had taken infants from incubators "and left the children to die on the cold floor."[9] Though invented, her resonant account of Iraqi brutality was crucial in authorizing the Bush administration's own story of a humanitarian crusade in the Middle East.

This story created an enduring obstacle for liberal antiwar filmmakers, including David O. Russell and Barry Levinson. While critical of the war's constructedness as a media event, Russell's *Three Kings* (1999) and Levinson's *Wag the Dog* (1997) are more ambivalent about how human rights fit into that criticism. When Bush constructed a resolution to the Vietnam War by reclaiming it as a noble cause—by kicking the Vietnam syndrome—he assimilated it into a new stage of permanent war that connected the end of the Cold War, the drug wars, and the beginning of the war on terror. But when the home video of white LAPD officers beating an unarmed Rodney King surfaced days after the cease-fire, it shook the state's newfound humanitarianism. Poet and activist June Jordan later wrote of the Gulf War, connecting it to racial violence at home, "All who believe only they possess / human being and therefore human rights / they no longer stood among the possibly humane."[10]

Humanitarian War in the Interregnum

The Gulf War was not the first time the United States had marshaled humanitarianism as a rationale for war. When the UN General Assembly signed the Universal Declaration of Human Rights in 1948, the Truman administration was in the middle of forming a new centralized defense and intelligence infrastructure that, though motivated by Soviet communism and the Chinese Civil War, sought to present the United States as a defender of human rights around the world. The Cold War state and human rights were intertwined from the start, with officials treating communists as human rights abusers and human rights abusers as communists. Truman modeled this marriage of anticommunism and humanitarianism during the Korean War by describing the nation's enemy not as a sovereign state but as "Communist slavery."[11]

But human rights did not move out of the shadow of anticommunism and become a dominant value in the United States until after the defeat in Vietnam. That war marked the breakdown of containment as a framework for knowing the world and remaking it by force. Americans were no longer willing to believe that installing anticommunist governments in distant countries was critical either to national security or to the benefit of the people living under those governments. The United States needed a new way of seeing itself in the world with which Americans as well as Asians, Africans, and Eastern Europeans might agree. Over the next two decades, human rights, decoupled from anticommunism, moved to the center of the defense establishment. While humanitarian militarism has been associated with the ensuing wars in the Balkans, the Gulf

War launched this new era through a careful revision and assimilation, rather than erasure, of the war in Southeast Asia. Three years after the end of the Vietnam War, commemorating the signing of the Universal Declaration of Human Rights, President Jimmy Carter declared human rights to be "the soul of our foreign policy."[12] Though dismissed by Reagan as a naive understanding of a dangerous world, Carter's words would have an enduring effect. Over time, Vietnam was transformed into a testament to, rather than a negation of, the nation's commitment to human rights.

Twelve years after Carter declared the United States a humanitarian state, as Bush readied the nation for a new war, Americans believed that the Vietnam War had been ended at least in part by the humanitarian sentiment of those watching on television at home. This revisionist account redeemed the defeat as a moral success. After the war in Southeast Asia, ethnic studies scholar Neda Atanasoski writes, "documentaries and photographs depicting the horrors of war allowed U.S. audiences to experience outrage at having caused the suffering of Vietnamese women, children, and civilians, affirming the ability of U.S. citizens to distinguish right from wrong."[13] Americans embraced images of wartime atrocities, including Eddie Adams's "Saigon Execution" (1968) and Nick Ut's "Napalm Girl" (1972), as evidence of the nation's self-reckoning, transforming them into icons of their own national trauma and rehabilitation. Somehow images thought to condemn the state's death-dealing in Southeast Asia— intended to elicit anger and humanitarian affect from Americans at home—formed the foundation of future wars, beginning with Bush's war in the Persian Gulf.

The figure of the Vietnamese refugee was at the center of this humanitarian-minded rehabilitation of the Vietnam War. Reagan himself recognized the usefulness of the refugee to rationalizing war as a human good, seeing the arrival of "boat people" from Southeast Asia as evidence of the rightness of the war fought there and the need to "do a better job of exporting Americanism" in the future.[14] When he declared the Vietnam War a noble cause, Reagan asked, in effect, how could it not be, when Vietnamese refugees had fled their communist-governed homeland for the shores of freedom-loving America? Critical refugee studies scholar Yen Le Espiritu argues that the success of some Vietnamese refugees has been used to grant the United States a kind of retroactive "win" in Southeast Asia. Through the rehearsal of stories of "good refugees," defenders of the war maintain that it was worth it in the end because thousands of

Vietnamese were "saved" from an illiberal social world.[15] The figure of the successful Vietnamese refugee is assumed to validate the state's role as an advocate for human rights and to serve as an illustration of what Vietnamese life would look like now if the United States had seen the war through as a humanitarian cause. Like the state's anticommunist and antidrug agendas before it, humanitarianism functioned after the Vietnam War as an instrument of liberal antiracism with which the state distinguished legitimate, assimilable forms of difference (the good refugee) from illegitimate, unassimilable forms (the unconverted), while masking its role in forming new racial categories and divisions by articulating them in the deracinated language of beliefs and behaviors (the human rights abuser).

When Bush set out to kick the Vietnam syndrome in the Persian Gulf, officials, writers, filmmakers, and activists had been struggling to remake the meaning of the war for more than a decade through stories of Southeast Asian refugees, POW/MIA activism, Maya Lin's Vietnam Veterans Memorial, and Hollywood movies, big and small.[16] While much of the cultural work of the Reagan years focused on recentering and rehabilitating the traumatized white veteran, the Bush administration extended that work in the Persian Gulf by reclaiming the soldier as a liberal humanitarian actor who could at last rescue Vietnam by liberating Kuwait. This idea of humanitarian rescue was founded on an ahistorical account of Vietnamese refugees "taken in" by the United States and the humanitarian ethic of an earlier generation of war resisters. The state reasserted itself as a defender of human rights through testaments to the humanitarian crises it had created in Southeast Asia, obscuring the origins of an American-made disaster in the act of retelling it.

If the Vietnam syndrome is understood in Reagan's original usage as the belief that the United States acted out of self-interest in Vietnam, then kicking it meant deflecting attention from what the nation stood to gain from a war in the Middle East. Although most of the soldiers who fought in the Gulf War were Americans, Bush was careful to describe the war as being waged by an international coalition against a rogue state. This was a war fought not by the United States but by an alliance of right-minded governments armed with twelve UN resolutions. Gone was the three-worlds model of the Cold War in which the United States and the Soviet Union vied for influence in and access to the markets of the decolonizing world.[17] Instead, the first Bush administration framed the Gulf War as a moral errand undertaken by a unified world in defense of liberal freedoms.

Fukuyama, Bush, and others believed that the end of the Cold War meant that liberal democratic values had won out. We were all, or would be, liberals now, and the Gulf War signaled the commencement of that new world order. Bush and his allies advertised the Soviet Union's involvement in the coalition as heralding a new liberal consensus founded on human rights. When a White House reporter asked him if by declaring an end to the Vietnam syndrome he was forecasting a new era of interventionism, the president responded that he believed the threat of war alone would be enough, after the US-led coalition's dominant showing in the Persian Gulf, to force nonaligned states to conform to liberal democratic internationalism. "I think when we say something that is objectively correct, like don't take over a neighbor or you're going to bear some responsibility, people are going to listen, because I think out of all this will be a newfound—put it this way, a reestablished credibility for the United States of America," Bush stated.[18] Unlike in Vietnam, he recognized, there would no longer be an ideological counterweight—communism—to challenge the nation's belief in the goodness of its government's wars. Bush imagined a world where all nations subscribed to his government's account of what was "objectively correct," whether by choice or by the threat of force. His administration had kicked the Vietnam syndrome by reestablishing defense as the governing idea of the wars in Southeast Asia, the Middle East, and wherever else the United States invaded next. The humanitarian Gulf War built on earlier iterations of the idea of defense—anticommunist, anti-drug, anticrime—that, like it, assumed the military to be an instrument of antiracism by which the United States defended the world against forms of government that it deemed illegitimate, illiberal, backward, and racist.

But the union of human rights and militarism introduced a troubling contradiction—creating humanitarian crises in the course of alleviating them—that the state tried to resolve with stories of new "clean" and "smart" war technologies. CNN and other news media celebrated these technologies, including guided munitions and surface-to-air Patriot missiles, for how they limited human error and reduced civilian casualties. Whereas the bombing of Southeast Asia had been indiscriminate, killing hundreds of thousands of civilians—as iconized by the image of Phan Thi Kim Phúc running from a napalm attack on her village in 1972—the coalition's bombing of the Persian Gulf was imagined as a series of targeted strikes on faceless infrastructure. Fewer than one in ten bombs detonated were laser- or satellite-guided, though, and the high-tech missiles didn't fare much better than unguided, or "dumb," bombs, hitting their intended

KICKING THE VIETNAM SYNDROME WITH HUMAN RIGHTS

targets less than half the time. But broadcasters internalized coalition commander Norman Schwarzkopf's memorable term for the bombings he ordered: they were "surgical strikes."[19]

This assent to the state's account of the war is satirized in *Wag the Dog* when communications adviser Conrad Brean (Robert De Niro) describes the Gulf War as a Hollywood-made event, asking, "What did you see day after day? The one smart bomb falling down the chimney."[20] Though untrue, the idea of the war as a clean, mechanized conflict stuck with Americans. All they remember is that "one smart bomb" that demonstrated, they were told, the precision of the rest. The technologies of the US-led coalition forces were seen as humane because they hid the bodies of the dead and humanizing because they corrected for the "unclean" violence of the Iraqi Army. When 147 Americans died in the Gulf War—far fewer than commanders had predicted—some at defense agencies received this as evidence that a "revolution in military affairs" had begun, imagining a future in which technological advances would allow wars to be waged from a distance and with no American casualties.[21] While this future was never realized, the idea of a bloodless war in the Persian Gulf, of that "one smart bomb falling down the chimney," would facilitate the waging of humanitarian wars in Somalia, Bosnia, and Kosovo under the Clinton administration.

Humanitarian war is based on a belief that liberal rights are inherent in all human beings and that when those rights are obstructed by an illiberal state, it is in the interest of all to intervene and restore them. Like earlier wars to combat communists and alleged drug traffickers, it is assumed to be a kind of nonwar against a belief or behavior rather than a legitimate antagonist. Although Bush did not shrink from describing the conflict in the Persian Gulf as a war, the humanitarian state that he inaugurated articulated itself as answering a higher calling than regular war by securing liberal freedoms around the world. The universal language of human rights disguises the fact that war, even when it is fought under the banner of humanitarianism, is founded on and reinforces one kind of human being above all others. Liberal war creates and fortifies the boundaries of the universal, the human, and the good. It is not universal or antiracist. It is a racial regime. The humanitarian state does not, Slovenian philosopher Slavoj Žižek writes, set out to transform victims of human rights abuses into self-governed individuals, since "the Other to be protected is good *insofar as it remains a victim*; the moment it no longer behaves as a victim but wants to strike back on its own, it suddenly, magically turns into a terrorist/fundamentalist/drug-trafficking Other."[22]

   Yet the Gulf War coincided with the beginning of a decade that is remembered as an interregnum between the Cold War and the war on terror.
Human rights—the humanitarian Gulf War—bridged anticommunism
and counterterrorism and sustained the empire of defense in the absence
of Soviet communism. Bush's ecstatic declaration that his administration
had "kicked the Vietnam syndrome" in the Persian Gulf imagined an end
to one war and launched another. He regarded the liberation of Kuwait
to be his government's obligation as the leader of the free world, a title
confirmed, in his mind, by the downfall of the Soviet Union. This was an
imaginative ending to the Vietnam War, but it was also a new beginning,
because the union of human rights and war was authorized by the humanitarian feeling of the antiwar movement that had rebelled against the
war in Southeast Asia. The militarization of human rights is the link that
binds the Vietnam War to a new stage in the defense era, and it was facilitated by a young Kuwaiti girl named Nayirah. Her orchestrated testimony
shows the interregnum to be part of, rather than a break from, an age of
permanent war that stretches from the formation of the Department of
Defense into the twenty-first century.

The High Road to War

The Gulf War did not begin as a battle for human rights. On the morning
of August 2, 1990, after learning that the Iraqi Army had invaded Kuwait,
President Bush was unsure what to tell Americans about his administration's intentions in the Persian Gulf. He did not know at the time whether
military force would be needed, but he wanted to have that choice available if it were. This, he knew, would mean convincing Americans, most of
whom had never heard of Kuwait, that intervening in the region was vital
to the nation's interests. Writing later in a book he coauthored with his
national security adviser, Brent Scowcroft, Bush acknowledged, "We had
a big job ahead of shaping opinion at home and abroad and could little
afford bellicose mistakes at the start."[23] But for the next two months, Bush
struggled to communicate why the events in the Middle East should matter to Americans. At first, he stressed that allowing Hussein to control so
much of the world's oil reserves could destabilize the region and endanger
the United States. With Kuwait's oil wells, the Hussein government would
govern a fifth of known oil resources and, as Bush told Congress, have
"the economic and military power, as well as the arrogance, to intimidate

and coerce its neighbors—neighbors who control the lion's share of the world's remaining oil reserves."[24] He made the case that the United States couldn't run the risk of letting Hussein overrun Saudi Arabia and gain access to the lion's share of a resource on which the United States depended.

Going to war for oil didn't resonate with most Americans, who, by early October, remained skeptical about the need for a war in the Persian Gulf.[25] Bush's secretary of state, James Baker, made matters worse by suggesting that the administration was waging a war in the Middle East for the American worker, stating, "The economic lifeline of the industrial world runs from the Gulf, and we cannot permit a dictator such as this to sit astride that economic lifeline. And to bring it down to the level of the average American citizen, let me say that means jobs. If you want to sum it up in one word, it's jobs."[26] In the first months after the Iraqi invasion, the Bush administration came across as if it were running for office, framing the conflict in terms of gas prices and jobs, rather than preparing the nation for war. The president was going to great lengths to avoid mentioning the Vietnam War, and he had not yet used human rights as a call to arms. Although Bush and his team continued to cite rising oil costs as a reason for intervening in Kuwait throughout the fall and winter, it was clear that gas prices alone wouldn't convince Americans of the need for war. Bush didn't discover the high road to war until a Kuwaiti girl named Nayirah gave him a focusing event through which he could build a new story—a human rights story—about the war in the Persian Gulf.

Two months after the invasion of Kuwait, on October 10, the Congressional Human Rights Caucus held a hearing on human rights abuses allegedly committed by the invading Iraqi soldiers. Founded and cochaired by Congressmen Tom Lantos, a California Democrat, and John Edward Porter, an Illinois Republican, the Human Rights Caucus is a loose association rather than a formal committee of Congress. It conducts itself much as a committee would but doesn't require that testimonies be delivered under oath, meaning witnesses are not vulnerable to legal action should they lie. Lantos and Porter heard testimonies from dozens of witnesses and human rights advocates that day, but none were as moving as that given by Nayirah, a fifteen-year-old Kuwaiti girl who did not give her full name, the congressmen said, for fear of inviting retaliation against her family. Before the caucus and a television audience, Nayirah recalled how, in the second week after the invasion, she had been volunteering at the al-Addan hospital in Hadiya when it was ransacked by Iraqi soldiers. "I saw the Iraqi soldiers come into the hospital with guns," she testified, struggling to hold back tears. "They took the babies out of the incubators, took the incubators, and left the children to die on the cold floor."[27] She went on to describe how the Iraqis had tortured her friend and burned entire neighborhoods, but the story of babies being removed from incubators was the one that everyone remembered, defining for Americans the brutality of the Iraqi Army.

After Nayirah had finished, Porter closed the hearing by noting that, in the caucus's eight-year history, he had never heard "a record of inhumanity, brutality, and sadism [comparable with] the ones that the witnesses have given us today. I don't know how the people of the civilized countries of this world can fail to do everything within their power to remove this scourge from the face of our Earth."[28] That night at a White House event, Bush told Porter that he had watched the caucus hearing on CNN and was shocked by what he had seen. Five days later, Bush told Nayirah's incubator story at a Dallas fund-raiser for gubernatorial candidate Clayton Williams, referring to Hussein for the first time as "Hitler revisited."[29] He went on to cite the story at least six more times at events that fall. The war was no longer about oil. It was, Bush asserted, about saving babies from a Hitler-like menace.

Only after the war did Americans learn that Nayirah's testimony was fabricated. Ten months after the cease-fire, journalist John MacArthur revealed in a *New York Times* editorial that Nayirah was not your average Kuwaiti teenager. She was the daughter of the country's ambassador to the United States, Saud Nasir al-Sabah, who had been sitting four seats down from her, unacknowledged, at the caucus hearing.[30] Nayirah never volunteered at the al-Addan hospital. She had visited only once and, during that visit, had not witnessed babies being taken from incubators by looting soldiers, because it had never happened. The incubator story was a myth that had been circulating among Kuwaitis in Britain and the United States since the late summer and was treated as fact by the London *Daily Telegraph* and the *Los Angeles Times*. Nayirah's decision to assume the story as her own was a result of coaching by the public-relations firm Hill and Knowlton for its client, Citizens for a Free Kuwait, a US-based organization bankrolled by the Kuwaiti government to advocate for the United States to intervene on behalf of Kuwait. Acting under CFK's direction, Hill and Knowlton chose and advised the witnesses who testified during the Human Rights Caucus hearing.[31]

Although there is no way of measuring what effect Hill and Knowlton's efforts may have had on the nation's attitude toward Kuwait, the reason-

ing behind their decision to represent the conflict as a humanitarian crisis foreshadows the strategies later used by the Bush administration. Hill
and Knowlton's method was a new style of strategic communication that
takes account of the insights of human behavioral sciences and a studied
knowledge of the client's targeted cultural environment.[32] On the basis of
social scientific and cultural research, the firm determined that it needed
to do two things to convince Americans of the need to intervene in the
Persian Gulf. First, it had to encourage them to see Kuwait as a nation
committed to democratic values and women's rights. It stressed, for example, that Kuwaiti women were allowed to drive. (It avoided mentioning
that women couldn't vote.) Second, Hill and Knowlton discovered that
Americans took to the idea of Hussein as a villain, as an enemy of human
rights everywhere.[33] This was the unambiguous story Hill and Knowlton
set out to tell that fall: Kuwait was a democratic nation and an advocate
for women's rights, while Hussein was a brutal dictator threatened by and
striving to overrun liberal Kuwait.

Nayirah was the ideal candidate through whom to communicate this
message. Before the Human Rights Caucus hearing, Hill and Knowlton
instructed its "witnesses" on how to dress, and Nayirah wore an embroi-
dered sweater with her long hair in a braid. She looked like any American teenager might, and by testifying on behalf of her country, she embodied Kuwait's alleged commitment to women's rights. Her testimony
underscored the callousness of the Iraqi Army by communicating that it
had ended her generation's dream of a brighter future for Kuwait. "We
are children no more," she told Lantos and Porter. As a stand-in for her
country, Nayirah's American-style dress and manner attested to Kuwait's
assimilation into the liberal West, whereas her testimony underscored
that its invading neighbor could not be assimilated and sought to destabilize post-Soviet liberal internationalism. Under the coaching of Hill and
Knowlton, Nayirah invited Americans to see their own government as
the solution to the Hussein government's illegitimate violence, which, she
suggested, encroached on women's rights and on the freedoms of ethnic
and religious minorities. The public-relations firm constructed an imagined scenario in which the United States rescued assimilable, modern
women from unassimilable, backward Muslim men. Their star witness's
testimony validated the state's already well-established practice of sorting the world into liberal humanity (the West), those on whom liberal
freedoms may be "conferred" (Kuwaitis), and those against whom freedoms must be defended (Iraqis). Nayirah's orchestrated words reframed

the war in the Persian Gulf as the new liberal struggle for humanity after the fall of Soviet communism.

The effectiveness of Nayirah's account of human rights abuses by the Iraqi Army did not go unnoticed by the Bush administration. Within days, the president began referencing the incubator story at fund-raisers, rallies, and military bases across the country. At the Dallas event, for example, Bush described the "horrible tales" he had heard from Kuwaitis, all of which echoed testimony given before Lantos and Porter, and told of how "newborn babies [were being] thrown out of incubators and the incubators then shipped off to Baghdad." These atrocities, he remarked, were reminiscent of Nazi Germany. "But remember, when Hitler's war ended, there were the Nuremberg trials."[34] This was the first time Bush alluded to Nayirah's much-discussed testimony, and it was also the first time he characterized Hussein as analogous to Hitler. The president's words suggested that he had recognized what Hill and Knowlton had earlier discovered. To convince Americans of the need to intervene in the Middle East, he needed to foreground the moral stakes of the war. This meant telling a black-and-white story of innocent victims (Kuwaiti children) and an unambiguous villain (Hussein). Bush's allusion to the Nuremberg trials, which established the tribunal as a basic instrument of international human rights law, reinforced the idea that what was at issue in the Persian Gulf was his government's mandate to defend the rest of the world against human rights abuses. He based his case on the image of newborn babies being thrown from incubators.

It took only three months for the incubator story to go from rumor to documented fact. On November 27, the UN Security Council held a hearing on the Iraqi invasion of Kuwait for which Hill and Knowlton organized witness testimony. The story of babies taken from incubators by Iraqi soldiers was recounted at the hearing, this time by a doctor (using an assumed name) who testified that he had overseen the burial of 120 infants, including 40 he had buried himself.[35] Two days later, the National Security Council issued a resolution authorizing the use of military force if the Iraqi Army did not retreat by January 15. Three weeks later, on December 19, Amnesty International, the world's best-known human rights NGO, released an eighty-four-page report on human rights abuses in occupied Kuwait. It confirmed that Iraqi soldiers had looted incubators from at least three hospitals in Kuwait City, resulting in the deaths of 312 infants.[36] Although Amnesty would later retract the report, the damage was done.

The incubator myth had been confirmed by a renowned human rights organization, and Bush ran with it. On January 9, with coalition forces readied for war, the president wrote a letter to college students in which he described the conflict as "unambiguous—right vs. wrong" and cited Amnesty's findings as his evidence. "Each day that passes," he concluded, is "another day of atrocities for Amnesty International to document."[37] The letter was sent to 460 college newspapers. With the Vietnam War on his mind, Bush understood that large-scale antiwar demonstrations could transform the conversation surrounding the war effort. With an assist from Amnesty International, Bush's letter mobilized the humanitarian ethic of the antiwar movement to military ends. The United States was, he contended, on the side of humanity in the Persian Gulf, and every college student who resisted that effort was enabling further human rights abuses against Kuwaiti children. The point he tried to make with the Amnesty-authenticated incubator story was that in the post–Cold War era the liberal collegian should welcome rather than resist war as a humanitarian cause.

While the Nayirah testimony may not have changed the course of the Gulf War, it introduced the idea of humanitarian defense through which the United States would fight future wars. This transition was achieved by connecting the Iraqi invasion of Kuwait not only to the Holocaust but also to the Vietnam War. The Human Rights Caucus hearing made Nayirah and the fictitious dead infants the symbolic victims of the conflict. The story of murdered babies and a refugeed Asian girl summoned the visual legacies of the My Lai massacre and of Phúc running from a napalm attack on her village. Unlike in Vietnam, however, the United States had not caused their suffering, and by coming to the Kuwaitis' rescue, it was able to revise the memory of the war in Southeast Asia by transferring those human rights abuses from American soldiers in Vietnam to the Hussein regime in Kuwait. Although the Nayirah testimony was broadcast live on CNN and shown on other news channels in the following weeks, it never delivered an enduring visual icon in the mold of Robert Haeberle's My Lai photos or Ut's "Napalm Girl." Instead, it lived on as a story that, without its own visual material, drew on that of the war in Southeast Asia and the idea of national "innocence lost" that it signified in the United States—but with a new distribution of trauma, guilt, and virtue. This absence of a visual icon meant that the Nayirah testimony rewrote rather than erased the icons of the Vietnam War. It kicked the Vietnam syndrome.[38]

But when Bush decided not to continue to Baghdad and oust the man he had labeled the new Hitler, he found himself facing the same criticism that he had earlier used to shame the antiwar left.[39] For some humanitarian internationalists, Bush had not gone far enough. Among the

president's critics, the conservative *New York Times* columnist William
Safire scolded Bush for having "abandoned tens of thousands of Kurdish
fighters to death and their families to starvation" and forfeited the nation's
"newfound pride as a superpower that stands for the right."[40] This is part
of the reason the Gulf War is remembered not as a humanitarian war but
as a war waged for oil and staged on live television. When Bush refused
to enter Baghdad, fearing a Vietnam-like entanglement, he lost control
of the humanitarian narrative with which he had convinced Americans
of the need to intervene. This humanitarian criticism of a humanitarian
war is a source of confusion for the movies made later that decade about
the war in the Persian Gulf. While they satirize Bush's good-versus-evil
rhetoric, they struggle to address the rise of human rights as an instrument of military violence at the end of the Cold War. The last decade
of the twentieth century felt to some like an interregnum because of the
humanitarian containment of the antiwar movement.

The Humanitarian Satire of Hollywood's Gulf War

The Gulf War never attracted much attention from movie studios. This
has been attributed to CNN's entertainment-minded broadcast of the war,
which gave audiences what felt like a forty-two-day, blow-by-blow military
thriller. When asked in 1991 if he thought that the Gulf War would generate enduring art, Robert Stone, the author of the Vietnam War novel
Dog Soldiers (1974), admitted, "When I think of the cultural impact of the
Persian Gulf War, what I end up with literally is commercials on CNN."
Director Oliver Stone reflected, "In a sense, Tom Cruise already did the
Persian Gulf War in *Top Gun*."[41] This attitude suggests why Hollywood
movies about the Gulf War—*Courage Under Fire* (1996), *Wag the Dog*,
Three Kings, Demme's remake of *The Manchurian Candidate*, *Jarhead*
(2005)—tend to concentrate on how and to what ends the war was staged
by the government and government-regulated media. The Gulf War itself
is beside the point in these films. Did it even take place?

Hollywood's Gulf War looks much like that imagined by French philosopher Jean Baudrillard, who wrote three essays about the war for the
French newspaper *Libération* before, during, and after the six-week air
war. Baudrillard gave the essays the controversial and somewhat mislead-
ing titles "The Gulf War Will Not Take Place," "The Gulf War: Is It Really
Taking Place?" and "The Gulf War Did Not Take Place." He argued not

that a material event in Kuwait and Iraq had not taken place but that what Western viewers watched on their television screens and called the Gulf War had no relation to that material event in the Middle East. The war on television was detached from the war on the ground. It signified nothing but itself. Television, he argued, was a "medium without a message." Viewers were watching not live coverage of a war but "the image of pure television."[42] The United States and its allies were simulating a war, Baudrillard believed, for no other reason than to demonstrate that war could still take place at the end of the twentieth century. "Unlike earlier wars, in which there were political aims either of conquest or domination, what is at stake in this one is war itself: its status, its meaning, its future," the philosopher wrote. "It is beholden not to have an objective but to prove its very existence."[43] But Baudrillard got it backward. The United States didn't set out to demonstrate that it could still wage war but that it had put war, including the Vietnam War, behind it. This time it had the world on its side, and it would defend that new world at all costs. Western viewers were watching a simulation not of war but of humanitarian defense.

But Hollywood filmmakers, including a young David O. Russell, embraced Baudrillard's argument, imagining the Gulf War as a television war. Russell's *Three Kings*, the highest-grossing Gulf War movie, follows four American soldiers who, after the cease-fire, go in search of gold bullion that had been stolen from Kuwait during the invasion. The soldiers are tracked by a frustrated cable newswoman, Adriana Cruz (Nora Dunn), who, constrained by military regulations, is forced to recite clichés to her television audience. "They say you exorcised the ghosts of Vietnam with a clear moral imperative," she tells a crowd of soldiers, causing them to break into a rowdy rendition of Lee Greenwood's "God Bless the USA."[44] While the film challenges the military-media relations that allowed the war to look so sanitized on television, it also reinforces a belief in the military's role as an institution with the authority to defend human rights anywhere the United States deemed necessary. When the gold heist devolves into chaos, the Americans get entangled with a village of Iraqi Shia refugees and help them flee the country. Their greed is overcome by the humanitarian obligation to rescue the villagers, and Russell's film comes to endorse the "clear moral imperative" it had earlier treated as an idea deserving of satire, condemning Bush's war on the basis that it had not lasted long enough to violently humanize the Middle East.

After the war, Bush was attacked from the right and the left for not entering Baghdad and overthrowing Hussein, instead declaring a cease-fire

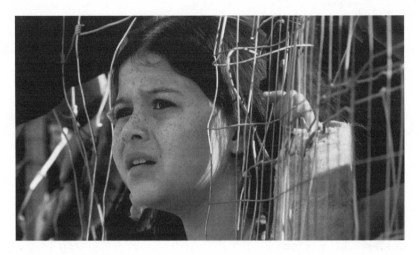

FIGURE 4.1. *Three Kings* (1999).

and suggesting that Iraqis "put him aside" themselves.[45] The criticism that
Bush instigated a rebellion and then abandoned the rebels to be crushed
by Hussein resurfaces in *Three Kings*, a film released in the wake of the
US-led NATO air strikes in Kosovo. Having located the Kuwaiti gold in a
bunker outside Karbala, the Americans are ready to return to base when
they witness the murder of a woman at the hands of the Iraqi Republican
Guard. She had rebelled against the Hussein government, as Bush had
advised, and dies begging the Americans to defend her village. Her young
daughter (Alia Shawkat), who wears casts on two broken arms, runs to
her body screaming. Acting on instinct, the Americans break the cease-
fire and rescue the remaining villagers from the guard. Later, the husband
of the murdered woman, Amir Abdulah (Cliff Curtis), admonishes the
Americans for stealing gold when he and other Iraqis are struggling to
overthrow Hussein. "What good is [saving our lives] if you leave us here
to be slaughtered, huh?" he asks. "The big army of democracy beats the
ugly dictator and saves the rich Kuwaitis." Making a case for why the
Americans should escort them to the Iranian border, Amir confronts major Archie Gates (George Clooney). "You saw what happened to my wife.
Look at my daughter," he demands. The camera turns to Amir's daughter,
who sits with her broken arms held out and her eyes wide. Moments later,
Archie agrees to Amir's demands.

Although the soldiers had set out to make themselves rich by stealing
Kuwaiti gold, once they witness the civilians' suffering, they are transformed

into human rights crusaders. They are reluctant to take on this role, but Amir's monologue welcomes them to his country as invited guests rather than self-interested invaders. Questioning the coalition's rationale for saving "the rich Kuwaitis," he asks Archie to make good on the promise of humanitarian war by seeing the refugees to the border. The film's antiwar message is not anti-imperialist but humanitarian. It echoes Reagan's revisionist account of the Vietnam War: that American soldiers would have won that war on humanitarian grounds had the government only let them. It is not the refugees who are being defended but the disaffected white soldier, Archie. A Vietnam veteran, he embodies the norm around which liberal empire is organized and earns a heightened liberal consciousness through acts of humanitarian violence.

The moviegoer is invited, through Archie, to gaze at the suffering of the girl. Amir reminds the major that his daughter's mother was killed earlier that day and that, by abandoning them to Hussein's men, he would be sentencing her to death, too.[46] Although the mother takes a leading role in the villagers' resistance, before being shot by the Republican Guard, the negotiation of the meaning of her death and her daughter's life is conducted by two men, with the white American officer deciding the value of their lives. The scene illustrates why humanitarian war-making was able to achieve broad-based consent at the end of the Cold War. Human rights allowed lawmakers to reframe war as a moral cause—an effort to mediate foreign worlds of indiscriminate, irrational violence—rather than a political struggle conditioned by colonialism, race, religion, and debt. The Bush administration, in delegitimizing the violence committed by the Hussein regime, as earlier administrations had done with the governments of Kim Il-sung in Korea and Ho Chi Minh in Vietnam, distanced the war in the Persian Gulf from a real war against a legitimate state. Hussein was a criminal actor, the president suggested, making the US-led coalition's campaign a mission to order a disordered region rather than a war waged to convert an existing order to a new one more amenable to Western interests.

The soldiers' decision to guide the refugees to the border and risk their new fortunes reflects the humanitarian state's ethic of self-sacrifice. When their commanders arrest the AWOL Americans within sight of the border, leaving the refugees to be corralled by the Iraqi Army, Archie bargains with his commanding officer, trading the location of the gold for the refugees' freedom. Thanks to Adriana's coverage of these events, the redeemed Americans don't face charges afterward. The ending endorses the idea that the true calling of the armed forces is to defend liberal rights by humanizing illiberal social worlds and that the ideal function of American media is to alert domestic viewers to the suffering occurring in these worlds and to advocate war as the commonsense solution. While at first ridiculing the idea of "a clear moral imperative" in the Persian Gulf, Russell's film concludes with an image of the humanitarian armed forces as an antiracist institution, defending ethnic and religious minorities from the racist violence of the Hussein government.

The soldiers' actions in *Three Kings* are not unlike those taken by the Bush administration after the Gulf War, when it established refugee settlements for ethnic Kurds along the Turkish border and barred aircraft in the northern and southern regions to defend the region's disenfranchised Kurdish and Shia communities. This flight ban was maintained by the United States for seven years. When announcing the establishment of the refugee settlements in April 1991, Bush drew on human rights visual activism, stating, "No one can see the pictures or hear the accounts of this human suffering—men, women, and most painfully of all, innocent children—and not be deeply moved."[47] He understood the usefulness of humanitarian affect in framing the Gulf War as a moral crusade. Though critical of the Bush administration's conduct in the Middle East, Russell's movie arrives at the same conclusion, endorsing the war as a humanitarian act that transcended all other considerations.[48] *Three Kings* demonstrates the challenge of telling a story of humanitarian defense. It finds a straightforward ending to the Gulf War while acknowledging, in the margins, that the United States never left the Middle East. It hung around to fight an unending nonwar for human rights.

The film also intimates a connection between the US-led war in the Persian Gulf and racial policing in the United States. When sergeant Troy Barlow (Mark Wahlberg) is caught by the Republican Guard, he is taken to an underground bunker, where he is interrogated by the Iraqi captain Said (Saïd Taghmaoui). Trained by American advisers to the Iraqi Army during the Iran–Iraq War, Said is a reminder of the state's earlier dealings with Hussein, dealings motivated less by virtue than by self-interest. He begins the interrogation by asking Troy about pop star Michael Jackson's cosmetic surgeries. He wants to know why the United States made the singer "chop up his face." When Troy counters that Jackson underwent these surgeries by choice, Said tells him that he doesn't understand his meaning. "It is so obvious," he muses, "a black man make the skin white and the hair straight, and you know why? Your sick fucking country make the black man hate himself just like you hate the Arab and the children you bomb over here." Troy sees Jackson's surgeries as the singer's choice and unrelated to race or the Gulf War. Said's comments foreground the challenge of accusing the state of racism in the waning years of the Cold War. Bush's new world order, having subsumed the liberal antiracism of human rights, frustrated critics attempting to show how race continued to structure the government's wars in the Middle East. The Bush administration was careful to describe the war in the Persian Gulf as Arab-on-Arab violence that the United States was obliged to mediate as a model of racial and religious tolerance. Said tries to communicate to Troy that racism is not limited to individual behaviors and choices. He observes that Jackson's desire to have white skin and straight hair is governed by a racial order that maintains, extends, and forms hierarchies of human value based in part on attributes like skin color and hair texture. Jackson lives in a culture in which whiteness has been valued and blackness devalued. The government's decision to bomb Baghdad—a decision that led to the destruction of infrastructure on which civilians relied for food, water, and medical care—was influenced by the same differential valuation of human life. The coalition forces would never, Said suggests, do the same to a white, Christian nation.

The connection between the Gulf War and antiblack racism is further reinforced by the film's inclusion of the video recording of white LAPD officers beating an unarmed Rodney King. When Archie, Troy, and Chief Elgin (Ice Cube) first enter the bunker where the gold is hidden, they find Iraqi soldiers reveling in consumer goods stolen from Kuwait. Said is seated on a recliner watching the King video on television. The camera lingers on the television screen for a moment, and Chief, a black staff sergeant, registers what Said is watching. Two days after Bush had declared the Vietnam syndrome kicked, on March 3, 1991, King was tased and beaten on the Foothill Freeway in the San Fernando Valley. The incident was filmed by George Holliday, a local resident who later shared the video with a regional news station. Holliday's footage became a media sensation and incited outrage across the country.

Whereas news coverage of the Gulf War rendered it a clean war by removing violence from the visual field, the out-of-focus amateur video of the King beating reintroduced that violence. After the King video was released, as cultural historian Donald Pease observes, the story of the war began to change. Images of the liberation of Kuwait receded as news media turned their attention to accounts of abuse, friendly fire attacks, and

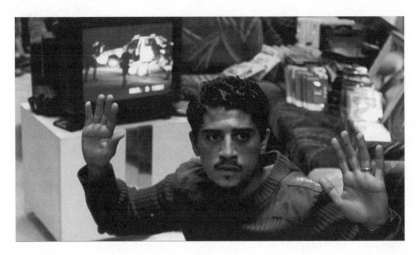

FIGURE 4.2. *Three Kings* (1999).

the technological assistance the Hussein government received from the Bush administration before and after the war. "The composite of these reversals in the symbolic fortunes of the official state fantasy irretrievably damaged the Bush administration's efforts to accrue the moral capital" of a good war in the Persian Gulf, Pease writes.[49] The King video embodied the ideological limits of Bush's new world order and highlighted the racial divisions aggravated and created by the war waged against black, brown, and poor people within the nation's borders and couched as a defense against narcotics and crime. Having watched the LAPD officers beat an unarmed black man, Said, once an ally, recognizes the falseness of the state's claim to be defending human rights in Kuwait, Los Angeles, and elsewhere. Chief's awareness of what Said is watching acknowledges, for a moment, the continuities between race-making in Los Angeles and war-making in Baghdad. It also alludes to the actor Ice Cube's vocal criticism of police violence against black men as a member of the rap group NWA and in his solo music career. (He famously wrote the 1988 hit "Fuck tha Police" for NWA.) While subscribing to the humanitarian argument for the war in the Persian Gulf, Russell's film introduces an alternative account of the liberal state that reconnects race to "universal" human rights.[50]

Bush knew that kicking the Vietnam syndrome meant reclaiming his government's standing as a moral leader in the world, and its claim to this role since World War II has been founded on a belief that America had reckoned with and redressed its racial sins. The idea that the nation had overcome racism grew out of a selective account of the civil rights move-ment—an account that dwells on the "classical phase" or "short civil rights movement"[51]—in which the state "solved" racism with the Civil Rights Act of 1964 and the Voting Rights Act of 1965. Its overcoming of racial intoler-ance at home authorized it, officials suggested, to resolve ethnic and reli-gious conflicts elsewhere. The state's status as a defender of human rights was founded on a revisionist account of the Vietnam War—wherein the war was brought to an end by the humanitarian affect of good-hearted Americans—but also on a strategic retelling of the civil rights movement. The video of white officers encircling and beating an unarmed black man contradicted the idea of the United States as a humanitarian state that had defeated the racism of earlier generations to serve as the leader of the free world. But the film concludes by suggesting that Bush should have held out longer, ousted Hussein, and established a liberal democratic government that would have safeguarded the rights of Kurds and Shiites. This is, of course, what the next Bush administration decided to do twelve years later. After that administration declared a war on terrorism and returned to the Middle East with full force, Russell rereleased *Three Kings* in theaters and on DVD with a new, thirty-minute segment about the new wars there. The military had by then already settled in to the humanitarian state-building that Russell's film had advocated five years earlier.

Whereas Russell's film tries to get underneath the sanitized media cov-erage of the war, Barry Levinson's *Wag the Dog* is a war movie without a war. After the president of the United States is accused of making advances on an underage girl, his communications adviser Conrad Brean, seeking to distract voters from the scandal, hires famed Hollywood filmmaker Stanley Motss (Dustin Hoffman) to construct a fake war with Albania. While Levinson's film became associated with Bill Clinton's handling of the Monica Lewinsky scandal, it is based on Larry Beinhart's Gulf War novel *American Hero* (1993), in which a fictional George Bush, concerned with his flagging ratings, enlists a Hollywood director to stage the Gulf War. Like the novel on which it was based, *Wag the Dog* understands war as a made-for-television event. Conrad and Stanley see the war with Albania as one more story to be written and sold, and the best way to sell a war story at the end of the Cold War, they realize, is with human rights. The stakes of the war they invent are unclear. The only information they release is a studio-made video of a refugee girl fleeing from a terrorist-abetting regime. Amer-icans must see the military as antiracist and self-sacrificing, and Conrad and Stanley understand that the refugee is the ideal figure through whom to communicate the humanitarian ethic of war. While it shines a critical light on how the state militarized human rights, *Wag the Dog* refuses to see war as more than a benign media construct. Conrad may distract Americans from a sex scandal with an artificial war, but the idea of war as nothing but artifice distracts from the actual devastation caused by humanitarian violence.

Conrad and Stanley's success in fabricating a war with Albania is founded on the idea that Americans assign meaning to their nation's wars based on the iconic images associated with those conflicts. Conrad reminds Stanley that, for the average American, the Gulf War was nothing but the CNN footage of "one smart bomb falling down the chimney." Wars are remembered by their icons, he argues, and so the two filmmakers set out to define the icon by which the war in Albania will be remembered. They settle on an image of a blonde-haired, blue-eyed teenage girl—an actress named Tracy Lime (Kirsten Dunst)—fleeing from Albanian terrorists. Wearing a headscarf and a wool dress, Tracy is filmed in front of a blue screen with a bag of Tostitos. Studio technicians then transform the footage, substituting the blue screen for a burning village, adding sounds of screaming and gunfire, and inserting a white calico kitten where the Tostitos had been. The video doesn't offer information about what led to the violence in Albania. But Stanley insists that details of this kind are irrelevant. Before shooting, he observes, "Young girl in rubble. She was driven from her home by Albanian terrorists, okay? It's her we are mobilizing to defend." Stanley argues that most Americans are convinced of the goodness of war not by abstract ideas but by a resonant individual story that accesses a genre already familiar to them. That genre in the 1990s was the trauma narrative, and, in the context of the fictional war with Albania, it is used to authorize war on an affective level. Americans are sold on the story of the unnamed refugee fleeing from terrorists, the film suggests; that is who the state is "mobilizing to defend." Like Nayirah's account of Kuwaiti infants taken from their incubators, the refugee video reveals the degree to which a focalizing image may be used to circumscribe and revise the meaning and memory of war.

The fabricated footage of Tracy fleeing a burning village draws on but also remakes the story of national "innocence lost" through which Americans understand the iconic image of Phúc running from a South Vietnamese bombing. Earlier in the film, Conrad recalls World War II and the Vietnam War as a reel of images, recounting, "Naked girl covered in Napalm. V for victory. Five marines raising the flag, Mount Suribachi. You'll

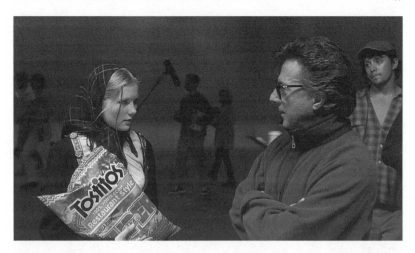

FIGURE 4.3. *Wag the Dog* (1997).

remember the picture fifty years from now, but you'll have forgotten the war." For a man hired to invent a war, Ut's Pulitzer Prize–winning photograph of Phúc is an icon to avoid, a reminder of the violence committed or facilitated by the United States in a losing effort in Southeast Asia. The iconic images of World War II—Winston Churchill flashing the "V for victory" sign and five marines raising a flag on Iwo Jima—comprise a far easier archive with which to sell a war. But the effectiveness of the refugee video lies in the way it draws on the memory of Ut's image of American-aided violence. The video of Tracy reminds the viewer of Phúc running from a cloud of smoke in Vietnam, but their government's role has shifted from aggressor to welcomed savior. It satirizes the rehabilitation of national innocence carried out by Hollywood films from *The Deer Hunter* (1978) to *Platoon* (1986) but also the idea of humanitarian rescue promoted by the Bush administration in 1990 and 1991. Rather than inserting itself into the tradition of the "good war" by reference to Churchill or the flag raising, the staged scene rewrites the Vietnam War. With their studio-made video, Conrad and Stanley invite their viewers to return to Southeast Asia, reclaim the nation's durable sense of its own innocence, and rescue Phúc from an aggressor that is no longer their own military. Reimagining the United States as humanitarian rescuer was a useful and necessary revision to make at the beginning of the decade if Bush was to realize his vision of ushering in a new world order governed by universal human rights. The state needed to absolve itself of its own human

FIGURE 4.4. *Wag the Dog* (1997).

rights abuses in Southeast Asia and establish itself as a steadfast defender
against those abuses. That transformation was achieved not through a
substitution for but the revision of the memory of the Vietnam War.

Levinson's film satirizes how the Bush administration tried to revise
the state's image through stories of humanitarian crisis and liberation. But
unlike in the Gulf War, Conrad and Stanley choose a light-skinned girl for
humanitarian rescue. When *Wag the Dog* was released in December 1997,
the wars of the former Yugoslavia had been ongoing for close to a decade.
During the US-led NATO occupation of Bosnia, news media presented
Muslim Bosnians as white. The Bosnian refugees shown on television and
in news magazines were almost always light-skinned women and children.
This allowed the United States to define itself through and against the
Balkans, associating the region with a kind of racism from which the nation had, the media coverage suggested, long ago advanced. The United
States and its NATO allies, Atanasoski writes, "displaced ongoing racial
anxieties by opposing their humanitarian presence in the Balkans to the
premodern barbarism of 'ethnic cleansing,' for which the region came to
be known."[52] Levinson's film reveals how the United States transferred

its own racial violence onto the Balkans, as Atanasoski argues, but also onto the Hussein government in the first years of the decade. Beginning in the Persian Gulf, the humanitarian wars of the 1990s rewrote the Vietnam War twice over, celebrating it as a moral achievement and then reassigning the violence committed by the United States to other regimes, whether that of Hussein, Serbian President Slobodan Milošević, or "Albanian terrorists."[53]

But Tracy troubles the whiteness of humanitarian rescue. Though light-skinned, her costume includes a headscarf that would suggest that she, like most Albanians, is Muslim. At the end of the Cold War, Islam was racialized in much the same way that communism had earlier been used to categorize and differentiate human value.[54] With the Soviet Union in crisis at the time, Islam, seen as an illiberal form of religious faith, succeeded communism as the ideological antithesis to liberal democratic values. The humanitarian wars fought in the Persian Gulf, Somalia, Bosnia, and Kosovo were founded on a belief that Islam was an unreformed, backward religion that encouraged intolerance and denied individual freedoms. So while Tracy may look white to viewers, her headscarf alludes to how religion animated racial divisions by the time of the Gulf War. Humanitarianism, which the West defined against Islam, bridged anticommunism, anticrime, and counterterrorism as a new iteration of a racial regime that differentiates the human, the deferred human, and the nonhuman, whether by skin color or by belief.

While Conrad and Stanley's studio-made video rewrites the Vietnam War, it also restages the Holocaust. As the studio technicians edit the raw footage, the lead technician remarks, "You know what might be good is ooh-ah sirens. . . . You know, ooh-ah ooh-ah. Anne Frank." The technician is referring to the air-raid sirens used during World War II and featured in stage and film versions of Anne Frank's Holocaust diaries, including the Academy Award–winning movie *The Diary of Anne Frank* (1959). Stanley likes the technician's idea, and when the "Anne Frank sirens" are added, comments, "That's chilling. That's giving me goose bumps." The drafting and signing of the Universal Declaration of Human Rights was motivated by revelations of the atrocities committed by Nazi Germany. Ever since, human rights abuses have been understood in relation to the Holocaust. While historians and news media criticized Clinton's allusions to the Holocaust in authorizing the US-led NATO air strikes on Kosovo, Bush had years earlier instituted this rhetoric during the Gulf War, describing Hussein as "Hitler revisited" and stressing that the United States must intervene on Kuwait's behalf, or there would be a second Holocaust in the Middle East.[55] Conrad and Stanley recognize that there is nothing off limits, including the Holocaust, when it comes to selling the nation a new war.

Levinson's film embodies the virtues and shortcomings of satirizing the orchestrated media coverage of the Gulf War. It identifies how the Bush administration mobilized human rights to create a right–left consensus behind a war in the Middle East, a consensus that his Democratic successor, Clinton, would use in Somalia, Bosnia, and Kosovo later that decade. But in rendering human suffering as something staged by filmmakers, *Wag the Dog* distracts from the real violence committed by the United States in the decade that followed the end of the Cold War. When Conrad tells Stanley that, for most Americans, the Gulf War was nothing more than "one smart bomb falling down the chimney," he adds, "The truth: I was in the building when we shot that shot." His contention is not that the Gulf War was faked but that we have no way of knowing what is and is not true. If truth is constructed, he contends, then why not construct it in a way that benefits you? This is the trouble with movies like Russell's and Levinson's that condemn the constrained domestic coverage of the conflict. When the media war in the studio receives more attention than the actual war in the Persian Gulf, CNN starts to look like the real combat zone. Forgotten are the humanitarian wars—rationalized by the kind of stories told by Conrad and Stanley—that were not merely news cycles for the people who lived them.

This Is Vietnam, Jack

While writers, filmmakers, and activists struggled to cut through the sanitized news coverage of the war in the Persian Gulf, Bush's new world order could not contain the war at home. As his administration launched a new iteration of defense grounded in one-world humanitarianism, the state's wars on drugs and crime began to break down. One year after Bush declared the Vietnam syndrome kicked, the LAPD officers who had beaten King on the Foothill Freeway were found not guilty on charges that they had used excessive force in tasing, kicking, and striking King more than forty times. The verdict set off a week of riots that resulted in fifty-four deaths and the destruction of more than eight hundred buildings in South Central Los Angeles and the surrounding area. Mayor Tom Bradley instituted a dusk-to-dawn curfew. Bush sent in the National Guard and, soon after, the army and the marines.

The continuities between the Gulf War and the policing of South Central were not lost on its residents. The Bush administration used some of the same methods and elite task forces in Los Angeles that it had used in Iraq and in the invasion of Panama. But as one veteran of the 1965 Watts riots told historian Mike Davis, "That ole fool Bush think we as dumb as Saddam. Land Marines in Compton and get hisself re-elected. But this ain't Iraq. This is Vietnam, Jack."[56] The man recognized that, while Bush may have controlled the story in the Persian Gulf, he could not achieve the same result in Los Angeles, where the lie of the state as an arbiter of antiracism and human rights could not be maintained. It was out of his control. It was "Vietnam, Jack." The South Central resident's words challenged not only Bush's humanitarian case for waging war in the Persian Gulf but also his rewriting of the war in Southeast Asia by comparing it to the racial policing of black and Latina/o communities in California. While his administration may have, with the assistance of the Human Rights Caucus, reframed the visual icons of the Vietnam War in the Persian Gulf, it could not contain the image of uniformed officers beating an unarmed black man in Los Angeles. June Jordan made a similar argument in a *Progressive* article about the Bush administration's handling of the riots, writing, "We would be oblivious to brutal colonial attitudes if we did not note and decry that the overwhelming state response [to the King verdict] has been paramilitary, at best."[57] War-making in Kuwait and law enforcement in South Central were, she argued, intertwined and motivated by the same "colonial attitudes."

Before the release of the King video—and the verdict, riots, and city-wide shutdown that followed—Jordan had emerged as one of the country's most vocal critics of the Gulf War. As a professor at the University of California, Berkeley, she founded Poetry for the People, a collective that teaches verse writing as an instrument of activism and community building; organized the nation's first "teach-in" on the Gulf War; and led antiwar rallies around the Bay Area. At an event in Oakland organized by the Middle East Children's Alliance, she noted that the war was costing the government a billion dollars a day and suggested that the Bush administration instead devote a billion dollars a day for seven days to Oakland schools, health care, and community services. "It's a bargain!" she declared. "Seven billion dollars on the serious improvement of American life in Oakland versus $56 billion for death and destruction inside Iraq."[58] Throughout the war and its aftermath, Jordan asked Americans to recognize how the war in the Middle East drew on and fed racial divisions within the United States. At an event in Hayward, California, on February 21—the day of Malcolm X's assassination—she lamented the fact that the United States had "desecrated" Martin Luther King's memory by launching an aerial assault on his birthday and noted that he and Malcolm X had been targeted by the FBI after denouncing the Vietnam War. Jordan told the crowd that black Americans disagreed with the war in larger numbers than the rest of the country, because they understood, as King and Malcolm X had of Vietnam, that the state's conduct in the Middle East was determined by an unwillingness to recognize the legitimacy of nonwhite, non-Western, and non-Christian self-government. Challenging the president's humanitarian claim, she stressed again and again to her Hayward audience that "this war has not saved one human being."[59]

While Russell's film mounts a liberal humanitarian challenge to a liberal humanitarian war, and Levinson's film treats the Gulf War as nothing more than a media event, Jordan's long poem "The Bombing of Baghdad" (1997) shows how war reinforces and introduces, rather than mends, breaks in humanity, how it could not by definition be antiracist or serve a universal good. The poem launches from the title right into the first line ("began and did not terminate for 42 days") and for the next thirty-two lines catalogs all the places in Baghdad that the coalition forces bombed, from bridges and streets to schools and air-raid shelters. She uses the word *bombed* thirty-two times in those thirty-two lines and stresses that Baghdad is "a city of 5.5 million human beings" to underscore the human toll of the coalition's clean and smart bombs that commanders described as "collateral damage." But, while she refuses to let her reader ignore the extent of the devastation caused by the bombing of Baghdad, she also situates the Gulf War in relation to settler colonialism in North America by returning to battles between Indian forces led by Oglala Lakota warrior Crazy Horse and the Seventh Cavalry Regiment of the United States— "Custer's Next-To-Last Stand," she calls it. Jordan writes that she can "hear Crazy Horse singing as he dies" and in it "the moaning of the Arab world."[60] While eliding significant historical differences, of course, the poem's back-and-forth movement between the Gulf War and the American Indian Wars draws attention to how state violence serves a race-making function, as a means of defining and distinguishing the people, places, and beliefs to be defended from the people, places, and beliefs to be converted or decimated. The war in the Persian Gulf did not save lives so much as further differentiate them through the racial regime of defense.

In "The Bombing of Baghdad," Jordan reverses the liberal humanitarian terms on which the coalition waged its war. The poem concludes by addressing the false universalism of human rights and suggesting that war could not be conducted without the uneven inclusions, exclusions, and assimilations of liberalism:

> And all who believed some must die
> they were already dead
> And all who believe only they possess
> human being and therefore human rights
> they no longer stood among the possibly humane
> And all who believed that retaliation/revenge/defense
> derive from God-given prerogatives of white men
> And all who believed that waging war is anything
>   besides terrorist activity in the first
>   place and in the last
> . . . .
> All who believed these things
> they were already dead
> They no longer stood among the possibly humane[61]

Jordan acknowledges how "human being" and "human rights," while assumed to be inalienable and universal, have organized the differential valuation of human life on the basis that "some must die" to ensure the security of others. A person's freedom to "possess" their human being derives from the denial of others' freedom to do so. This is the founding logic of modern war, and it is, Jordan suggests, a mechanism of racialization by which the West has rationalized the "retaliation/revenge/defense" of white liberal freedoms. While she includes herself in the "we" that bombed Baghdad, she distances herself from the "they" who authorize war as a form of self-defense. It is they, rather than Iraqis, who are "already dead" and no longer stand "among the possibly humane." Jordan's antiwar activism and writing unsettled the humanitarian basis for waging war in the Persian Gulf by connecting it to histories of state violence against American Indians and the black and Latina/o residents of South Central Los Angeles. She identified how, as Bush embraced a new world order, old racial orders—settler colonialism, the social control of antidrug and anticrime agendas—continued to trouble the state's claim to be leading a free world.

After sending tanks to South Central Los Angeles rather than Baghdad, the Bush administration could no longer maintain its story of humanitarian rescue in the Persian Gulf. Americans would instead remember
a war for oil broadcast live on CNN. But Bush's humanitarian war had
an enduring effect on post–Cold War liberal imperialism and offered a
blueprint for the wars to follow in Somalia, Bosnia, Kosovo, and elsewhere. With the Soviet Union on the verge of dissolution, his administration substituted liberal humanitarianism for the declining rhetoric of
anticommunism and found a new way to wage war that could reconstitute
the state's role as an antiracist model for the world. The Gulf War was a
transitional event for the empire of defense as the first humanitarian war
by which Americans could reimagine the nation's character in relation to
the Vietnam War. And, with the Vietnam syndrome kicked, it would not
be the last.

CHAPTER FIVE

The Craft of Counterinsurgent Whiteness

It was the end, some thought, of a long war. On the night of May 1, 2011, a team of Navy SEALs entered a safe house in Abbottabad, Pakistan, and killed al-Qaeda leader Osama bin Laden. In the United States, news of his death set off days of flag-waving celebrations and led commentators to wonder whether the war on terror might be nearing its end. One month later, Matt Gallagher, a former army captain and Iraq War veteran, wrote an *Atlantic* article titled "Where's the Great Novel about the War on Terror?" in which he bemoaned the lack of fiction about the counterterror wars. "Almost a decade after the first bombs were dropped in Afghanistan," he wrote, "even the most avid bookworm would be hard-pressed to identify a war novel that could be considered definitive of this new generation's battles."[1] Gallagher, the author of the war memoir *Kaboom* (2010), observed that the literary market had been saturated with nonfiction accounts of the wars in Iraq and Afghanistan—from books by veterans like himself, Colby Buzzell, and Kayla Williams to those by journalists like Deborah Amos and Sebastian Junger. Editors and reviewers had begun diagnosing themselves with "war fatigue." But the wars had yet to generate a great novel.

Gallagher attributed this absence to the growing military-civilian divide in American life and readers' desire to forget the country's wars rather than devote an evening to reading about them. Perhaps, he thought, a "great war on terror novel" could mend that divide by delivering the "definitive" story of the counterterror wars, a story that must, he suggested, be authored by an American veteran and about an American soldier. Gallagher concluded that the greatest obstacle to writing that novel was that Americans had served in different countries and in different years. "Some doubt whether a war so widespread and so disparate in experiences can ever be fully represented in just one book—how can there be a definitive GWOT [global war on terror] novel when there's no definitive GWOT experience?" he asked. "One service member's war in 2003 Iraq couldn't be more different than another's in 2010 Afghanistan."[2] Gallagher did not acknowledge that Iraqis and Afghans might have their own stories to tell. Instead, he assumed that the great war on terror novel was the exclusive terrain of the American warrior-scribe.

When he wrote these words, Gallagher knew that the lack of new war fiction wouldn't last long. He was at work on his own Iraq War novel, *Youngblood* (2016), and was at the center of a community of ambitious, MFA-trained veteran-writers that included Kevin Powers (*The Yellow Birds* [2012]), Phil Klay (*Redeployment* [2014]), and Roy Scranton (*War Porn* [2016]). Two years later, Gallagher and Scranton coedited *Fire and Forget: Short Stories from the Long War* (2013), a collection that show-cased some of the best new veteran writing. In 2014, after Klay won the National Book Award for Fiction, *New York Times* book critic Michiko Kakutani wrote a feature article that celebrated "the extraordinary out-pouring" of war fiction since the drawdown in Iraq. Her article ran on the front page under an image of five white men, including Gallagher and Klay, and one white woman, Kayla Williams.[3]

Gallagher had gotten what he wished for. The wars in Iraq and Afghanistan had become the material of best-selling, award-winning fiction. But why would a writer whose memoir had received admiring reviews in the *New York Times* and the *Washington Post* and launched his career be so eager to see his military service translated into fiction instead? What would a war on terror novel achieve that a war on terror memoir could not? Gallagher argued that fiction, with its greater creative license, could lend structure to the war as a whole by abstracting its larger meaning from individual stories of violence and loss. Taking James Michener's Korean War novel *The Bridges at Toko-Ri* (1953) as his model, he wrote, "For any novel to meet the nebulous and loaded term 'definitive,' it seems, tran-scending the matters of specific time, place, and experience is the inher-ent challenge involved."[4] Whereas the nonfiction writer faces the generic demands of sticking to what is knowable and verifiable, the novelist might, Gallagher argued, sacrifice the narrow fact for the broader truth. His dubi-ous model, *The Bridges at Toko-Ri*, which Michener wrote before the 1953 armistice agreement, reduces the anticolonial, intranational, and unending Korean War to one botched bombing run through which the American hero confronts the follies of war. One month after bin Laden's death had occasioned conversations about an end to the war on terror, Gallagher called for a novel that could transcend "matters of specific time, place, and experience" and tell a concise, coherent story about an endless war.

Although he acknowledged Williams's and Amos's writing, Gallagher cast the great war novel as the domain of white men. He began his article with a letter written by Ernest Hemingway to F. Scott Fitzgerald in 1925, in which Hemingway remarked that "war is the best subject of all" and then cited email and Twitter exchanges between himself and his white veteran friends—Eric Cummings, Alex Horton, and Scranton—about the state of the genre in 2011. The article represents war fiction as a conversation among white men, who write it, read it, review it, and discuss it in letters, emails, and on social media. Scranton even suggested, in an email to Gallagher, that women readers were the reason editors weren't interested in war novels. Advised by editors, agents, and teachers to write a memoir rather than a novel, Scranton wrote, "I was told that women buy novels and they aren't interested in war novels."[5] He and Gallagher assumed war fiction to be a white, masculine form that had been devalued by a feminine literary market and a civilian culture that would rather not think about the wars it had authorized.

Gallagher envisioned the great war on terror novel as a cultural bridge between the veteran-writer and the disengaged civilian reader. But he also conceded that it may never be written. He concluded his article by comparing the "brushfire wars" in Iraq and Afghanistan to the Philippine–American War, which he described as "a protracted guerilla war [that] happened at the edges of both the American empire and the national consciousness, and lasted far longer than official ceasefire declarations would suggest."[6] That war lacked a "classic" novel, and perhaps, he admitted, the counterterror wars would, too. This comparison runs even deeper than Gallagher acknowledged. The wars in Iraq and Afghanistan marked a return to counterinsurgency doctrine, a theory of "irregular" war that the United States first embraced at the end of the nineteenth century and forged in the Philippines. Counterinsurgency combines conventional military means with political and cultural methods intended to isolate insurgents from unaffiliated civilians and encourage the establishment of liberal democratic institutions in a region that may be otherwise hostile to Western forms of government and foreign interference. It demands that field officers learn, navigate, and revise the cultural narratives that have fueled local resistance to the United States and its allies. Achieving that kind of consent can be difficult because, as Gallagher indicated, counterinsurgent wars are by definition protracted imperial occupations. They do not lend themselves to the kind of concise story that he imagined for the great war on terror novel. Counterinsurgency resists Gallagher's ambition to write a great war on terror novel, but it may also form the basis of that ambition.

There has been no lack of attention to how President George W. Bush's declaration of a war on terror changed the nation.[7] The Bush administration's aggressive, unilateral actions after the 9/11 attacks on New York City and Washington, DC, threatened to undermine the racial regime of defense through which the United States had rationalized decades of war by delimiting who could execute legitimate violence, who might be "saved" by that violence, and who must be contained or killed through the use of "defensive" force. But as revelations of torture and sexual abuse emerged from Abu Ghraib and other overseas military prisons and "black sites" in the mid-2000s, the state underwent another transition through which it sought, yet again, to reassert itself as a humane actor in the world. After Defense Secretary Donald Rumsfeld authorized the Coalition Provisional Authority order that disbanded the Iraqi Army in May 2003, the United States faced an insurgency constituted in part by out-of-work, armed ex-soldiers. Facing an escalating crisis, the defense establishment turned to counterinsurgency devotees Conrad Crane, David Kilcullen, John Nagl, and David Petraeus for answers.

Their work culminated in December 2006 with the release of the Army/Marine Corps Field Manual 3-24, *Counterinsurgency*, the first official statement on counterinsurgency by any branch of the armed services since 1986. Like earlier forms of defense, the new counterinsurgency doctrine embraced a long-war model while representing counterinsurgency as nonwar ("nonkinetic activities") waged in self-defense and for the good of humanity. The manual's humanitarian ethos made counterinsurgency a consensus agenda among American lawmakers, as evidenced by conservatives' and liberals' shared adoration for General Petraeus. But a belief that war can be waged more humanely may only facilitate its continuation. The argument that large-scale state violence can serve a universal good, political scientist Laleh Khalili writes, relies on racial divisions to resolve "the tensions between illiberal methods and liberal discourse, between bloody hands and honeyed tongues, between weapons of war and emancipatory hyperbole."[8] The revised counterinsurgency doctrine of the second Bush and Obama administrations reflected the defense establishment's ongoing commitment not to ending war but to making it more palatable to Iraqis, Afghans, and, perhaps most of all, Americans at home. Of all the forms the idea of defense has taken since the formation of the Department of Defense under the Truman administration—from anticommunism and antidrug to humanitarianism and counterterrorism—counterinsurgency may be the most ingenious and the most dangerous for how it turns permanent war into a lesson in cultural studies.

The new counterinsurgency weds the humanitarian militarism of the 1990s to the academic humanities, reframing war as a form of cultural exchange. Under the guidance of Petraeus and other PhDs, war got a college education, and it got a good liberal arts one at that. The military's revised counterinsurgency field manual stressed that "the most important cultural form for counterinsurgents to understand is the narrative" because narratives organize a person's identity, community, and values. The counterinsurgents' mission is to undermine the insurgents' narrative and replace it with an alternative cultural narrative that better lends itself to Western interests—"a single narrative that emphasizes the inevitability and rightness of the COIN [counterinsurgency] operation's success."[9] The manual underscored that insurgent culture is changeable, while assuming the relative stability of liberal counterinsurgent culture. Some of the most acclaimed new veteran-writers—Gallagher, Klay, Powers—served in counterinsurgent forces, and their writing reflects the doctrine's utilitarian understanding of cultural narrative. That these writers are all white men is not a coincidence, because whiteness has continued to be a condition for conducting defense (counterinsurgency), as a means of dictating the uneven distribution of life chances (racialization) in the counterterror era. Even as American culture centers the white soldier, stories of indefinite detention and torture at military prisons, including Guantánamo detainee Mohamedou Ould Slahi's *Guantánamo Diary* (2015), unsettle the liberal humanitarian story told by counterinsurgents. His memoir, with its twenty-five hundred black-bar redactions, reveals the violent extremes to which the empire of defense has gone to control the contradictions of permanent war.

Back to the Counterinsurgent Future

Although news media and reviewers hailed the 2006 counterinsurgency field manual as charting a "radical" new direction for the twenty-first-century military, counterinsurgency was nothing new in North America.[10]

White settlers used counterinsurgent methods against American Indians throughout the nineteenth century, and, as the United States set its sights on overseas territories at the turn of that century, those settler colonial wars formed the basis of the first formal articulations of counterinsurgency doctrine. West Point textbooks of that era held that "the laws of war did not apply" to Indians because "savages" did not abide by those laws, while stressing the need for "Christian charity" to ensure that academy-trained officers did not descend to "the level of their enemies."[11] Officers could do whatever they wanted to Indian "insurgents," as long as they maintained the moral high ground. Academy textbooks taught the young men of the future officer class that the American Indian Wars were not wars at all but missions to police unlawful people. The army was responding to and containing disorder, they asserted, not creating it. Students were taught that insurgency (criminality) created the need for counterinsurgency (police). The earliest counterinsurgencies against American Indians constituted whiteness as the right to police not crime but criminal *being*—the right to define the boundaries between the legal and the illegal, the righted and the rightless. It is common sense, critical race theorist Nikhil Singh writes, to believe that crime is violence that threatens the social order, and policing is the counterviolence that limits that threat. "Yet," he argues, "this presumed normalcy partakes of a shadow lineage in which human incommensurabilities became the means of licensing and retroactively justifying extraordinary violence."[12] That shadow lineage reveals whiteness as a condition for converting war against people of color into policing—into counterinsurgency, into defense.

Beginning with the American Indian Wars, counterinsurgency traveled and grew with the emerging American empire—from the Philippines (1898–1906) and Cuba (1906–09) to Haiti (1915–34), the Dominican Republic (1916–24), and Nicaragua (1927–33). A black soldier serving in the Philippine–American War wrote a letter to the editor of the black newspaper the *New York Age* in 1900, in which he noted the continuities between policing at home and war in the Philippines. Soon after arriving, white soldiers "began to apply home treatment for colored peoples," he wrote, describing how they behaved like rogue police, stealing from civilians and using antiblack racial slurs against Filipinos. "Expansion is too clean a name for [this war]," he wrote. It is a "highway robbery."[13] These imperial wars were the case studies that informed the 1940 *Small Wars Manual*, a work that remains a must-read among counterinsurgents and that the authors of the 2006 field manual listed as a counterinsurgency "classic."[14]

Counterinsurgency theorists continue to embrace colonialists David Galula, T. E. Lawrence, Robert Thompson, and Orde Wingate as their intellectual heroes, venerating these military theorists as "mavericks" and "Renaissance men" who dared to challenge the received knowledge of their times.[15] When considering the sordid record of the counterinsurgent wars, it is astonishing that these methods could be rehabilitated in Iraq and Afghanistan as a humane form of state violence. Even conservative writers like historian Andrew Bacevich acknowledge that counterinsurgency is the ugliest kind of war. "Although U.S. troops had repeatedly clashed with insurgents over the course of American history, little of that experience, ranging from the ethnic cleansing of Native Americans who impeded westward expansion to suppressing Asian or Latin American opposition to the rising American empire, had been positive," he writes. "The biggest of all American counterinsurgencies—the agonizing Vietnam War—had ended in abject humiliation."[16]

That "agonizing" defeat in Southeast Asia made counterinsurgency a last-choice course of action by the 1980s, when Petraeus wrote a dissertation at Princeton University on the "lessons" of that war, concluding that counterinsurgencies were a "very problematic proposition."[17] At the end of the Cold War, the Pentagon and defense think tanks turned their attention from the execution of ground wars to what became known as the "revolution in military affairs." Unlike counterinsurgency theorists, RMA advocates argued that technological change was remaking the nature of war itself and that it was essential that the United States invest in long-range weapons and information-based methods and emerging technologies. This "revolution" was led by Andrew Marshall, the longtime director of the Office of Net Assessment and a mentor to Donald Rumsfeld, future Vice President Dick Cheney, and future Deputy Secretary of Defense Paul Wolfowitz. In 1993, Marshall authored an eight-page memo, "Some Thoughts on Military Revolutions," to the soon-to-be Defense Secretary William Perry that outlined his vision for the future of American war. The document became a kind of manifesto for other "revolutionaries." Marshall saw the 1990s as "a period during which a major transition between regimes of warfare will take place" as had occurred between the world wars, with the emergence of blitzkrieg offensives, aircraft carriers, and submarines. It was critical, Marshall wrote, that the defense establishment direct its resources to the advancement of "long-range precision-strike operations" and "information warfare" and recognize the Gulf War as "something like Cambrai"—the first battle in a long revolution in military technologies and organization.[18] The Gulf War signaled, for Marshall and his disciples, that war could and would be fought by machines in the next century and therefore with limited American casualties.

After the 9/11 attacks, Rumsfeld turned to his former mentor and his team of revolutionaries in the Office of Net Assessment, located in the innermost of the Pentagon's five ring corridors. On September 27, 2001, the defense secretary wrote an editorial in the *New York Times* titled "A New Kind of War," in which he suggested that "the uniforms of this conflict will be bankers' pinstripes and programmers' grunge just as assuredly as desert camouflage." Twenty-first-century war, he wrote, would even have a different vocabulary. "When we 'invade the enemy's territory,' we may well be invading his cyberspace. There may not be as many beachheads stormed as opportunities denied."[19] The following month, Rumsfeld established the Office of Force Transformation and named Arthur Cebrowski, an RMA believer known for coining the term *network-centric warfare*, as the government's first "transformation czar." Cebrowski built the new office with a mandate to "prepare [the] armed forces for the threats and challenges of this new century" by anticipating rather than responding to those threats and challenges.[20] The counterterror wars would be won, Rumsfeld and Cebrowski believed, by maintaining their government's edge in long-range missile systems and information technologies while building a leaner, more flexible organization capable of adapting to new conditions as they emerged. But when the Iraqi insurgency began in May 2003, the Pentagon's revolutionaries had no answers. In October 2006, two months before his resignation, Rumsfeld dissolved the Office of Force Transformation.[21]

As lawmakers lost faith in Rumsfeld's efforts to revolutionize the armed forces, they turned to a man with a different vision for the twenty-first-century military. David Petraeus had commanded the 101st Airborne Division in the initial invasion of Baghdad and then led his forces in securing and governing the city of Mosul, using classic counterinsurgency tactics. He became known in Mosul as *Malik Daoud* (King David) and emerged as a star in America, thanks in part to the writing of embedded journalist Rick Atkinson, whose 2004 bestseller *In the Company of Soldiers* painted a glowing portrait of the then–lieutenant general. After returning from his tour, Petraeus commanded the Combined Arms Center at Fort Leavenworth, Kansas, from 2005 to 2007, where he assembled the writing team for the new counterinsurgency field manual.

The idea for the manual originated at a conference at the Carr Center for Human Rights Policy at Harvard University in November 2005, during which Petraeus, Lieutenant Colonel John Nagl, and others met at a Cambridge bar and outlined a new counterinsurgency doctrine on a cocktail napkin. Soon after, Petraeus enlisted Army War College administrator and military historian Conrad Crane to serve as his lead writer, and Crane recruited Kilcullen, Nagl, and others to contribute to a draft of Field Manual 3-24. Petraeus showed himself to be a master of consensus formation by convening a vetting conference at Fort Leavenworth in February 2006, in which human rights official Sarah Sewall, *New Yorker* staff writer George Packer, and anthropologist Montgomery McFate were invited to read a draft and suggest revisions. "Sewall and her center [the Carr Center] co-sponsored the event," Crane recalled, "and she brought in a number of colleagues from the human rights community and NGOs. The conference featured open discussions with no holds barred, and active participation from Sewall and Lieutenant General Petraeus up front."[22] The defense establishment's brain trust had relocated from the high-security inner sanctums of the Pentagon to human rights conferences and roundtable discussions with journalists who were treated as co-creators of military doctrine. Petraeus had defanged Rumsfeld's liberal critics.

Published online in December 2006, the field manual was a hit. It was downloaded more than one and a half million times in the first month. Samantha Power, the founding executive director of the Carr Center, reviewed it for the *New York Times Book Review*, declaring it a "landmark" and "paradigm-shattering" document.[23] *Newsweek* named Crane to its list of "people to watch" for 2007 for his "innovative" contribution to military thought.[24] The University of Chicago Press republished the manual in an army-green edition with a new foreword by Nagl and an introduction by Sewall. Never before had an armed forces instructional document received this kind of attention from critics and readers outside of the military community. This wider audience was, it seems, something Petraeus had in mind when he took on the assignment. As he stated on the back cover of the Chicago edition, in what amounted to a blurb for his own book, "Surely a manual that's on the bedside table of the president, vice president, secretary of defense, 21 of 25 members of the Senate Armed Services Committee and many others deserves a place at your bedside too." In an era of an all-volunteer force and anxious discussions of a growing military-civilian divide, Petraeus sought and found a wider civilian audience for a three-hundred-page army field manual loaded with acronyms and appendices. Field Manual 3-24 stated that "victory is achieved when the populace consents to the government's legitimacy."[25] That line refers to civilians living amid an insurgency, but it could just as easily refer to Americans with *Counterinsurgency* on their beside tables.

Like earlier iterations of defense, counterinsurgency formed a consensus among lawmakers and news media by attracting liberal intellectuals to a military agenda. The leading contributors to the field manual arrived at Fort Leavenworth with academic credentials in tow. Petraeus earned his PhD in international relations from Princeton; Conrad, in history from Stanford University; Nagl, in international relations from Oxford University; and Kilcullen, in politics from the University of New South Wales. These soldier-scholars, through their writing and their academic backgrounds, cast counterinsurgency as the thinking man's war. In *Learning to Eat Soup with a Knife* (2002), a book that began as his Oxford dissertation and takes its title from Lawrence's *Seven Pillars of Wisdom* (1922), Nagl stressed that successful counterinsurgency necessitates that the military overcome its "mechanical adherence to the letter of orders" and function as a "learning institution" that welcomes intellect and innovation.[26] Nagl's ideas on "structured learning" animated Field Manual 3-24, and he wrote in his foreword that it was the first doctrinal manual to include an annotated bibliography, seeing this as "key evidence of the Army's acceptance of the need to 'Learn and Adapt' to succeed in modern counterinsurgency operations."[27] After the manual's release, Conrad noted that, unlike most field manuals, which are written at a high-school level, *Counterinsurgency* targets a college-level reader. He and Petraeus, he remarked, "felt that this more elevated discussion was necessary because of the complexity of the topic."[28] This new generation of counterinsurgents had re-intellectualized and re-humanized American war through the militarization of cultural studies.

Militarizing the Cultural Terrain

After agreeing to coordinate the new counterinsurgency field manual, Crane flew to Fort Leavenworth to meet with Petraeus, who was then formulating his theory of irregular war in a series of fourteen "observations" for a *Military Review* article. The lieutenant general wanted to see his observations reflected in the field manual, and Crane, an admirer of his former West Point classmate, made them the backbone of the manual's first chapter.[29] The article, published two months later as "Learning Counterinsurgency: Observations from Soldiering in Iraq," envisioned

THE CRAFT OF COUNTERINSURGENT WHITENESS

the counterinsurgent as a kind of combat-zone ethnographer. Petraeus described his time in Iraq as if he were conducting field research for a dissertation rather than commanding an infantry division. "The institutional structures for capturing lessons are still dependent on Soldiers' thoughts and reflections," he wrote. "Indeed, my own pen and notebook were always handy while soldiering in Iraq."[30] Advocating on-the-ground cultural intelligence gathering, Petraeus stressed that the soldier's "pen and notebook" were a critical part of the military's arsenal. Counterinsurgents must immerse themselves in local culture and get to know tribal leaders, because *"cultural awareness is a force multiplier,"* he wrote. "Knowledge of the cultural 'terrain' can be as important as, and sometimes more important than, knowledge of the geographical terrain." Whereas Petraeus had once toed the RMA line—admonishing officers in 1997 to "never send a man when you can send a bullet"[31]—he now recommended that soldiers act as community-level cultural ambassadors. This observation formed the basis of one of the field manual's "paradoxes" of irregular war, that "some of the best weapons for counterinsurgents do not shoot."[32]

Field Manual 3-24 promoted what military theorists call "population-centric" counterinsurgency. Unlike "enemy-centric" war, in which the military targets its enemies with "kinetic" (lethal) force, population-centric counterinsurgency focuses on winning the consent of unaffiliated civilians through a combination of "offensive, defensive, and stability operations."[33] Modeling their doctrine on a revisionist account of the "valuable and successful" Civil Operations and Revolutionary Development Support program conducted in South Vietnam from 1967 to 1973, the authors argued that, by integrating civilian and military operations, counterinsurgents could persuade the population to align with the United States and its local allies by offering safer streets, more resources, and a less corrupt government than the insurgents could offer.[34] This population-centric method offered the state a way to "rebrand" the war on terror by returning to the humanitarian message that the first Bush and Clinton administrations had used in Kuwait, Somalia, Bosnia, and Kosovo in the 1990s. In their foreword to the manual, Petraeus and Marine Corps General James Amos stated that counterinsurgents must "be ready to be greeted with a handshake or a hand grenade" and serve as "nation builders as well as warriors," suggesting that American soldiers and marines shake hands and distribute aid until insurgents force them, against their will, to use lethal force—that they are nation builders first and warriors second.[35] But counterinsurgents do not research the cultural terrain for innocent reasons. "A key objective" of cultural awareness in Iraq and Afghanistan, geographer Derek Gregory writes, "was to generate actionable intelligence about insurgency to inform lethal targeting, so that cultural knowledge was not only a substitute for killing but also a prerequisite for its refinement."[36] Petraeus and Crane's counterinsurgency doctrine was not an agenda for ending the war on terror but a way to guarantee its continuation by reframing it as carefully administered liberal defense.

From efforts to contain "communist slavery" in Asia to the protection of ethnic minorities and women's rights in Iraq, the empire of defense has maintained a state of permanent war by imbuing large-scale violence with a liberal antiracist ethos. The state has modified and revitalized that racial regime in the twenty-first century by defining counterinsurgency as what Kilcullen calls "armed social work."[37] The involvement of human rights officials and NGOs in the writing and revision of Field Manual 3-24 reinforced the idea that the state's ambition in the Middle East was to secure the rights of the region's poor and disenfranchised communities. Sewall, who had served in the Clinton administration as the first deputy assistant secretary for peacekeeping and humanitarian assistance, recruited leading members of the human rights community to Petraeus's cause by representing counterinsurgency as a form of humanitarian aid work. In her introduction to the University of Chicago Press edition, she wrote that success in counterinsurgency necessitated that civilian government agencies and humanitarian organizations work hand-in-hand with the military and align themselves with its agenda. "Counterinsurgents seek to expand their efforts along the rights continuum, beyond physical security toward economic, social, civil, and political rights," she stated. "Achieving a more holistic form of human security is important for overall mission success."[38] Conforming to the idea of defense first formulated during the Truman administration, she and her coauthors described counterinsurgency as unending nonwar ("nonkinetic," humanitarian activities) while also anticipating its victorious end (the attainment of local consent).

Sewall, offering her endorsement as the director of a leading human rights center, praised the new counterinsurgents for charting a program of humanitarian sacrifice in the Middle East. She identified the manual as "radical" because it put the rights of Iraqis and Afghans ahead of the safety of American soldiers, who must assume more immediate risk in on-the-ground, population-centric missions. The new doctrine "countermands decades of conventional military practice," she wrote, by telling soldiers that they must defend civilians first and themselves second. The success of counterinsurgency depends on the willingness of American soldiers to sacrifice their bodies and their lives for the future of the country in which they are serving. Sewall acknowledged that this inversion of military priorities may doom counterinsurgency, that the manual's call for humanitarian self-sacrifice may be its "political Achilles' heel."[39] But it may also, she suggested, offer a moral cure for the military's racial Achilles' heel by reframing the wars in Iraq and Afghanistan—defined at this time by images of torture and abuse at Abu Ghraib—as acts of white humanitarian sacrifice in which the lives of Iraqis and Afghans are valued above those of white soldiers. She didn't acknowledge it, but the audience for this radical message was not the army's officer class but Americans at home, who must believe that the wars they authorize are good and honorable.

While Sewall insisted that humanitarian ambassadors must serve alongside counterinsurgents, the manual also instructed counterinsurgents to behave as humanitarian ambassadors. Military theorists valorize the British colonialist T. E. Lawrence ("Lawrence of Arabia") for how he immersed himself in Bedouin culture during World War I and used that cultural knowledge to facilitate an Arab revolt against the Ottoman Empire. They embrace the Lawrence maxim "Better the Arabs do it tolerably than you do it perfectly" as an unofficial motto of counterinsurgency, the idea being that successful counterinsurgency relies on the cultivation of "tolerable" local clients whose collaboration with Americans distracts from their interference in the nation's internal affairs.[40] Kilcullen, a retired lieutenant colonel in the Australian Army whose influential essay " 'Twenty-Eight Articles': Fundamentals of Company-level Counterinsurgency" (2006) borrows its structure from Lawrence's own "Twenty-Seven Articles" (1917), hailed Lawrence as a model of "bi-cultural" soldiering. He argued that the failures of the war on terror can be attributed to Western militaries' lack of "cultural capability" in the Middle East, recommending that soldiers learn to " 'fit in' with local groups" and "perform effectively while immersed in local culture" so they can "use culture to generate leverage within an insurgent system." With even a small number of "bilingual and bi-cultural" individuals, he added, armed forces could, like Lawrence, "exploit cultural norms and expectations to generate operational effects."[41] Kilcullen and his coauthors suggested that their revised counterinsurgency doctrine would transform the Western soldier from a killer into a cultural ambassador conducting nonkinetic activities. Instead, as Kilcullen's determination to wield "leverage" makes clear, it treated culture as a resource for legitimating imperial violence as humane, multi-cultural, and welcomed by the communities on which it is inflicted.

Liberal humanitarians and defense consultants were not the only contrib-utors to the militarization of the cultural terrain. Petraeus and Crane also recruited social scientists to their writing team, including Yale University–trained cultural anthropologist Montgomery McFate. Having written a dissertation based on field research conducted among Irish Republican Army insurgents and British counterinsurgents, McFate authored the third chapter of the field manual, "Intelligence in Counterinsurgency," which Conrad called the "foundation" of the new counterinsurgency and the chapter that "had the most impact on broader institutional doctrine."[42] The chapter reflected her belief that insurgencies are maintained by in-timate social networks and that the United States could not defeat them without a "granular" understanding of the culture that founds and main-tains their networks.[43] McFate schematized culture as a "web of mean-ing" or, better yet, an "operational code" through which individuals find meaning in events, behaviors, and rituals and form a shared set of values. She stressed that culture is learned through social "enculturation" and is therefore "changeable," "arbitrary," and naturalized. Because most in-dividuals belong to more than one social group, they must reconcile dif-ferent, sometimes conflicting sets of learned values. To defeat an insur-gency, she wrote, the counterinsurgent must have the cultural awareness to locate these intergroup differences and "exploit these differences in values."[44]

Her chapter reads like critical theory that has been reverse engineered to reinforce rather than challenge hegemony. This may have been Mc-Fate's intention. In a series of articles written between 2004 and 2014, she criticized scholars in her field for having taken a once-influential "war-fighting discipline" and orchestrated a "plunge into the abyss of postmod-ernism." Led by thinkers who subscribe to "self-reflexive neo-Marxism" and wish to speak for the "subaltern," she wrote, anthropologists con-demned their own discipline as "the handmaiden of colonialism" and "began a brutal process of self-flagellation."[45] McFate advised scholars to instead share their "anthropological finesse" with the government so that it could wage war with a more sensitive understanding of "cultural dynam-ics" and "ethnic distinctions."[46] She recommended that the military form "an office for operational cultural knowledge" that could coordinate "the expedient use of adversary cultural knowledge."[47] Her vision was realized in 2007 when the army established the Human Terrain System program to connect military commanders with social scientists, a move denounced by the American Anthropological Association. McFate served as one of the program's first advisers. Under her guidance, the army declared itself to be aligned with liberal, university-based knowledge of cultural difference and fighting a war informed by that knowledge in the Middle East.

The thesis of the McFate-authored chapter of Field Manual 3-24—a thesis that resurfaces in American veteran fiction—is that successful counterinsurgency necessitates the militarization of cultural narrative. Informed by McFate's own academic work, the chapter called the narrative the "most important" cultural form for the counterinsurgent, defining it as "a story recounted in the form of a causally linked set of events that explains an event in a group's history and expresses the values, character, or self-identity of the group." Because cultural narratives are "the means through which ideologies are expressed and absorbed," commanders must "decode" insurgent narratives and mobilize "counternarratives" that legitimate the United States and its local allies.[48] McFate and her coauthors imagined counterinsurgency as fought on the cultural terrain through narrative, with insurgents telling one story and counterinsurgents telling another. Armed with the methods of cultural studies, the counterinsurgent seeks to remake the culture or "operational code" of the Muslim world by using its own values and identities against it. This culture-mindedness had the effect of making the wars in Iraq and Afghanistan look, to American eyes, like neutral humanitarian efforts—like nonwars. Counterinsurgency does not, however, mark the end of kinetic (lethal) activities but the militarization of nonkinetic activities. The new counterinsurgents, with the authority of social science behind them, converted culture into an instrument of liberal war.[49]

Guided by McFate's cultural anthropological contribution, the field manual acknowledged that cultural narratives are multiple and naturalized through social interaction, while seeking to center its own white Western narrative as the default "rational" account of human society and conflict. The authors encouraged the counterinsurgent to recognize that "American ideas of what is 'normal' or 'rational' are not universal" and to "avoid imposing their ideals of normalcy on a foreign cultural problem."[50] On the surface, Petraeus, Conrad, and their writing team communicated a sensitivity to cultural difference, encouraging soldiers to examine how their own understanding of what is "normal" may be learned and contingent rather than natural. Insurgents must be confronted on their own cultural terrain, not treated as aberrant and irrational. But, while the authors discouraged field officers from "imposing" American norms on Iraqi and Afghan communities, they urged them to marshal cultural narrative as a means of influencing locals to assent to those norms. One of the manual's central lessons is that counterinsurgent forces must "exploit a single narrative" that undermines the insurgents' narrative. Through careful research on the cultural environment, commanders should, the authors instructed, craft a story that "emphasizes the inevitability and rightness of the COIN operation's success." If American forces introduce that story "gradually" and through native clients, locals won't even recognize it as foreign; it will become normalized.[51] Although the military's new counterinsurgency doctrine, informed by cultural studies, announced itself as embracing a non-hierarchical, non-normative understanding of culture, it centered the white Christian male as the arbiter of cultural difference able to schematize, "decode," and remake non-Western cultures through the weaponization of storytelling.[52]

Counterinsurgency theorists understand cultural narrative as an instrument for securing consent at home as well, and the vehicle for securing that domestic consent is the counterinsurgent's own story of struggle and sacrifice. Petraeus is often described as the most media savvy general of his generation, a savviness that shows in Field Manual 3-24's instructions to commanders on how to engage embedded journalists and "help the media tell the story" of the nation's wars. Above all else, the manual's authors advised that, while senior officials will communicate the military's broader mission in formal press conferences, journalists should be given access to soldiers and marines in the field. "These young people nearly always do a superb job of articulating the important issues for a broad audience," they wrote. "Given a chance, they can share their courage and sense of purpose with the American people and the world."[53] The manual set out a program for managing news media that called for commanders to establish a unified story and for the on-the-ground counterinsurgent to serve as the vessel for and protagonist of that story. Like most military documents, the manual imagined the soldier as deracinated and degendered, but that absence of racial and gender identities, in the context of military culture, assumed the soldier's whiteness and maleness. Whiteness functions in counterinsurgency as the disavowed norm around which it is organized and through which it imagines and polices cultural difference. Petraeus, Nagl, Crane, Sewall, Kilcullen, and McFate recalibrated the idea of defense by mobilizing the methods of cultural studies to center, and further obscure, the whiteness of liberal war. They theorized a white male soldier—the unstated normative embodiment of the American military—who could accrue diverse cultural knowledge while never acknowledging or surrendering a belief in his own centrality. That ideal counterinsurgent studies the cultural terrain of the state's wars and distills it into a single narrative that contains the stories of people living under occupation. Field Manual 3-24 instructed the white military man to author a definitive account of the counterterror wars—to write what Gallagher, four years later, termed the great war on terror novel.

The Great War on Terror Novel

Three months before the release of Field Manual 3-24, in September 2006, Random House published *Operation Homecoming*, an anthology of short stories, private journals, letters, and emails by American soldiers, marines, airmen, and their families. Edited by military historian Andrew Carroll, the book grew out of the National Endowment for the Arts program Operation Homecoming, which, between 2004 and 2006, coordinated more than fifty writing workshops at twenty-five military bases in five countries. NEA chairman Dana Gioia conceived Operation Homecoming as a corrective to the "cultural snobbism" of which conservative lawmakers had accused the endowment, trading Robert Mapplethorpe exhibitions for accessible, soldier-authored literature.[54] He teamed with the armed forces in organizing the events, and convinced Boeing, the second largest military contractor in the world, to donate more than half a million dollars to the program. The *New York Times* celebrated Gioia for having brokered a truce in the culture wars and "won the Congressional approbation that eluded his predecessors" by giving voice to the country's fighting men and women.[55] But, while Gioia insisted that Operation Homecoming was "not about politics but about particulars," it reflected a counterinsurgent's recognition of the usefulness of cultural narrative as a mechanism for securing consent and containing resistance.[56] Like the field manual authors' advice that soldiers and marines be invited to "share their courage and sense of purpose with the American people and the world," defense officials and Boeing executives recognized that soldiers' stories of sacrifice and loss would not undermine, and might even facilitate, their ability to wage war and sell military aircraft.[57] As Petraeus's writing team put the finishing touches on *Counterinsurgency*, the *New Yorker* published excerpts of *Operation Homecoming* in its annual fiction issue, and filmmaker Richard Robbins adapted the book into an Academy Award–nominated documentary.

Gioia declared the program a success for having bridged America's military-civilian divide. "One of the tragedies of the Vietnam War is that no one wanted to listen to the vets when they came back," he told the endowment's in-house magazine. "If Operation Homecoming does anything, it creates a vehicle for conversations between the troops and their families and society."[58] Matt Gallagher would echo Gioia's words five years later when he argued that civilian editors and reviewers had neglected veteran fiction out of a desire to forget their country's wars. But veteran-writers had not been neglected—far from it, with government agencies like the NEA, publishers like Random House, and elite universities like Syracuse, Johns Hopkins, and NYU having incubated their careers through special programs, publishing contracts, and veterans' writing workshops. Gallagher himself holds an MFA from Columbia University, which has taken an active role in transforming war veterans into war writers. Veteran-writers may have more institutional resources available to them than any other group of emerging artists. So why do writers like Gallagher see the war story as a marginalized form? And why have government agencies sought to build a canon of new war fiction?

White veteran-writers may have recognized a strategic advantage to declaring their marginalization in American literary culture. The institutionalization of creative writing at universities since World War II has reordered American fiction into genres of what literary historian Mark McGurl calls "high cultural pluralism," a form of modernist writing that combines acts of authorial self-making with "a rhetorical performance of cultural group membership preeminently, though by no means exclusively, marked as ethnic." High cultural pluralists include black writers, Latina/o writers, regional writers, and "Veteran-American" writers whose "psychic wounds" and "authoritative experience of war" have, McGurl writes, formed the basis of their careers "in the same way that [Philip] Roth's Jewishness has" his.[59] An understanding of his own minoritization has allowed the white veteran-writer to reassert his relevance in an age of liberal multiculturalism. But Gioia's and Gallagher's claims that the veteran-writer has been ignored and must now be heard also function as a mechanism for further disremembering civilians killed and refugeed by American armed forces. Although veteran-writers Gallagher, Kevin Powers, and Phil Klay have been critical of the wars in which they fought, their fiction aligns with the state's militarization of cultural knowledge. This new generation of MFA-trained veteran-writers has internalized the counterinsurgent's ambition to "craft" a narrative of white humanitarian sacrifice (counterinsurgency) and Muslim backwardness (insurgency) that reveals whiteness as an enduring condition for the execution of defense.[60]

A year after Gallagher asked why he had yet to read a great war on terror novel, critics anointed their first candidate for that title by touting Kevin Powers's *The Yellow Birds* (2012) as "a classic of contemporary war fiction," "the first American literary masterpiece produced by the Iraq war," and "a fully realized work of imagination" and "brutal lyricism" that accesses and transcends the "American tradition of war writing."[61] Powers, a volunteer in the Virginia National Guard, served in Iraq from 2004 to 2005 as a machine gunner for an EOD (Explosive Ordinance Disposal) unit. His team arrived in Mosul as David Petraeus began conducting counterinsurgency operations in the city, fine-tuning a method that would form the basis of Field Manual 3-24 and govern the later stages of the war. Powers's novel, based on the author's own service in Mosul and derived from his MFA thesis at the University of Texas, follows army veteran John Bartle as he looks back on his tour and the loss of his close friend Daniel Murphy. In an interview with *PBS NewsHour*, Powers described it as one vet's reckoning with his own "powerlessness" through the invention of meaning amid a war that "seems to have a mind [of its own] and purpose beyond his ability to comprehend it."[62] Through Bartle's search for a memory with which he can live, the novel traces the counterinsurgent's struggle to transform cultural knowledge into a coherent, useable story that centers the white soldier's suffering and obscures non-American losses as the regrettable but necessary cost of that narrative formation.

In more than two hundred pages, the novel introduces just one Iraqi character by name—Malik, a translator—and he dies within three pages of being introduced. Stationed on a roof in the fictional city of Al Tafar, Malik informs Bartle and Murphy that he grew up in the neighborhood below and stands to point out the street on which his family had lived. The Americans advise him to get down, worried that he could "get silhouetted," that he could attract enemy fire to their location. Ignoring their warnings, Malik continues to tell them about an old woman who grew flowers in the neighboring field. Seconds later, he is struck by a bullet and killed. Afterward, Bartle and Murphy agree that Malik should not, as an Iraqi, be included in the official death count:

> We heard [the bullets] tear at the air around our ears and smack into the clay
> brick and concrete. We did not see Malik get killed, but Murph and I had his
> blood on both of our uniforms. When we got the order to cease fire we looked

over the low wall and he was lying in the dust and there was a lot of blood around him.

"Doesn't count, does it?" Murph asked.

"No. I don't think so."

"What're we at?"

"Nine sixty-eight? Nine seventy? We'll have to check the paper when we get back."[63]

While Sarah Sewall, in her introduction to Field Manual 3-24, described the military's embrace of counterinsurgency as a radical transformation, because it asked that soldiers and marines take on greater risk to save civilian lives, Powers's novel suggests more familiar relations of human value and valuelessness in which Iraqi deaths don't "count" and, as Bartle admits, even serve as "an affirmation of [American] lives."[64]

Although Malik, as their translator, grants the counterinsurgents access to linguistic and cultural knowledge that they would not otherwise have, they show themselves to be more attuned to Al Tafar than he, a local, is. As Malik describes the old woman's flower garden, Bartle remembers drinking tea in "the small clay hovels" on the street below and having his "hands wrapped in the thinly veined hands of the old men and women who lived in them."[65] Armed with the intimate knowledge of Al Tafar gained through community-based intelligence gathering, Bartle senses a threat and directs the translator to take cover. When Malik catches a bullet from a neighboring building, the counterinsurgent, a foreigner, comes across as more aware of the neighborhood than a man raised in it. Like the Vietnam War films of the 1980s, Powers uses civilian deaths as a mere device for communicating the American soldier's trauma. Bartle and Murphy don't see Malik die, but they wear his blood on their uniforms and recognize that they too "could be among the walking dead."[66] Their counterinsurgency tactics—having tea with elders, receiving briefings on "the social structures and demographics" of Al Tafar[67]—show the United States to be a humane actor in the Middle East while granting the veteran-writer the license to tell a balanced story of the war that acknowledges civilian life without decentering the white Western narrator.

Powers's novel tells the story of the making of a war story. Narrated by an older Bartle, years removed from his service, it ends with him incarcerated in a low-security military prison in Fort Knox, Kentucky, where he is serving a three-year sentence for an unidentified crime. He is innocent of the charges brought against him and confused by the events that led to his detainment. But the novel doesn't dwell on the details of his charges. Instead, it finds a resolution when Bartle settles on a story that he can understand. When a CID (Criminal Investigation Command) agent arrests him at his home in Richmond, Virginia, Bartle reflects, "I could not pattern it. None of it made sense. Nothing followed from anything else and I was required to answer for a story that did not exist." Four years later at Fort Knox, he has found a story that he can assimilate. "The details of the world in which we live are always secondary to the fact that we must live in them," he concludes. "I don't want to look out over the earth as it unfurls itself toward the horizon. . . . [I'd rather look out at] something manageable and finite that could break up and fix the earth into parcels small enough that they could be contended with."[68] The novel charts not Bartle's attainment of knowledge but his achievement of narrative order. It finds its resolution not in the revelation of Bartle's alleged crimes but with the veteran's coming-to-terms through the construction of his own "manageable and finite" story. Like an earlier generation of veteran-novelists, Powers received acclaim for how his writing reckons with the human costs of war and the traumas that the returning vet carries with him. But his novel also shows how such storytelling may hide as much as reveal those human costs. Bartle's years-long struggle to formulate a meaningful war story reflects his training as a counterinsurgent for whom narrative is part of the cultural terrain to be studied, weaponized, and won, in Iraq and at home.

Most veteran-writers, like Powers, devote as much attention to the soldier's homecoming as to the war itself, introducing the violence of battle through flashbacks that hang over the veteran as he tries to reconcile his military and civilian lives.[69] In February 2014, Phil Klay wrote an editorial in the *New York Times*, "After War, a Failure of Imagination," in which he lamented that most Americans reacted to his military service by conceding that they could never imagine what he had been through. "Believing war is beyond words is an abrogation of responsibility," he wrote. "It lets civilians off the hook from trying to understand, and veterans off the hook from needing to explain."[70] Klay, a former marine captain who served as a public affairs officer in Anbar Province, stressed that civilians must work harder to imagine war stories and that veterans must work harder to tell them. Two months later, he answered his own call with *Redeployment*, a collection of twelve short stories about the challenges veterans face in communicating something about the world to reverent but unlistening civilians. The book went on to win that year's National Book Award for

Fiction, with the judges declaring it "a kaleidoscopic vision of conflict and homecoming" that "stakes Klay's claim as the quintessential storyteller of America's Iraq conflict."[71] The twelve stories in Klay's effort to close the military-civilian divide by sharing the veteran's knowledge with the American reader reflect the Petraeus-led forces' understanding of the Middle East as an unstable but knowable otherworld that necessitates the counterinsurgent's learned administration of conflict and cultural difference.

Klay's stories feature teenage grunts, college-educated officers, bureaucrats, and veteran-students. "There's an incredible diversity of experience [in modern war]," he told Gallagher, whom he met through NYU's Veterans Writing Workshop, in an interview. "By using different perspectives, I wanted to open a place for readers to compare and contrast, to make judgments, to engage."[72] Of course, that "diversity" has its limits in Klay's book. All of the stories are narrated by male American soldiers and veterans. All but one of those narrators are white. In the title story, marine sergeant Price returns home to his wife in the suburbs of Jacksonville, North Carolina, wrestling with the memory of shooting wild dogs in Fallujah with his fellow marines ("we called it Operation Scooby"). The story culminates with Price shooting his own hobbled dog, Vicar, beside a stream near his house, an act that reminds him of killing an insurgent whom his men found hiding in a water cistern filled with human feces. "[Vicar] wagged his tail. And I froze. Only one other time I hesitated like that. Midway through Fallujah, an insurgent snuck through our perimeter. When we raised the alarm, he disappeared," he remembers, recounting the man's horrendous death in the cistern. Price describes how his military training had taught him to kill while inflicting minimal suffering, a method he executes in putting Vicar down. "I'd been trained to do it right. Sight alignment, trigger control, breath control. Focus on the iron sights, not the target. The target should be blurry. . . . Hammer pair to the body. A final well-aimed shot to the head."[73] Price's analogous thoughts about the insurgent and his dog allude to how the counterterror state has located Muslims at the limits of the human, whether as deferred humans ("civilians") or nonhumans ("insurgents"). But Price masks that racialization through the care with which he conducts the act of killing. He focuses not on the man's or even the dog's loss of life but on his own methodical administration of violence through which he mediates the animating contradictions—war and nonwar, racialization and antiracism—of the empire of defense.

Klay's fiction shows the effectiveness of, and trouble with, bringing the methods of counterinsurgency home. In "Psychological Operations," Waguih, an Arab American veteran and student at Amherst College, lands in the office of the Special Assistant to the President for Diversity and Inclusion after telling a black Muslim student, Zara, that he—being Christian rather than Muslim, as she assumed—had no misgivings about killing Muslims as a soldier. Waguih, having served as a specialist in Psychological Operations, recognizes that he can use his military training to deflect her accusation of anti-Muslim racism. "If I couldn't PsyOps my way out of this, I wasn't worth a damn," he thinks. When Zara tells the administrator that she and her friends felt threatened by his comments, Waguih counters with what he calls a "my hard little war" story. "Of course they feel threatened," he tells the administrator. "I'm a crazy vet, right? But the only mention of violence came from her. When she accused me of murdering Muslims." The administrator, not knowing what to do with two students of color trading grievances, decides on "a course of minimum liability" and dismisses the incident as a "teachable moment."[74] Waguih remembers how he had been instructed to use linguistic and cultural knowledge as "a weapons system" to "get inside [insurgents'] heads."[75] At Amherst, he discovers that his training as a counterinsurgent can also be used to divert attention from the racial violence of the war in which he had served. Accused of targeting Muslims, Waguih sees that his own status as an Arab vet can be used as a counteroffensive, an argument for his own—and by extension the military's—minoritization and studied management of racial and ethnic difference.

"Psychological Operations" is the rare veteran-authored story that addresses race in direct terms. But Waguih tells Zara that being a veteran at Amherst is more "alienating" than being an Arab soldier in the military, citing a racist white comrade who still, he believes, would have died for him in a heartbeat.[76] His meeting with the college administrator draws attention to how veteranness has been treated by universities, colleges, and the cultural industries as a form of diversity that mirrors and even subsumes racial difference. Waguih states that in the army he was first and foremost a fellow soldier, and that he finds his liberal arts college isolating not because of his skin color but because of his military service. His veteranness, he argues, transcends his Arabness. But, given the hegemonic status of whiteness in military culture, the alleged color blindness of the armed forces reinforces an unacknowledged white norm. "To have no identity at all is the privilege of whiteness, which is the identity that pretends not to have an identity, that denies how it is tied to capitalism, to race, and to war," novelist and ethnic studies scholar Viet Nguyen writes. "Victimization and voice become the markers of difference and identity for minorities, while whiteness becomes unmarked alienation, manifest in the supposedly universal experiences of loneliness, divorce, ennui, and anomie."[77] Klay's story brings to light how military whiteness has managed to straddle the center and margin of American culture by trafficking in the "unmarked alienation" of hegemonic whiteness while also claiming the "victimization and voice" of a minority culture. Waguih identifies the value of veteranness and a well-executed "my hard little war" story in rescuing himself from the charge of racism—a value that the defense establishment has recognized as well.

David Kilcullen sees these "PsyOps" strategies as part of the counterinsurgent's trained cultural intelligence. Kilcullen, a former Australian officer who served as a senior adviser to Petraeus in Baghdad, emerged as a lead architect of the revised counterinsurgency doctrine after moving to Washington, DC, in 2004 to assist in an internal assessment of the Pentagon's readiness to win the war on terror. A student of the colonial military theories of David Galula and T. E. Lawrence, he argued, in recounting his time in the Australian Army and with Petraeus in Iraq, that most insurgents don't subscribe to radical ideologies but have been "coopted" by a minority of extremists. These non-ideological insurgents constitute what he calls "accidental guerillas" who follow "folk-ways of tribal warfare that are mediated by traditional cultural norms, values, and perceptual lenses" and see themselves as resisting foreign intervention rather than advancing a radical cause.[78] Cavalier Western interference, he wrote, only strengthens an insurgency by creating accidental guerillas in a "rejection phase" that "looks a lot like a social version of an immune response in which the body rejects the intrusion of a foreign object, even one (such as a pin in a broken bone or a stent in a blocked blood vessel) that serves an ultimately beneficial purpose."[79] Like a stent, the counterinsurgent must, Kilcullen suggested, disguise his foreignness by blending in with the cultural environment to counteract the formation of accidental guerillas and to isolate extremists.

That struggle to win the consent of would-be accidental guerillas unfolds in Matt Gallagher's *Youngblood* (2016). No writer has been more engaged in defining the literature of the counterterror wars than Gallagher, who contributed to the *New York Times* blog *At War* while earning his MFA and has mentored fellow veteran-writers through the nonprofit organization Words after War. As a glowing *Washington Post* review acknowledges,

"Everyone who reads war lit knows Matt Gallagher."[80] Gallagher served as a cavalry officer in a village on the outskirts of Baghdad, leading his men in what he has described as "the drudgery of counterinsurgency life."[81] Set in the fictional village of Ashuriyah, his novel follows an army lieutenant, Jack Porter, tasked with managing that drudgery. Porter, a sensitive leader with a fondness for Lawrence's writing, struggles with his callous staff sergeant, Daniel Chambers, a veteran of four tours. Whereas Porter seeks to understand Ashuriyah on its own terms and even begins a romance with the daughter of a local sheik, Chambers resists what he calls the "counterinsurgency handholding bullshit" of the Petraeus-led coalition forces.[82] Although it shows the messiness of counterinsurgency on the ground, Gallagher's novel echoes the doctrine conceived by Kilcullen in which the United States chooses not whether to wage war but whether to wage it more or less humanely.

Gallagher's novel contends with the canon of counterinsurgency writing. "The most vivid description of COIN I ever got as a young lieutenant was 'You know, like British imperial occupation,'" he recalled in a 2016 interview. "It's about the long game, being a jack-of-all-trades immersed with the people, being beat cops and conducting electricity surveys and dealing with roadside bombs and snipers all at the same time."[83] His narrator, Porter, admires the Westerners who fought in the region before him. He reads and rereads Lawrence's *The Seven Pillars of Wisdom*, the British officer's account of fighting alongside Bedouins. As Porter investigates rumors about crimes committed by his staff sergeant and an American solider who had, years earlier, married the sheik's daughter before being assassinated by al-Qaeda, he hides the evidence he uncovers in the book, building his own story inside Lawrence's. When Chambers discovers *The Seven Pillars of Wisdom* beside Porter's bunk, he dismisses it as "self-aggrandizing bullshit" and recommends that he instead read Julius Caesar's *Conquest of Gaul*. "That's how an empire deals with the barbarians," he tells him. When Porter asks Chambers what he sees as their role in Ashuriyah, he laughs and tells him that he is "a simple cog in the machine" who doesn't "get paid to think." But he adds, "I'll be here for years after you leave. For three, four platoon leaders. It's all about the endgame."[84] Their argument over Lawrence's writing introduces the central conflict of the novel, with Porter toeing the counterinsurgency line and Chambers advocating the use of overwhelming offensive force. Porter, a graduate of Reed College, embraces the "thinking man's war" of Petraeus and Kilcullen, while Chambers sees counterinsurgency as the naive theories of ladder-climbing college graduates who will never stick around long enough to see their ideas fail. Their disagreement restages the animating conflict of Oliver Stone's film *Platoon* (1986), in which the liberal sergeant Elias (Willem Dafoe) contends with his men's gravitation toward the ruthless staff sergeant Barnes (Tom Berenger).[85] Like Stone's film, Gallagher's novel draws attention to the good-heartedness of the counterinsurgent by setting him against his less enlightened working-class comrade.

Even as Porter mocks commanders who drone on about the tenets of counterinsurgency, the novel validates the militarization of culture as a means of redeeming the counterterror wars. Following an American air strike on the village, civilians gather to demonstrate against the unwarranted attack. When Porter's commanding officer sends his team out to monitor the gathering, the demonstrators, who far outnumber the Americans, surround the soldiers and their vehicle. Chambers commands the men to fire, but Porter shouts, "Hold! Hold!" and, setting down his rifle, removes his helmet and lowers himself to one knee. The others follow his lead. "One by one, American soldiers took off their helmets, some cupping their hearts, others saying 'Salaam Aleichem' on repeat." Chambers orders them to stand, arguing that "soldiers don't kneel."[86] Porter answers that they are not kneeling but "taking a knee." The lieutenant's show of deference works. The demonstrators turn back, with some even convincing their more hostile neighbors to leave the disarmed Americans alone. Porter's insistence that he and his men are taking a knee suggests that theirs is a gesture not of submission but of listening. They acknowledge the demonstrators' suffering and hear their grievances, an act that allows them to fulfill their assigned task of ending the demonstration without firing a bullet. And by holding a hand over their hearts and saying "Salaam Aleichem," they signal their commitment to integrating cultural knowledge as an instrument of war. Porter leads his soldiers in an act of nonviolent mediation that staves off the "rejection phase" of which Kilcullen warned. The novel suggests that, while the racism of white working-class soldiers like Chambers (who sees Muslims as "barbarians") may have created "accidental guerillas," white middle-class counterinsurgents like Porter could reclaim the war effort as humane and principled, a testament to the armed forces' humanitarian ethos and readiness to manage cultural difference the world over.

Of course, Gallagher directed his book not to the Muslim world but to the American reader, as Powers and Klay did theirs. The ambition that

Gallagher laid out for them in "Where's the Great Novel about the War on Terror?" was to bridge the military-civilian divide in the United States by writing fiction that so transcended "matters of specific time, place, and experience" that it could correct for "a general lack of connection with the wars" among Americans, a small fraction of whom had served.[87] That divide has been a focus of their fiction and the lens through which critics have read it and imbued it with urgent social value. The state has also sought to close the gulf between its all-volunteer force and civilian Americans through arts initiatives like Operation Homecoming and by, as the authors of Field Manual 3-24 advised, giving journalists access to counterinsurgents in the field.[88] Powers, Klay, and Gallagher wade into that cultural war—a kind of domestic counterinsurgency—with novels that center the humane conduct and good intentions of the white counterinsurgent who struggles, most of all, to craft his own ordering narrative. Counterinsurgency doctrine holds that achieving consent from Iraqis and Afghans, as well as Americans, rests on the formation of a single narrative that makes sense of state violence and organizes one's encounters with it. But that single narrative has been challenged by the emergence of alternative stories from the furthest margins of the cultural terrain, where the cultural politics of permanent war surface and fail.

Empire of Redaction

On December 15, 2005, on the naval base at Guantánamo Bay, Cuba, Mohamedou Ould Slahi sat before the Administrative Review Board that the Bush administration had tasked with reviewing detainees' status as "illegal combatants." The board asked Slahi about his whereabouts on September 11, 2001, and the detainee described his life in his native Mauritania four years earlier. Part way through his answer—an answer he had given countless times before—he paused. "I just want to mention here that I wrote a book while in jail here recently about my whole story, okay? I sent it for release to the District [of] Columbia, and when it is released I advise you guys to read it," he told the board. "A little advertisement. It is a very interesting book, I think."[89] He then returned to his answer. That book would not be declassified until 2012 and would not be published, with more than twenty-five hundred black-bar redactions, until 2015. Slahi would not be released until 2016, fourteen years after the United States first rendered him to Guantánamo without a formal charge.

Slahi's case, his indefinite detention and torture, and his censored account of that detention and torture, troubles the idea of defense through which the state has waged nonwar against bodies and societies it has deemed illegitimate, from communists and drug traffickers to human rights abusers and insurgents. The lengths to which the counterterror state has gone to block Slahi from sharing his story suggests how much his handwritten memoir, and stories like it, threaten that idea. From the Cold War to the war on terror, the United States has cast its enemies outside the liberal world as illegal, as rightless, as something other than human.[90] This racial regime transforms the violent work of racialization into antiracism, the making of racial hierarchies into the safeguarding of human rights, war into defense. Slahi's memoir, a 122,000-word document that he wrote in English in the summer of 2005, asks how the United States has built an empire on these fundamental contradictions. Perhaps this is why the government held his memoir for seven years before releasing it, at last, with thousands of words hidden under black ink.

Even before the 9/11 attacks, government officials declared Slahi a terrorist by association. In 2000, he was detained en route from Canada to Mauritania and interrogated by the FBI in connection with the failed millennium plot to bomb the Los Angeles International Airport. The FBI ordered his detention on the basis that he had attended the same mosque, though never at the same time, as Ahmed Ressam, the architect of the plot, while living in Montreal; that his brother-in-law, Abu Hafs al-Mauritani, sat on al-Qaeda's Shura Council; and that he had fought with al-Qaeda in 1991 and 1992 in the Afghan Civil War to overthrow the communist-led government, an effort financed by the CIA. After three weeks, Mauritanian authorities released Slahi. The next year, on September 29, 2001, the Mauritanian government, acting at the behest of the Bush administration, detained him again, this time in connection with the September 11 attacks but without additional evidence. From there, the CIA rendered him to Jordan and then to Bagram Air Base in Afghanistan. On August 5, 2002, Slahi landed at Guantánamo Bay, where he would face a "special interrogation plan" that included sexual abuse, beatings, a mock execution, and long stretches in a freezing cell. Through the construction of a second-tier legal structure that has, as cultural historian Amy Kaplan writes, allowed the government to extend its extraterritorial carceral regime "while keeping itself immune from accountability and keeping prisoners from the safeguards of any [domestic or international legal] systems," the United States held him at the base for more than a decade because of the men he once knew or may have known.[91]

Slahi chronicles the first four years of his detainment in his memoir, which Little, Brown published, in redacted form, as *Guantánamo Diary* in 2015. The memoir details the interrogations he endured in Mauritania, Jordan, Afghanistan, and Cuba. Slahi asks all of his interrogators why he has been detained and what crime he has committed. When he asks an FBI interrogator why the United States believes him to be a terrorist, the man answers, "To me, you meet all the criteria of a top terrorist. When I check the terrorist check list, you pass with a very high score. . . . You're Arab, you're young, you went to Jihad, you speak foreign languages, you've been in many countries, you're a graduate in a technical discipline." When Slahi asks the interrogator how that constitutes a crime, he counters, "Look at the hijackers: they were the same."[92] Slahi has, he discovers, been detained for years not because of something he has done but because his skin color, age, religion, and education meet officials' "criteria" for terrorism. His candid exchange with the FBI interrogator reveals how being a terrorist has as much to do with who a person is as what a person does.

The interrogator bases his belief that Slahi is a terrorist on his Arabness, while extending and obscuring that race-based accusation by adding age, religion, language, and education to his "terrorist check list." His words indicate how the racial regime of defense has allowed the state to abstract its violence from color-line racial divisions by describing its enemies in the deracinated language of beliefs (Islam) and behaviors (terrorism, multilingualism, technical training). Being Arab and Muslim doesn't make one a terrorist, but it is, the interrogator acknowledges, a precondition for being identified as one. The subtext of his checklist suggests that being white and Christian insulates a person from the charge of terrorism, that even the most belligerent act of white violence cannot be dismissed as mere malice. The interrogator, whose name has been redacted, models how the counterterror state's indefinite detention and torture of Muslim men has been depoliticized through proceduralism. He sees his interrogation of Slahi not as part of a pattern of racial violence but as the meticulous administration of a checklist.

But, even as his interrogator assumes Slahi's guilt based in part on his faith, the United States has advertised its treatment of Guantánamo detainees as a testament to its commitment to religious freedom. On September 1, 2006, two months after three detainees died in what were deemed suicides, Secretary of Defense Donald Rumsfeld sent a memo to his undersecretary of policy, Eric Edelman, along with a five-page document titled "Guantánamo Bay: The Facts." "You ought to get these Guantanamo

Bay facts out widely," he instructed Edelman. After first stressing that the detainees held at Guantánamo are "dangerous men" and include bomb makers and some of Osama bin Laden's closest confidants, the document described the conditions of their incarceration as if they were on an extended vacation, with access to "volleyball and basketball courts, TV privileges, [and] workout equipment"; a library that featured Islamic books as well as the Harry Potter series; and "superb dental and medical care." The longest section of the document detailed religious accommodations that included "five daily calls to prayer," "a personal copy of the Koran," "special prayer rooms," and halal meat "flown in by a contractor." The mother of one detainee was claimed to have said that her returned son didn't want to leave Guantánamo because he "had human rights and good living standards there."[93]

Slahi's memoir contradicts the "facts" that Rumsfeld sent Edelman. At Camp Echo, where the military holds high-value detainees, he is denied access to a Koran and forbidden from reciting it. "The U.S. has always repeated that the war is not against the Islamic religion," he writes, "and back there [outside Guantánamo] the U.S. was showing the rest of the world how religious freedom ought to be maintained. But in the secret camps, the war against the Islamic religion was more than obvious."[94] Slahi directs his memoir to a Western audience and underscores that he doesn't believe that "the average American is paying taxes to wage war against Islam," but he identifies a contradiction that has defined the state's image of itself across the twentieth and twenty-first centuries. From the Truman administration to Slahi's detention during the Bush and Obama years, officials have transformed some of the government's worst acts of racial violence into evidence of its humanitarianism, making Guantánamo—a site of well-documented torture and abuse—a vehicle for "showing the rest of the world how religious freedom ought to be maintained."

Two thousand six, the year that the armed forces issued a field manual that militarized cultural narrative and the NEA launched an initiative to generate and circulate soldier-authored literature, was the first of seven years during which Slahi's handwritten memoir sat in a secure location in the Washington suburbs. When the memoir was finally released to his legal team in 2012, it contained thousands of single-word and single-sentence redactions that hid names, locations, and, oddly, all female pronouns. The censors also made three multipage redactions that concealed Slahi's account of two interrogations he underwent while wearing a lie-detection device—interrogations that indicated the truthfulness of his answers—and one poem he wrote from his cell.[95] Why would they single out these two interrogations and fifty-two lines of verse as threats to national security? Can a poem be so dangerous? Slahi's memoir draws out the cultural struggle to tell, and not tell, the story of permanent war. That struggle has been animated by anxieties and contradictions introduced by a national security establishment that has waged unending war as liberal defense. More than ever, since the revitalization of counterinsurgency, military and intelligence officials have recognized culture as the decisive terrain on which they fight and narrative as the means by which they win the war. Slahi's memoir, his poem, the validation of his account by the military's own lie-detection technologies—these tell a story of permanent war. Until we can read that story in full, we must read it in the redactions.

Epilogue: Defense in the Fifth Domain

With former Secretary of State Hillary Clinton and businessman Donald Trump entering the final months of their hobbled presidential campaigns, the Obama administration, late on a Friday, declassified its rules and procedures for using lethal force outside "areas of active hostilities," a document known internally as the drone-strike "playbook."[1] President Barack Obama had issued the eighteen-page document three years earlier, the day before he delivered a speech at the National Defense University in which he addressed critics of his administration's drone program. "My administration has worked vigorously to establish a framework that governs our use of force against terrorists—insisting upon clear guidelines, oversight, and accountability that is now codified in Presidential Policy Guidance that I signed yesterday," he announced that day in May 2013, referring to the playbook.[2] The White House released an abbreviated "fact sheet" describing the document, but it would take a Freedom of Information lawsuit filed by the ACLU for a redacted version of the guidelines to be made public three years later, in the waning months of the president's second term.

The Presidential Policy Guidance detailed a bureaucratic maze of legal vetting and committee reviews. The authorization to use lethal force originated with one of two "operating agencies," the Defense Department or the CIA, which "nominated" an individual for assassination. The nomination then moved to the National Counterterrorism Center, where intelligence officers assembled a macabre "baseball card" of the accused terrorist that was reviewed by legal teams from across the government's defense and intelligence agencies. It then advanced to the deputies committee and, if authorized, the principals committee of the National Security Council. With a green light from the NSC, the airstrike could be executed. If there was disagreement among committee members, then the strike had to receive the go-ahead from the president himself.[3] The declassification of the Presidential Policy Guidance followed the administration's release, a month earlier (and also late on a Friday), of its count of combatants and civilians killed by American airstrikes in Pakistan, Yemen, and elsewhere, numbers far lower than those reported by independent groups.[4] Ned Price, the NSC spokesperson, said of the releases, "Our counterterrorism actions are effective and legal, and their legitimacy is best demonstrated by making public more information about these actions."[5]

While Obama described the guidelines as a constraint on the remote use of force, the Presidential Policy Guidance bureaucratized and legalized rather than restrained the government's authority to kill those it deemed terrorists wherever and whenever it wanted. The procedure for authorizing a drone strike outside the state-designated combat zones in Iraq, Afghanistan, and Syria, while circuitous, was full of workarounds and ambiguities. "Absent extraordinary circumstances, direct action against an identified high-value terrorist will only be taken when there is near certainty that the individual being targeted is in fact the lawful target and located at the place where the action will occur," it stated. "Also absent extraordinary circumstances, direct action will be taken only if there is near certainty that the action can be taken without injuring or killing non-combatants."[6] The document gave no indication of what might constitute "extraordinary circumstances" or how the National Counterterrorism Center and National Security Council defined "near certainty" of a targeted individual's whereabouts and the absence of "non-combatants," another gray-area term. The Presidential Policy Guidance may have encouraged rather than inhibited the use of drone strikes by cloaking them in legal language and nonbinding checks and balances. Formalizing drone war normalizes it, makes it seem rational and humane—in Price's words, effective, legal, and legitimate.

The document's title, "Procedures for Approving Direct Action against Terrorist Targets," suggested that it was designed not to guide decision-making but to defend, after the fact, a decision to kill someone. Most of its eighteen pages outlined how defense and intelligence officials could build a case for the use of force, directing the National Counterterrorism Center to convene a team for "addressing issues" that could get in the way of a recommended strike. From the first line, the document confused procedure with policy. "This Presidential Policy Guidance establishes the standard operating procedures for when the United States takes direct action," it began.[7] The presidential policy was that officials execute the procedure. The procedure was the policy. That confusion stemmed from Obama's belief that the government had no better choice—that it must wage either a ground war or a remote war against terrorists, that *not* killing is not a viable alternative. "Neither conventional military action nor waiting for attacks to occur offers moral safe harbor," the president stated in 2013, "and neither does a sole reliance on law enforcement in territories that have no functioning police or security services—and, indeed, have no functioning law."[8] With reference to "the history of putting American troops in distant lands among hostile populations," he insisted that the United States had a choice to make. Either it could risk American and civilian lives in ground wars that could last for years. Or it could use drone and cyber technologies to target individuals who endangered the lives of Americans and people in their own communities. His administration's remote attacks were justified, he suggested, because they were conducted in countries already marked by lawlessness and death.

But are the choices so limited? Must the United States wage one kind of war or another, ground war or remote war? Is remote war, as Obama framed it, somehow more humane—a form of self-defense rather than war? The president argued that terrorism had become a part of the everyday life of the nation and would be for the foreseeable future. The government must therefore manage that new normal by maintaining a state of constant, violent readiness that he saw as humanitarian nonwar, or defense. But the idea of defense—enacted through drone and cyber technologies under Obama—has long created new unstable conditions that then become the cause for more war. It has formed and marshaled racial fear as the basis of modern state- building.[9] That ever-shifting fear has enabled the construction of new, war-minded state agencies geared toward the continuous identification of hostile societies. The empire of defense is founded on the normalization of liberal war as a counterbalance to illiberal beliefs and behaviors, a struggle to save lives rather than take them.

That idea—that well-executed state violence saves more lives than it takes—explains why Obama's effort to end the war on terror, including the drone-strike playbook, ended so little. His administration was disinclined to put an absolute limit on its ability to use lethal force. The Presidential Policy Guidance, for example, included the stipulation that

"nothing in this PPG shall be construed to prevent the President from ex-
ercising his constitutional authority as Commander in Chief . . . to authorize lethal force."[10] So the president must follow the rules, unless he decides otherwise. The weakness of the document is reflected in its form, the
administration having chosen to issue a presidential policy guidance—the
first of its kind—rather than a more traditional presidential policy directive. Obama told an audience at the University of Chicago Law School
in 2016, "My hope is that by the time I leave office there is not only an
internal structure in place that governs these standards [for remote war-
fare] that we've set, but there is also an institutionalized process whereby
the actions that the U.S. government takes through drone technology are
consistently reported on."[11] But there was nothing binding about that internal structure, leaving his successor, Trump, and future presidents to
use remote war technologies as they see fit.

This book begins and ends with Barack Obama, an antiwar presidential candidate who became a war president. Since Truman signed the National Security Act in 1947 and the National Security Act Amendments in
1949, the legislation that founded the national security state, lawmakers
and military commanders have refashioned modern war as methodical
and sensitive to cultural difference. They have redefined war as defense,
taking life as saving life, regime change as liberation, empire-building as
humanitarian assistance. This idea of defense was founded on the racial
liberal belief that anti-redistributive "equal opportunity," individual freedoms, and global markets were the solution to racism and therefore that
military violence, if administered in the interest of advancing liberal institutions, could serve an antiracist end by containing social worlds deemed
illiberal and backward. War became defense, and race-making violence
became antiracist. Obama's election as the country's first black president,
after the senator campaigned on his record of vocal opposition to the
Iraq War and a promise to bridge racial and partisan divides, signaled
the culmination—and, with the subsequent election of Trump, perhaps
crisis—of antiwar liberalism and liberal antiracism. While Obama drew
down the state's ground wars in Iraq and Afghanistan, he further militarized what defense officials call the "fifth domain" through drone and
cyber technologies, seeing remote attacks as more humane, less violent,
and not war at all. The Russian interference in the 2016 presidential election gave officials an event through which they could frame the state's
drone strikes and cyber attacks as necessary acts of defense. But before
Russia ever disseminated fake news to American voters or hacked the

servers of the Democratic National Committee, the United States had been waging defense in the fifth domain. Obama's transformation from antiwar presidential candidate to war president shows that the modern state was never built to end war but to refine and prolong it, to make it seem reasonable and good, defensive rather than offensive. Defense is the health of the state.

Politicians, scholars, and journalists continue to distinguish drone and cyber war from that fought on the ground, in the air, and at sea. Thomas Rid, a leading cyber war scholar, for example, argues that "cyber attacks are not creating more vectors of violent interaction; rather they are making previously violent interactions less violent."[12] But remote war cannot and should not be distinguished from conventional war. It should instead be recognized as the latest iteration of a racial regime of defense that has encouraged and obscured permanent war across the twentieth and twenty-first centuries by separating the people, places, and beliefs to be defended from those to be integrated or abolished. From the drone wars in Pakistan, Yemen, Somalia, and Libya to the Stuxnet cyber attack on Iran's nuclear facilities, the Obama administration's turn to remote technologies in the war on terror did not, as Rid suggests, result in less violence and fewer lives lost. Instead, emergent technologies have augmented the execution of state violence and, by removing American bodies from the battlefield, eased its continuation. The ongoing debate as to whether drone and cyber attacks constitute war—like the backlash to the proposed and then scrapped Distinguished Warfare Medal to honor drone pilots and cyber operators—restages the troubled cultural politics of unending war. Homeland Security chief Jeh Johnson's condemnation of the North Korea–affiliated hack of Sony Pictures, a hack motivated by the studio's satirical regime-change film *The Interview* (2014), as "an attack on our freedom of expression and way of life" suggests that the endurance of liberal war rests now as much as ever on the stories we tell about the permanent war we call national defense.[13]

The Nintendo Medal

On December 10, 2009, Obama delivered the Nobel lecture in Oslo, Norway, receiving the Peace Prize days after having issued an order to send thirty thousand additional soldiers and marines to Afghanistan. A White House staffer later referred to the speech as "a template to how [the president] approaches problems" and "a framework for how he thinks about US power."[14] In his thirty-minute lecture, Obama, to the embarrassment of the Nobel committee, justified why past American presidents had so often turned to military force as a means of "preserving the peace" and his own decision to escalate the war in Afghanistan. "Whatever mistakes we have made, the plain fact is this: The United States of America has helped underwrite global security for more than six decades with the blood of our citizens and the strength of our arms," he said. "America led the world in constructing an architecture to keep the peace: a Marshall Plan and a United Nations, mechanisms to govern the waging of war, treaties to protect human rights, prevent genocide, restrict the most dangerous weapons." Through "a gradual evolution of human institutions," he added, citing President John Kennedy, the country had averted a "Third World War."[15] Obama acknowledged his role as the leader of a nation at war and a government that had created international "mechanisms to govern the waging of war." But he insisted that these mechanisms had rallied the world around the ethic of defense and human rights, that peace had been achieved and must now be safeguarded through the careful administration of violence. Through "an architecture," "mechanisms," and "institutions," war turns into nonwar, into defense. In drone and cyber technologies, Obama found a vehicle for acting on his belief that "a just and lasting peace"—the title of his Nobel lecture—is best achieved not by ending war but by refining and reframing it.[16]

But the Obama administration could not, it learned, conceal its remote confrontations or the controversies they invited. On February 13, 2013, at the Pentagon briefing room, Defense Secretary Leon Panetta announced the establishment of a new military honor, the Distinguished Warfare Medal, to recognize individual achievements in drone and cyber war. Panetta, a former CIA director, stressed that he had "seen firsthand how modern tools, like remotely piloted platforms and cyber systems, have changed the way wars are fought." The medal would honor those who have made contributions that "directly impact on combat operations" but had not engaged in combat themselves. "This award recognizes the reality of the kind of technological warfare that we are engaged in in the twenty-first century," Panetta said.[17] The defense secretary's announcement was met with immediate criticism from all sides. Editorialists dismissed it as a "drone medal," "Nintendo medal," and "armchair medal."[18] Antiwar activists argued that it institutionalized remote killing. And veterans' organizations contended, when Panetta's staff revealed that the Distinguished

Warfare Medal would outrank the Bronze Star and the Purple Heart, that it degraded the service of soldiers, marines, sailors, and airmen in the field. "This new medal—no matter how well intended—could quickly deteriorate into a morale issue," John Hamilton, the head of Veterans of Foreign Wars, said in a statement the day after Panetta's announcement.[19] Bills were introduced in both houses of Congress to downgrade the medal, and an online petition to cancel it received more than eighteen thousand signatures within a day.[20] Panetta, set to retire two weeks later, didn't know what hit him.

The backlash against the Distinguished Warfare Medal, while on the surface about valuing the service of those who risk life and limb in combat, also grew out of a collective discomfort with what the medal suggested about how wars would be fought, recounted, and remembered in the twenty-first century. Combat-medal citations take a distinct form, introducing a hero and describing how that hero faced and overcame a challenge with courage and self-sacrifice. The citation is a concise, formulaic, and clear-cut genre. There is no gray area, no ambiguous ending. In a *New York Times* editorial, Jacob Wood and Ken Harbaugh, veterans of the war in Afghanistan, wondered what the Distinguished Warfare Medal would do to this form. "We took for granted that humans on the front lines would always play the lead role," they wrote. "Those on the front lines require real courage because they face real danger. But if a drone overhead gets hit, a monitor somewhere might go fuzzy, and its operator might curse his poor luck for losing an expensive piece of equipment." Wood and Harbaugh argued that this shift—from stories told by front-line soldiers to images beamed from drones—would lead Americans to lose "a true appreciation of the cost of war" and to send more "sons and daughters" into combat.[21] But they failed to acknowledge that the combat stories they valorized had not slowed the nation's march to war. Panetta's acknowledgment of drone and cyber attacks as war forced Wood, Harbaugh, and others, it seems, to confront war as a norm rather than an event and then refute that norm by defending the value of discrete combat stories.[22]

Two months after Panetta introduced the Distinguished Warfare Medal, his successor, Chuck Hagel, himself the recipient of two Purple Hearts, cancelled it. Hagel issued a memo in which he stated that, having heard from concerned veterans and consulted with the Joint Chiefs of Staff, he would be replacing the Distinguished Warfare Medal with a "device" that could be affixed to existing medals. "Utilizing a distinguishing device to recognize impacts on combat operations reserves our existing combat medals for those Service members who incur the physical risk and hardship of combat, perform valorous acts, are wounded in combat, or as a result of combat give their last full measure for our Nation," he wrote.[23] Veterans of Foreign Wars released a statement praising Hagel for "taking this issue on so early in his tenure" and defending the meaning and value of combat.[24] That afternoon, Chechen brothers Tamerlan and Dzhokhar Tsarnaev detonated two pressure-cooker bombs near the finish line of the Boston Marathon. The debate about combat-service medals and remote war vanished from the headlines.

Three years later, Ash Carter, who succeeded Hagel as defense chief, authorized the *R* (remote) device to honor the achievements of drone pilots and cyber operators. Unlike Panetta's and Hagel's announcements regarding the Distinguished Warfare Medal, Carter made no public statement about the new device. Instead, his staff issued a dry, three-page document titled "Military Decorations and Awards Review Results" that led with news that the military would be reexamining all decorations for valor in combat awarded since September 11, 2001, with plans to upgrade some and downgrade none, and establishing a new *C* (combat) device "to further emphasize the value placed on meritorious service under combat conditions." Buried at the bottom of the document, and in the shortest section, was the announcement of the *R* device "to specifically recognize remote but direct impact on combat operations."[25] News media took no notice of the new device that in 2013 had made headlines as a sign that the government was institutionalizing remote killing. Historian Matt Delmont writes that the drawdown of the ground wars under Obama and his simultaneous escalation of remote war minimized media attention on the counterterror wars. "Drones draw their deadly power from these twin claims to visual superiority: the ability to see and to resist being seen," he writes.[26] And drones must, Carter's staff understood, resist being seen not only by the Pakistanis, Yemenis, and Somalis they track but also by the Americans they are thought to defend.

But the technologies that allow drone and cyber attacks to go unseen can also, as some activists have demonstrated, be harnessed to document them. In late 2012, "data artist" Josh Begley, a graduate student at New York University, designed an iPhone app that mapped all of the government's drone strikes in real time and employed push notifications to inform users when a new strike had been executed. Apple blocked Begley's app, Drones+, from its App Store for content that it considered "objectionable

and crude." Begley was surprised, since Drones+ did little more than com-
pile reports from the London-based Bureau of Investigative Journalism
and place them on a map. "If the content is found to be objectionable, and
it's literally just an aggregation of the news, I don't know how to change
that," he told *Wired* magazine.[27] On his fifth try, Begley changed the name
to Metadata+ and submitted the app without content. Apple accepted it,
and Begley restored the content.

Metadata+ used the same geolocation technologies that the Defense
Department and CIA used to locate and assassinate alleged terrorists in
what are called "signature strikes"—attacks based on cell-phone metadata rather than human intelligence. The intelligence for these attacks
came from an NSA program called Geolocation Cell, or Geo Cell. Meta-
data+ made the drone strikes visible to iPhone users with some of the
same tools that made them invisible to Western media. It showed how
drone and cyber technologies, far from ending or taming war, had mediated how state violence was seen and obscured. Begley wanted to use
cell-phone metadata to create a "different kind of seeing" than the one
marshaled by armed drones. "If the folks on the other side of our missiles are presented to us in the same places we see pictures of our loved
ones or communicate with our friends, might that nudge me to learn a
little more about the contours of covert war?" he asked.[28] Metadata+ and
its associated Twitter account, @dronestream, offered a different kind of
seeing and a different kind of storytelling. With push notifications and
tweets, Begley found a way to tell a permanent story about a permanent
war. That story revealed that the United States had, in all likelihood, been
conducting "double tap" strikes, in which a location is bombed twice minutes apart, so that rescuers get caught in the second bombing, a tactic that
the United Nations had declared a war crime.[29] Seven months after Meta-
data+ went live, Apple banned it—again. But the tech giant did not catch
heat from news media for censoring Begley's news aggregator. Instead,
all eyes were on Seth Rogen, James Franco, and their toilet-humor film
The Interview, which, after the North Korea–orchestrated hack of Sony
Pictures, became a First Amendment cause.

Kim Jong-un's Exploding Head

On the morning of November 24, 2014, executives, filmmakers, and staff
arrived at the Sony Pictures lot in Culver City, California, to find an omi-

nous message on their computer screens. "We've obtained all your internal data including your secrets and top secrets. If you don't obey us, we'll release data shown below to the world." The data below consisted of five links to what turned out to be the studio's internal records, including thousands of social security numbers and millions of emails. The message was signed #GOP and illustrated with a blood-red skeleton and crude, zombified drawings of Michael Lynton, Sony Pictures' CEO and chairman, and Amy Pascal, the studio chief. A group calling itself Guardians of the Peace had hacked into the studio's network and erased the data stored on more than three thousand computers and eight hundred servers. Soon after, it began leaking the stolen data to news media, which unearthed some damning revelations about the film industry's treatment of women and actors of color. On December 8, Guardians of the Peace clarified their demand. It wanted Sony to cancel the Christmas Day release of the Seth Rogen vehicle *The Interview*, which, it was known, culminated with a CIA-orchestrated assassination of the North Korean leader Kim Jong-un. "Stop immediately showing the movie of terrorism which can break the regional peace and cause the War!" the group wrote to Sony's staff. On December 16, after Lynton refused to budge, Guardians of the Peace threatened to attack theaters showing the film. "Remember the 11th of September," it wrote. "We recommend you to keep yourself distant from the places at that time." The next day, after theater chains began backing out, Sony announced that it was cancelling the opening and had no plans to reschedule it.[30]

The criticism of the company's decision was harsher than Lynton could have imagined. Actors, directors, and other celebrities berated Sony on Twitter for caving to the hackers' demands. The FBI issued a press release in which it attributed the hack to the North Korean government and an affiliated group known as DarkSeoul. "North Korea's actions were intended to inflict significant harm on a US business and suppress the right of American citizens to express themselves," the press release stated.[31] Even Obama weighed in. At his end-of-the-year press conference, he told reporters that he believed Sony had "made a mistake" by pulling the film. "I wish they had spoken to me first. I would have told them, do not get into a pattern in which you're intimidated by these kinds of criminal attacks," the president said, adding that his administration would "respond proportionally" and "in a place and time and manner that we choose."[32] The press conference marked the first time that a sitting president had attributed a cyber attack to another state and declared plans to retaliate.

A week after the Senate Intelligence Committee declassified its investigation of the CIA's Detention and Interrogation Program, which concluded that the agency had tortured detainees under the Bush administration, Obama was fielding questions about Seth Rogen and James Franco. The Senate Intelligence Committee report did not come up once during the hour-long press conference. Later that day, Jeh Johnson, the secretary of Homeland Security, released his own statement. "The cyber attack against Sony Pictures Entertainment was not just an attack against a company and its employees," he wrote. "It was also an attack on our freedom of expression and way of life."[33]

The attack on Sony Pictures was far from the first directed at an American business. Retailers, banks, and defense contractors had been suffering similar attacks for years. Why would the president and the intelligence establishment take a stand on this of all hacks? An attack brought on by a Hollywood comedy? The FBI, Obama, and Johnson all addressed the DarkSeoul hack as a First Amendment issue. The hackers sought to "suppress the right of American citizens to express themselves," to "start imposing censorship here," and to undermine "our freedom of expression and way of life." The president and intelligence officials took a stand in defense of Sony and *The Interview* because that stand aligned with the racial regime of defense through which the state has long governed the line between liberal and illiberal social worlds, legitimate and illegitimate violence. The hack allowed officials to reinforce the narrative advanced by Rogen's film in which North Korea was an illiberal regime and therefore any act of violence against it, including assassinating its leader, could be construed as a countermeasure—the defense of liberal humanity rather than an act of war. In 2008, the United States and Israel had marshaled that discourse to rationalize launching a cyber attack on Iran's Natanz nuclear facilitates, installing malicious software that caused thousands of uranium-enriching centrifuges to crash. Iran was an illiberal state building a nuclear arsenal for the execution of illegitimate violence, making the United States and Israel's attack an act of self-defense—and, officials believed, a humane one because it was less brutal than bombing Natanz.

Some journalists doubted that North Korea was behind the Sony hack, but the FBI had good reason to feel confident in its attribution. While the bureau told news media that it had connected DarkSeoul to the hack by matching the group's "signatures" (lines of code, data-deletion methods, IP addresses) to attacks it had carried out in South Korea, it did not disclose that, years earlier, the NSA had penetrated the North Korean networks, giving it wide-ranging access to the government's online activities.[34] If DarkSeoul's hack of Sony Pictures' networks was a violation of a human right, then what was the NSA's hack of North Korea's networks? The comparison reveals how liberal universals have been wielded as a mechanism of racialization, distinguishing between the human and the nonhuman, the righted and the rightless, the defended and the defended against.

Rogen and his writing partner, Evan Goldberg, first had the idea to make a film about the assassination of the North Korean leader in 2010, a year before the death of Kim's father, Kim Jong-il. "[He] was the perfect villain, not just because of how unusual he was, but because no rational person would every try to defend him," Rogen and Goldberg later wrote. "North Korea has one of the worst human rights records on earth and no freedom of speech whatsoever. Once we began researching in earnest, the idea of in some way shedding light on this situation became incredibly appealing." After Kim Jong-il died, the filmmakers turned their attention to his son. Their working title for the film was *Kill Kim Jong-un*.[35]

Sony Pictures executives, knowing that the film could attract a hostile reaction from North Korea and unnerve their Japanese parent corporation, sought reassurances from the defense establishment. Lynton sat on the Rand Corporation's board of trustees and had moderated a panel two years earlier at its Politics Aside conference titled "How Hollywood Affects Global Policy," featuring *24* showrunner and *Homeland* creator Howard Gordon.[36] The executive's hacked emails reveal that, months before the cyber attack, Lynton had reached out to Rand senior defense analyst Bruce Bennett for guidance on the film. "I thought a bunch more about the ending," Bennett wrote Lynton, referring to a scene in which Kim's head explodes in slow motion. "I have to admit that the only resolution I can see to the North Korean nuclear and other threats is for the North Korean regime to eventually go away." So he advised Lynton, "While toning down the ending may reduce the North Korean response, I believe that a story that talks about the removal of the Kim family regime and the creation of a new government by the North Korean people (well, at least the elites) will start some real thinking in South Korea and, I believe, in the North once the DVD leaks into the North (which it almost certainly will). So from a personal perspective, I would personally prefer to leave the ending alone."[37] Later that day, Lynton responded, "Bruce, Spoke to someone very senior in State (confidentially). He agreed with everything you have been saying. Everything."[38] That official turned out to be Daniel Russel, the assistant secretary of state for East Asian and Pacific affairs.[39] The next day, Bennett added that he had consulted with Robert King, the government's special envoy for North Korean human rights issues, who corroborated his assessment.[40] Sony had received the go-ahead from the Rand Corporation and the State Department and even been told that *The Interview* could hasten Kim's downfall and the installation of a Western-facing government in North Korea.

Bennett, author of the book *Preparing for the Possibility of a North Korean Collapse* (2013), had good reason to encourage the film's ending. After airheaded talk-show host Dave Skylark (Franco) and his producer, Aaron Rapaport (Rogen), land an interview with Kim (Randall Park), the CIA recruits them to assassinate the North Korean leader. After much misadventure, Dave and Aaron steal a Soviet tank—a gift from Joseph Stalin to Kim's grandfather, Kim Il-sung—and kill Kim by shooting down his helicopter. The assassination sets off a revolution, and the film ends with North Korea holding democratic elections. Rogen and Goldberg see the Kim government as a regime that "no rational person would ever try to defend" and represent the North Korean people as brainwashed by state propaganda, believing, as Dave puts it, that Kim "doesn't pee or poo."[41] The assassination of Kim, the film suggests, echoing Bennett, could draw North Korea into the rational world. But Rogen and Goldberg, trusting that no right-thinking person could disagree with them, fail to see how their film does cultural work on behalf of their own government. "When it comes to Hollywood's North Korean regime-change narratives, the line between fact and fiction, not to mention the distinction between freedom of expression and government propaganda, is revealingly thin," ethnic studies scholar Christine Hong writes. The state authorization of *The Interview* should, she adds, "remind us that culture, when it comes to U.S. enemies, has always been a terrain of manipulation and war."[42] The consensus in the United States that North Korea is absurd and backward allows Americans to forget how their own ideas about freedom and human rights are informed by state ideologies transmitted through mass culture, including Seth Rogen comedies.

After Obama called Sony's decision to cancel the film a mistake, Lynton struck deals with Google and Microsoft to release it through their digital distribution services, and hundreds of independent theaters agreed to show the film on Christmas Day. *The Interview* had been transformed from a vehicle for fart and poop jokes into an affirmation of the First Amendment. "The president—yes, it's that important—should convene all the players who make billions from the free and unfettered display of content and broker a deal that gives Americans the opportunity to watch the film," David Carr, the *New York Times* media columnist, wrote at the time. "The industry, old and new, digital and analog, should step across a line together, holding hands with consumers and letting the world know that we prize our goofy movies, along with the important ones, and the freedoms that they represent."[43] The right-wing Human Rights Foundation announced plans to smuggle DVDs of the film into North Korea by balloon drop, the foundation's president said, to undermine "the monopoly of information that the Kim regime has successfully been able to deploy for so long."[44] The First Amendment defense of Rogen's regime-change film reveals how universal liberal ideals can be marshaled to create, rather than counteract, racial divisions and the uneven distribution of life chances. The North Korean government's human rights record excuses, for some, the making of an anti-Asian racist film. The film's defenders even believe that it takes an *antiracist* stand by goading a government that the West sees as an illegitimate anachronism, a hermit kingdom. The embrace of *The Interview* on First Amendment grounds and the "Je Suis Charlie" movement that arose two weeks later, after the shootings at the *Charlie Hebdo* offices in Paris, reflect how the idea of defense excludes as much as it includes, normalizes as much as it liberates, and weaponizes free speech as much as it champions it.

The *New* New Normal

In a 2009 *Joint Forces Quarterly* article, Stephen Korns, a senior director at Cyber Command, declared that "a new normalcy is ascendant in cyberspace." Korns argued that the defense establishment needed to undertake a radical restructuring to prepare for an age of cyber conflict. "Borderless cyber operations confounding border-based paradigms are not a deviation," he wrote. "It is cyber new normalcy."[45] But Korns was far from the first defense official to announce a new normal. In 1953, White House aide James Lambie, who coordinated public information campaigns for the Eisenhower administration, penned a memo in which he stressed the need to convince Americans of the imminent "threat to our national existence and way of life" posed by nuclear war. This threat, he wrote, "will continue as far ahead as anyone can foresee. We cannot return to 'normalcy.' This is the 'new normalcy.' "[46] Fifty years later, in

November 2001, Tom Ridge, who two months earlier had been named the
first director of Homeland Security, described his new role in the Bush
administration as addressing "the new normalcy" of global terrorism.[47] In
2012, Peter Singer, a think-tank defense strategist, insisted that "we must
now accept that technologies that remove humans from the battlefield
[such as drones] are becoming the new normal in war."[48] Throughout the
defense era, the national security state has continually identified *new* new
normals that, officials have argued, warrant the unending growth of military and intelligence infrastructure. There is nothing new about the new
normal. The idea of the new normal acknowledges permanent war (normal) while erasing its long past (new). It fails to register that all of these
new normals—nuclear proliferation, communism, totalitarianism, drug
trafficking, terrorism, insurgency—are related, are part of an old normal.

The continuities between anticommunism, narcotics control, humanitarianism, and counterterrorism have been obscured by, but are also revealed in, the stories we tell about race and defense. On September 28,
1951, historian and activist W. E. B. Du Bois, who was then facing a federal indictment for his role as chairman of the antiwar Peace Information
Center, addressed the Community Church in Boston. "Peace is dangerous," he began, "not to all folks but certainly to those whose power and
standard of living depend on war." But peace is not dangerous because
Soviet and Chinese communism must be met with force, he argued.

> Is it true that expanding communism is threatening our way of life? Or, on the
> contrary, is it the maintenance of our industrial methods which is threatening
> to keep the mass of the world's people not only below our standard of living,
> but even below the life of ordinary decency and sheer survival? It is this aspect
> of world war which America is today refusing to discuss, indeed is often not
> permitted to discuss.

Peace is dangerous for some Americans, Du Bois told the church, because it threatened to end the uneven distribution of life chances that had
existed under colonial rule and from which they profited. The Cold War
offered a way to extend that colonial order through the continued looting
of labor, land, and resources from Asia, Africa, and Latin America, while
imbuing that theft with an anticolonial ethos. This form of world war, he
explained, restored "the essentials of colonialism under the name of Free
Enterprise and Western Democracy."[49] Du Bois, in the first years of the
Cold War, identified how Americans either refused or were forbidden to

acknowledge the contradictions of the idea of defense: war as nonwar, racial violence as antiracist, war as an event and a new normal. This book has told the story of those contradictions and their endurance in the decades since Du Bois first declared peace to be the greatest danger to the empire of defense. Peace is dangerous. That is what the idea of defense tells us.

But to say that war is the new (and old) normal in the United States is not to say that war is inevitable. Efforts to make war more ordered, humane, and sensitive to racial difference assume that war does not and cannot end, that all we can do is manage it and refine the technologies with which the state doles out violence. The belief that we have a choice to make between bad war and better war has underwritten the state's military growth since the formation of the national security state, from the anticommunism of Du Bois's day through the drug wars and humanitarian crusades of the late twentieth century to the counterterrorism of the twenty-first. Since the beginning of the Cold War, the United States has, as Obama stated in his Nobel lecture, led the world in constructing "mechanisms to govern the waging of war."[50] But the mechanisms that it constructed have also ensured war's continuation by building a government geared toward the administration of racial defense on a world scale. The modern state has not been built to end war. War is what it does best. But governing war also means governing the stories we tell about it, and that has been a site of constant struggle and failure for the national security state and its critics. Sometimes it is where stories fail that the most important stories get told.

Acknowledgments

This book has many coauthors. It would not exist without the brilliance, guidance, and good humor of Cathy Schlund-Vials, who taught me what it is to be a scholar and how to be serious about my work without being too serious about myself. Meeting Cathy, and somehow persuading her to take me on as a graduate student, was the greatest stroke of luck of my professional life. At the University of Connecticut, where I completed my PhD, Clare Eby and Chris Vials read every page of my early work, which couldn't have been easy, and generously and patiently showed me the way forward as a young scholar and young person. Wally and Chris Lamb gave me a home away from home and reminded me—when I needed reminding—to slow down, have fun, and laugh. Some of my fondest grad school memories are of evenings at the Nathan Hale bar with Gordon Fraser, whose friendship sustained me through some long months. I met Maria Seger in my first week at UConn, and I have benefited from knowing her every day since. I owe her for reading draft after draft of this book and for so much else.

This work would not have been possible without the support of my colleagues at Texas Christian University. David Colón has been a mentor and friend since my first day on campus, and Joddy Murray and Karen Steele, my department chairs, have been tireless advocates for me, my work, and our discipline. Thanks to Theresa Gaul, Dan Gil, Anne Frey, Jason Helms, Regina Lewis, Stacie McCormick, T. J. McLemore, Celeste Menchaca, Sarah Robbins, Merry Roberts, and Ann Tran for their inspiring work and friendship. Thanks, as well, to Max Krochmal, the founding director of the Comparative Race and Ethnic Studies Department, for building a second departmental home for me and so many others. I'm also grateful to the Office of Sponsored Programs for a Junior Faculty Summer Research Program grant and to my dean, Andy Schoolmaster, for his support.

Sean Goudie and Priscilla Wald, the directors of the First Book Institute at Pennsylvania State University, taught me how to turn a half-written manuscript into a book. I don't know how they do all that they do, but I know they have had a transformative effect on me and my writing, for which I am so grateful. I also thank Ting Chang, Tina Chen, Jon Eburn, and my comrades in first book writing: Kelly Bezio, Brianna Burke, Danielle Christmas, Gordon, Kya Mangrum, Matthew Schilleman, and Lindsay Thomas.

I completed this book at the University of California, Irvine, where I spent a year as a Mellon Sawyer Seminar fellow, a year of research I owe to the brilliant Carol Burke and Cécile Whiting. Thank you. And thanks to those who made a welcome home for me in Irvine: Christine Balance, Chris Fan, Olivia Humphrey, Saeid Jalalipour, Jim Lee, Julia Lee, Ted Martin, Annie McClanahan, Amanda Swain, Michael Szalay, Linda Võ, David Woods, and Judy Wu. I learned the most that year from Sam Gailey, whose intelligence and flair for debate reminded me why I love what I do and that it is meant to be shared. The second I met her I knew that nothing like this, all evidence to the contrary notwithstanding, had ever happened to anyone before. I'm looking forward to writing more books so I can dedicate them to her.

I thank those friends and colleagues who read papers and chapter drafts for their criticism, insight, and encouragement, including Steve Belletto, Dan Grausam, Keith Feldman, Mai-Linh Hong, Alex Jacobs, Dinidu Karunanayake, Juliet Nebolon, Naomi Paik, Don Pease, Mari Yoshihara, and Jim Zeigler. John Rowe, whom I first met at the Futures of American Studies Institute at Dartmouth College, has been the most generous of mentors and a model scholar.

Thanks to my editor at the University of Chicago Press, Doug Mitchell, for seeing what this book could be and showing me how to get there, and to Kyle Wagner for shepherding it along. I'm grateful to the two readers whose careful attention to my writing and thoughtful advice made this book better. Mary Corrado and Nick Murray turned my manuscript into this book with their sharp and generous editing. I thank Nick, my scrupulous and patient copyeditor, for improving my writing from top to bottom. Thanks also to Jimmy's and the Curtis Black Quartet—the man behind the drums most of all. An earlier version of chapter 3 appeared as "Dispatches from the Drug Wars: Ishmael Reed, Oscar Zeta Acosta, and the Viet Cong of America" in *Modern Fiction Studies* 64, no. 1 (2018), and an earlier version of chapter 4 appeared as "Kicking the Vietnam Syndrome Narrative: Human Rights, the Nayirah Testimony, and the Gulf War" in *American Quarterly* 69, no. 1 (2017). I thank the journals and their publisher, Johns Hopkins University Press, for permission to reprint parts of those essays here.

I'm fortunate to have good friends in my life. Thanks to Alex Cargol, Nick Ferron, Gordon, Ted, T. J., Sean McPherson, and Nate Windon for being there and for years of listening to me talk about this book. I apologize in advance for the next one. And thanks to Cathy Day, who first taught me the pleasure of reading and talking about books. I have always been lucky to have the support and humor of my brothers, Zack and Sam Darda, and my parents, Dave Darda and Patty Garvey-Darda. Zack and Sam are the smartest, funniest—and because they grew up with me— most patient people I know. I thank them for making me think and making me laugh. This book is dedicated to my parents, who, for thirty-one years, have made me feel at home in this world.

Notes

Introduction

1. Obama, "National Defense University."
2. Obama, "Iraq War."
3. *New York Times* Editorial Board, "End of a Perpetual War."
4. Obama, "National Defense University."
5. Critical race theorist Howard Winant identifies the years after World War II as a "racial break" in which the world underwent a crisis of racial formation set off by the war, migration, decolonization, and antiracist movements. But the break was partial, half-finished at best. "For all their achievements," Winant writes, "the insurgent movements of the break period were unable to realize a full-scale repudiation of the past, were incapable of destroying white supremacy, were inadequate to generate an anti-racist, anti-colonial revolution" (*World Is a Ghetto*, 145). The result instead was incorporation and reform, and the transition from war to defense was part of that incorporation.
6. Truman was far from the first to present the United States as an anticolonial empire. Cultural historian John Carlos Rowe writes in the first sentence of *Literary Culture and U.S. Imperialism*, which ends where this book begins, in 1945, "Americans' interpretations of themselves as a people are shaped by a powerful imperial desire and a profound anticolonial temper" (3). The United States had long seen itself as a champion of anticolonial resistance when it began making that case to the former colonies of Asia and Africa in the years after World War II.
7. Obama, "National Defense University."
8. In 1993, cultural historian Amy Kaplan kicked off the "transnational turn" in American studies by acknowledging some glaring absences: "the absence of culture from the history of U.S. imperialism; the absence of empire from the study of American culture; and the absence of the United States from the postcolonial study of imperialism" ("Left Alone with America," 11). Scholars have been answering Kaplan's call for a long time now. But most continue to treat the Cold War,

the drug wars, the humanitarian wars, and the war on terror as separate imperial ventures rather than stages in a permanent war waged as national defense. See also Kaplan, *Anarchy of Empire*.

9. Du Bois, *Souls of Black Folk*, vii.

10. Du Bois, "Fifty Years After," 208.

11. Obama, "National Defense University."

12. Obama, "Democratic National Convention."

13. Gerdau, "Obama's Speech on Counterterrorism."

14. Rosenberg, "Tracking the Hunger Strike."

15. Ethnic studies scholar Naomi Paik sees the detainee hunger strikes at Guantánamo as a radical form of protest through which the detainees announced their rightless condition, unable even to choose whether to live or die. "The prisoners have attempted to seize their own form of habeas corpus, taking their bodies back from the U.S. camp regime, by inflicting self-harm," she writes. "Enduring a state defined by unfreedom, the prisoners seek a form of negative freedom from life—from life that is unlivable, that is not life at all" (*Rightlessness*, 191).

16. United Nations Human Rights Office of the High Commissioner, "Indefinite Detention at Guantánamo."

17. Bourne, "State," 71.

18. Bourne, 69.

19. Bourne, 77.

20. Truman, "State of the Union."

21. Baldwin, "Forrestal Faces Trials."

22. Hogan, *Cross of Iron*, 24.

23. Truman, "National Security Act Amendments."

24. Baldwin, *Price of Power*, 322.

25. Truman, "State of the Union."

26. Foucault, *"Society Must Be Defended,"* 15–16.

27. Foucault, 47.

28. Dudziak, *War Time*, 15.

29. Bush, "Combat Operations Have Ended."

30. Obama, "End of Combat Operations."

31. Political philosopher Giorgio Agamben argues that permanent war threatens to erode the constitutive tension between normal law and the "state of exception," a concept he borrows from German jurist Carl Schmitt. Agamben suggests that the Bush administration's conduct after September 11, 2001, inaugurated "a situation in which the emergency becomes the rule, and the very distinction between peace and war (and between foreign and civil war) becomes impossible" (*State of Exception*, 22). This book argues that, as yet another form of imperial defense, there was nothing exceptional about Bush's state of exception.

32. Buck, *American Unity in Asia*, 29.

33. For more on the entangled histories of racial liberalism, the Cold War, and black freedom struggles, see Dudziak, *Cold War Civil Rights*; Plummer, *Rising Wind*; and Von Eschen, *Race against Empire*.

34. Quoted in Myrdal, *American Dilemma*, ix.

35. Myrdal, xlvii.

36. Myrdal, 928.

37. Lynd, "Prison for American Genius," 5.

38. Keppel, foreword to *American Dilemma*, vi.

39. Myrdal, *American Dilemma*, 1021.

40. For more on *An American Dilemma* and the world-facing politics of racial liberalism, see Melamed, *Represent and Destroy*, 56–63; and Singh, *Black Is a Country*, 142–51.

41. Lowe, *Intimacies of Four Continents*, 7.

42. Ethnic studies scholar Neda Atanasoski argues that the Cold War occasioned a racial reorientation from biological racism to cultural or ideological racism. The United States, distancing itself from the empires it replaced, she writes, "reconfigured the European imperial *spatialization of race relations* as the *racialization of belief and ideology* mapped onto those previous spatializations" (*Humanitarian Violence*, 7). Critical race theorist Jodi Melamed also contends that racial liberalism extended and obscured color-line racial divisions by introducing "alternate criteria for distinguishing forms of privilege and stigma arising from a liberal model of race as culture" (*Represent and Destroy*, 58). This book argues that the idea of defense orchestrated that racial reorientation and governed those alternate criteria for legitimate being.

43. Truman, "State of the Union."

44. United Nations General Assembly, "Universal Declaration of Human Rights."

45. Myrdal, *American Dilemma*, 784.

46. Hughes, "Memo to Non-White Peoples," 456–57.

47. Scholars disagree about whether Hughes retreated from the left in his later career. Hughes' biographer Arnold Rampersad suggests that the poet withdrew "from the far left toward the black center" in the 1940s and 1950s (*Life of Langston Hughes*, 55), while literary historian James Smethurst insists that Hughes never abandoned radical politics and, as a mentor to young black writers, "served as a bridge between different generations of radical black artists" (*Black Arts Movement*, 8–9). Cultural historian Mary Helen Washington argues that Hughes and other black writers struggling against the onslaught of McCarthyism "carried the resistant traditions of the Black Popular Front of the 1930s and 1940s into the 1950s and became a link to the militant politics and aesthetics of the 1960s and 1970s" (*Other Blacklist*, 12). His "Memo to Non-White Peoples," which Hughes published in 1957, reflects this tradition.

48. Truman, "Executive Order 9981."

49. Myrdal, *American Dilemma*, 422, 422–23.

50. Hemingway, letter to F. Scott Fitzgerald.

51. O'Brien, "Responsibly Inventing History," 23–24.

52. Lederer and Burdick, *Ugly American*, 121.

53. Lederer and Burdick, 284, 285.

54. Ferguson, *Reorder of Things*, 195.

55. *Platoon*.

56. *Casualties of War*.

57. Wheeler, *Touched with Fire*, 16.

58. Winant argues that the racial reforms of the 1960s gave rise to a fractured, dualistic white racial politics in which whiteness is imagined as, "on the one hand, egalitarian, on the other hand, privileged; on the one hand, individualistic and 'color blind,' on the other hand 'normalized' and besieged" ("Behind Blue Eyes," 52). The white Vietnam veteran, treated as a deracinated universal and minoritized outsider, embodies the white racial dualism of post–civil rights America.

59. Truman, "President's News Conference."

60. Johnson, "President's Commission on Law Enforcement."

61. Nixon, "State of the Union."

62. Legal scholar Cheryl Harris argued in 1993 that white settlers and slave owners justified the settlement of indigenous lands and the enslavement of black people by making whiteness a precondition for property rights. A person had to first possess whiteness before he could own land and profit from his labor. "Whiteness and white identity were sources of privilege and protection," she wrote; "their absence meant being the object of property" ("Whiteness as Property," 1721). It also meant being the object of police, the object of defense.

63. Singh, *Race and America's Long War*, 37–38.

64. Sloane, "Dogs in War," 388.

65. US Marine Corps, *Small Wars Manual*, 1, 3, 28.

66. US Marine Corps, 19, 23.

67. US Marine Corps, 1, 9. The National Security Council, which authored NSC 68, advocated that the Truman administration "change the world situation by means short of war" (45), a line it used five times, through the containment of Soviet communism.

68. Phillips, foreword to *Small Wars Manual*.

69. US Department of the Army, *Counterinsurgency*, AB-1.

70. Lee, *Race Riots Aren't Necessary*, 15, 21.

71. President's Committee on Civil Rights, *To Secure These Rights*, 155.

72. For more on how racial liberals promoted policing as an engine for rather than an obstacle to the achievement of black civil rights, see Hinton, *War on Poverty*; and Murakawa, *First Civil Right*.

73. Johnson, "Law Enforcement Assistance Bills."

74. In 1978, cultural theorist Stuart Hall and his colleagues at the University of Birmingham published an investigation of mugging and the rise of law-and-order

politics in Britain. Hall and his coauthors argued that law-and-order policies were a response not to a new form of street crime called mugging but to militant anti-racist and labor movements and a growing economic crisis. The government was not policing crime, they concluded, but "policing the crisis" (*Policing the Crisis*, 332). The idea of defense in the United States, paralleling law and order in Hall's Britain, has never been about combating communism, crime, authoritarianism, or terrorism but about containing crises of race and war.

75. In 1993, postcolonial scholar Edward Said argued that imperialism is mediated, justified, and challenged through narrative. "The main battle in imperialism is over land, of course; but when it came to who owned the land, who had the right to settle and work on it, who kept it going, who won it back, and who now plans its future," he wrote, "these issues were reflected, contested, and even for a time decided in narrative" (*Culture and Imperialism*, xii–xiii). Novelist and ethnic studies scholar Viet Nguyen identifies the dangers of letting soldier and veteran stories stand in for war. "Thinking of war as an isolated action carried out by soldiers transforms the soldier into the face and body of war, when in truth he is only its appendage," he writes. The war story should also, he argues, "tell of the civilian, the refugee, the enemy, and, most importantly, the war machine that encompasses them all" (*Nothing Ever Dies*, 225, 224).

76. Berlant, *Cruel Optimism*, 6, 9–10, 10.

77. Obama, "National Defense University."

78. Lederer and Burdick, *Ugly American*, 117, 129.

79. Lederer and Burdick, 122.

80. Acosta, *Revolt of the Cockroach People*, 200.

81. Quoted in Wong, "Gang of Four," 71.

82. King Jr., "Time to Break the Silence," 240.

83. *Surname Viet Given Name Nam*.

84. *Surname Viet Given Name Nam*.

85. Newton, "Reply to William Patterson," 175–76, 176. The Panthers, Singh writes, as a "small and relatively poorly trained and equipped band of urban black youth," never could have done more than minor material damage to state institutions. But their performance of state power—naming Newton their minister of defense, for example—posed a deeper threat to the government. "By challenging the police and aligning themselves with the Vietnamese, the Panthers did not so much challenge the government's monopoly on physical violence," Singh writes, "as disrupt its monopoly on legitimate symbolic violence" (*Black Is a Country*, 204).

Chapter One

1. "Korea: The 'Forgotten' War," 21.

2. Halberstam, *Coldest Winter*, 2.

3. Cultural memory studies scholars have conducted thorough examinations of the structured forgetting of the Korean War in the United States. Much of their research identifies how Korean American writers, artists, and activists have reintroduced the forgotten war to historical consciousness and cast it in relation to the Cold War state's broader ambitions in decolonizing Asia. See, for example, Cho, *Haunting the Korean Diaspora*; Hong and Em, eds., "Unending Korean War"; and Kim, *Ends of Empire*.

4. "Korea: The 'Forgotten' War," 21.

5. "Korea: The 'Forgotten' War," 21.

6. See Sparrow, *Warfare State*, 122–33.

7. LaFeber, *America, Russia, and the Cold War*, 96.

8. Quoted in Johnston, *Hegemony and Culture*, 84.

9. Quoted in Young, "Revisiting NSC 68," 24.

10. O'Brien, "How to Tell a True War Story," 213.

11. Hemingway, *Farewell to Arms*, 161.

12. Stone, *Hidden History*, xxii.

13. Quoted in May, ed., *American Cold War Strategy*, 121.

14. US National Security Council, "NSC 68," 40.

15. Quoted in US Department of State, *Foreign Relations of the United States*, 195.

16. Quoted in US Department of State, 197–98.

17. Acheson, *Present at the Creation*, 374.

18. X [George Kennan], "Sources of Soviet Communism," 567, 576.

19. Quoted in Thompson, *Hawk and the Dove*, 113.

20. Quoted in Thompson, 114.

21. US National Security Council, "NSC 68," 45.

22. US National Security Council, 97.

23. Chow, *Age of the World Target*, 38–39.

24. US National Security Council, "NSC 68," 39.

25. US National Security Council, 40.

26. US National Security Council, 41.

27. This emergent racial regime also drew on entrenched color-line racial knowledge. Asian American studies scholar Jodi Kim shows how in Kennan's "Long Telegram" and other state documents the Soviet Union was racialized as "Asiatic" and communism imagined as an "oriental" ideology. She argues that the idea of communism as a kind of disease relied on its racialization as oriental, writing, "The figuration of racialized bodies as the very embodiment of disease, and the concomitant fear that they have the ability to cross multiple boundaries— particularly of space, race, or class—build on an enduring historical discourse of the 'yellow peril'" (*Ends of Empire*, 45).

28. For more on the convergence of Cold War and civil rights interests, see Dudziak, *Cold War Civil Rights*.

29. Queer studies scholar Chandan Reddy describes modern American governance as a "freedom with violence" by which "the modern state establishes itself in and through practices and their apparatuses that . . . generate the conditions for the expression of legitimate violence, seeking to conserve those apparatuses for the state exclusively." He adds that the state claims "a monopoly on legitimate violence" by forging "the conditions for the universalization of a specific expression of reason or rationality" (*Freedom with Violence*, 38). Liberalism is that form of reason, and the state authorizes itself to conduct legitimate violence against governments and societies that don't subscribe to it.

30. Truman, "Presidential Directive," 33.

31. Nitze, "Grand Strategy of NSC-68," 13.

32. Acheson, *Present at the Creation*, 374.

33. Quoted in Thompson, *Hawk and the Dove*, 111.

34. Hammond, "NSC-68," 361.

35. Quoted in Johnston, *Hegemony and Culture*, 84.

36. Quoted in Thompson, *Hawk and the Dove*, 124.

37. *Supplemental Appropriations Bill*, 20.

38. Truman, "Situation in Korea."

39. Truman.

40. US National Security Council, "NSC 68," 48, 63–64.

41. Melamed, *Represent and Destroy*, 13.

42. Nichols, *Breakthrough on the Color Front*, 3, 8.

43. Nichols, 9.

44. Nichols, "Secret War against Racism."

45. Truman, "Executive Order 9981."

46. Marshall, "Fashioned in Battle."

47. Nichols, Humphrey, and Marshall were not alone in making a war-minded case for domestic racial integration. Officials in the Truman and Eisenhower administrations, critical race theorist Nikhil Singh writes, recognized "white supremacy [as] the 'Achilles heel' of U.S. foreign relations" and advocated for civil rights reforms with the Cold War on their minds. "From the highest levels of government and social policy, it appeared that the stability of the expanded American realm of action in the world was linked to the resolution of the crisis of racial discord and division at home," he observes (*Black Is a Country*, 7).

48. Quoted in Young, "Revisiting NSC 68," 8.

49. Patner, *I. F. Stone*, 61.

50. Straight, "Fictive Report," 21; Ball, "Some Questions on Korea," 14; "Recent Books," 167.

51. Rovere, "History in the Stone Age."

52. Stone, *Hidden History*, xxi–xxii.

53. Stone, xxi.

54. Stone, "Familiar Chill," 43.

55. Truman, "Situation in Korea."

56. Stone, *Hidden History*, 1, 2, 4, 8.

57. Stone, 22. Stone later steered clear of suggesting that South Korea might have baited North Korea into crossing the thirty-eighth parallel, reflecting in 1988, "It's hard to believe that the *South* provoked the war. Maybe they did, I don't know; but if they *did*, it's very odd that the North was able to get all the way down to the end of the peninsula within a few days" (quoted in Patner, *I. F. Stone*, 65).

58. "Korea: The 'Forgotten' War," 21.

59. Hong, "Pyongyang Lost," 137, 142.

60. US National Security Council, "NSC 68," 45.

61. Stone, *Hidden History*, 143.

62. Stone, "Familiar Chill," 43.

63. Stone, *Hidden History*, 346, 348.

64. Cumings, preface to *Hidden History*, xv.

65. United Nations General Assembly, "Universal Declaration of Human Rights."

66. Civil Rights Congress, *We Charge Genocide*, 3.

67. Patterson, *Man Who Cried Genocide*, 182.

68. Truman, "Situation in Korea."

69. Historian Carol Anderson recounts how state officials argued that the United Nations had jurisdiction to prosecute human rights violations in the Soviet bloc because of the peace treaties that the governments of Bulgaria, Hungary, and Rumania had signed after World War II. "By emphasizing treaty rights, rather than the UN's human rights instruments, the United States had established a principle by which it could attack the Communists while shielding its 'Negro problem' from UN scrutiny," she writes (*Eyes Off the Prize*, 191).

70. Patterson, *Man Who Cried Genocide*, 172.

71. "Patterson Is Jailed."

72. White, "Progress Report," 9.

73. Quoted in Anderson, *Eyes Off the Prize*, 192.

74. Stone, "Is the Way We Treat Negroes 'Genocide'?"

75. Civil Rights Congress, *We Charge Genocide*, 7.

76. Quoted in Civil Rights Congress, 32.

77. Civil Rights Congress, 4.

78. Cultural historian Penny Von Eschen shows how the Cold War state countered the radical black internationalism of activists like Du Bois, Patterson, and Robeson by sending black artists and musicians to Asia and Africa as goodwill ambassadors and "symbols of the triumph of American democracy." But Louis Armstrong, Dizzy Gillespie, and other jazz ambassadors "didn't simply accept the way they were deployed by the State Department," Von Eschen writes, but "slipped into the breaks and looked around, intervening in official narratives and playing their own changes on Cold War perspectives" (*Satchmo Blows Up the World*, 4, 25).

79. Kennedy, "Police Restrain House Georgian."

80. Quoted in "Stigmatizing Witness Admitted by Lanham." See also Horne, *Black Revolutionary*, 139.

81. Phillips, *War!*, 156.

82. Civil Rights Congress, *We Charge Genocide*, 8.

83. Civil Rights Congress, 27.

84. Black studies scholar Alexander Weheliye argues that centering blackness—as "a changing system of unequal power structures that apportion and delimit which humans can lay claim to full human status" (*Habeas Viscus*, 3)—reveals how racialization organizes genres of the human that include rather than form the limits of Western man. Like Patterson years earlier, Weheliye contends that a more just and less violent future depends not on the gradual conferral of full human status embodied by Western man to excluded groups but on a "radical reconstruction and decolonization of what it means to be human" (4), a reconstruction not bound to a white Western norm.

85. Patterson, foreword to *We Charge Genocide*, vii, ix.

86. Patterson, x.

87. Clinton, "Korean War Veterans Memorial."

88. US Commission of Fine Arts, minutes.

89. Of the Korean Memorial's dehistoricized content, cultural historian Kristin Hass writes that the celebration of the fighting man's sacrifice "allows the soldier to represent war and allows the work that the war might have done in the world, the global implications of the war and the challenges that it might have presented to U.S. nationalism, to recede out of sight and therefore out of both the past and the present that the memorial constructs" (*Sacrificing Soldiers*, 57–58).

90. Quoted in Schwartz and Bayma, "Commemoration," 955.

91. Quoted in Purdum, "War in Korea."

92. American Battle Monuments Commission, "Korean War Memorial."

93. Cultural historian Melani McAlister argues that the Bush administration's war effort in the Persian Gulf benefited from news stories celebrating the multicultural character of the "new army." These stories, she writes, authorized the war by suggesting that "the diversity of its armed forces made the United States a world citizen, with all the races and nations of the globe represented in its population," even as the Middle East was constructed as the constitutive "outside" to that multicultural nationalism (*Epic Encounters*, 250, 259).

94. Clinton, "Korean War Veterans Memorial."

95. Purdum, "War in Korea."

Chapter Two

1. Herr, *Dispatches*, 188.

2. Herr, 188.

3. Herr contributed Benjamin Willard's (Martin Sheen) voiceovers in *Apocalypse Now* and wrote *Full Metal Jacket* with Kubrick and novelist Gustav Hasford.

4. Bryan, "Different War."

5. Herr, *Dispatches*, 210.

6. Pearson, "Joseph Heller Dies."

7. Herr, *Dispatches*, 65.

8. Pratt, "Yossarian's Legacy," 92–93.

9. Cultural historian Marita Sturken, for example, shows how the cultural memory of the Vietnam War shifted from "rupture" to "closure" throughout the late 1970s and 1980s as Hollywood films about self-searching American soldiers revised and obscured news media images that had foregrounded Southeast Asian suffering. "Despite their role as fictional narratives, these films rescript the war and subsume documentary images," she writes, noting that "many deliberately restage documentary images, blurring the boundaries between the reenactment and the original event" (*Tangled Memories*, 94). See also Chong, *Oriental Obscene*; and Nguyen, *Nothing Ever Dies*.

10. Esslin, "Theatre of the Absurd," 5.

11. Trinh, "All-Owning Spectatorship," 101.

12. O'Brien, "Nobel Prize–Winner Camus."

13. Camus, *Rebel*, 174.

14. Camus, 305, 4.

15. O'Brien, "Nobel Prize–Winner Camus."

16. Camus, *Myth of Sisyphus*, 53.

17. Medovoi argues that the new attention to identity in the 1960s originated amid, and was animated by, the anticommunism of the 1950s, when the *Partisan Review* and other liberal anticommunist magazines began celebrating individual rebellion as a defining characteristic of American culture that distinguished it from the alleged uniformities of communist societies. This new regard for rebellion, he writes, "hinged on an ideological reciprocity between literature and politics" in which critics read such novels as J. D. Salinger's *The Catcher in the Rye* (1951) as national allegories dramatizing "America's political culture as [having] a young and rebellious identity." Writers contrasted that rebelliousness with Soviet culture but also, as Heller's novel demonstrates, with the "American landscape of Fordist conformity" (*Rebels*, 56–57).

18. Camus, *Myth of Sisyphus*, 58.

19. Camus, 60–61.

20. Heller's novel-in-progress became more absurdist as Camus's fame in America grew throughout the mid- to late 1950s. When he first introduced Yossarian in a 1955 short story titled "Catch-18," the "catch" of the title named a rule that officers censoring outgoing mail must sign the letters they censored. It hadn't yet become the absurd situation—a catch-22—for which the novel would later be known. See Heller, "Catch-18."

21. Esslin, "Theatre of the Absurd," 4.

22. Calder, "Martin Esslin"; Gussow, "Martin Esslin."

23. Daugherty, *Just One Catch*, 289–92.

24. Esslin, "Theatre of the Absurd," 14.

25. Esslin, 6.

26. Pratt, "Yossarian's Legacy," 89.

27. Stern, "Bombers Away."

28. Algren, "Catch," 358.

29. Daugherty, *Just One Catch*, 149–50.

30. Simon and Schuster, "Happy Birthday *Catch-22*."

31. Brickner, "Unrequired Reading."

32. Newfield, "New Left."

33. Lehmann-Haupt, "Trying to Novelize Vietnam."

34. Pratt, "Yossarian's Legacy," 89.

35. Witkin, "Antiwar Slate."

36. Shenker, "Joseph Heller."

37. Heller, "*Playboy* Interview," 160.

38. Quoted in Seed, *Fiction of Joseph Heller*, 85.

39. Heller, *Catch-22*, 16.

40. Homberger, "Joseph Heller."

41. Heller, *Catch-22*, 7.

42. Heller, 440.

43. Nguyen, *Gift of Freedom*, 15.

44. Heller, "Impolite Interview," 18.

45. Literary scholar Steven Doloff suggests that the name Yossarian might signal the character's unstated Jewishness. Heller's mother's first language having been Yiddish, the author's childhood nickname would have been, Doloff concludes, "Yosef" or "Yossi." He wonders whether Heller derived the name Yossarian from his childhood nickname, leaving "a perceptible, if unintentional, ethnic fingerprint of some significance on Heller's protagonist" ("What the Hell Kind of Name Is Yossarian?," 304).

46. Cultural historian Timothy Melley situates the novel's individualism within the wider "agency panic" of the Cold War. Amid the rise of mass media and the growth of the federal government, he suggests, Americans feared they were losing control of their own thoughts and behaviors. Of Yossarian, Melley writes, "His refusal to associate himself with the national project or with the collective body under attack leaves him with only one way of comprehending an attack on his unit: it is an attack on him personally" (*Empire of Conspiracy*, vii, 65). But Yossarian's rebellion also serves the Cold War state by modeling the liberal freedoms it announced itself to be defending in Asia.

47. Heller, *Catch-22*, 11.

48. Literature scholar Michael Szalay identifies a wide range of post–World War II American writing that reflects this white fetishization of black outsiderness—what he

considers a kind of "dematerialized" blackface for the modern liberal set. He sees the white authoring of blackness as motivated by a desire among white office workers to liberate themselves from the conformities of their middle-class suburban lives. These authors, Szalay suggests, use blackness to remove themselves from "the white communities of which they are a part as if they are from the outside and possessed of a black second skin" (*Hip Figures*, 8, 117).

49. Heller, *Catch-22*, 259.

50. "Vietnam-Book Boom."

51. Reagan, "Peace."

52. "Reagan Gets Idea from *Rambo*."

53. Hinson, "Vietnam."

54. *Platoon*.

55. Black studies scholar Roderick Ferguson argues that universities and colleges contained student demands for structural antiracist changes by substituting representation for redistribution and elevating the white liberal who "seemingly embraces matters of diversity but eschews visions for structural redistribution" ("Distributions of Whiteness," 1101). Post–civil rights multiculturalism, he writes, "enables whiteness to perform *publicly and privately* as an expression of liberal appreciation for diversity and multiculturalism while allowing it to proceed *structurally* as a beneficiary to racial disenfranchisement" (1104).

56. Halberstam, "Two Who Were There."

57. Schlund-Vials, *War, Genocide, and Justice*, 77.

58. Stone and Boyle, Platoon *and* Salvador, 70.

59. Norman, "*Platoon* Grapples with Vietnam."

60. Herr, foreword to *Full Metal Jacket*, vi.

61. *Full Metal Jacket*.

62. Herr, foreword to *Full Metal Jacket*, v.

63. Hinson, "Vietnam."

64. See Jeffords, *Remasculinization of America*; Lipsitz, *Possessive Investment in Whiteness*; and Winant, "Behind Blue Eyes."

65. Reagan, "Peace."

66. Sociologist Jennifer Pierce locates the emergence of two interrelated white racial narratives amid the new right's efforts to roll back affirmative action. While news media circulated stories of white male innocence and grievance, Hollywood studios, she writes, made films about "antiracist white heroes" who "underwent a transformation from racial innocence to racial understanding and become advocates who fought for racial justice" (*Racing for Innocence*, 45). The Vietnam War movies of the late 1980s feature "antiracist white heroes" who also reflect the innocence and grievance of the former narrative.

67. Daugherty, *Just One Catch*, 223.

68. Chong, *Oriental Obscene*, 27, 129.

69. *Surname Viet Given Name Nam*.

70. Feminist scholar Lan Duong writes that Trinh acts as a "traitor to the production of knowledge about women" and forms the basis for a collaborative "trans-Vietnamese feminism"—a trans-Vietnamese feminism that troubles the "monstrous" heroism of Vietnamese nationalism and the victimhood of the American soldier's bildungsroman (*Treacherous Subjects*, 124, 125). Scholars have also called attention to the film's double movement between, in film scholar Peter Feng's words, "a desire to make cinema speak the truth of Vietnamese American women's lives" and a critical awareness that "cinematic convention traffics not in truth but in truth effects" (*Identities in Motion*, 199). Film scholar Glen Mimura shows how *Surname Viet Given Name Nam* functions as "simultaneously a documentary and a critique of the form" (*Ghostlife of Third Cinema*, 76). Ethnic studies scholar Jodi Kim stresses that the film's "political responsibility is embedded within, and not eclipsed by, the film's critique of the apparatuses of representation" (*Ends of Empire*, 227).

71. *Surname Viet Given Name Nam*.

72. Trinh, "All-Owning Spectatorship," 101.

73. *Surname Viet Given Name Nam*.

Chapter Three

1. Steinbeck IV, "Importance of Being Stoned," 34.

2. Steinbeck IV and Steinbeck, *Other Side of Eden*, 109.

3. Steinbeck IV, "Importance of Being Stoned," 33–34.

4. Steinbeck IV, 35.

5. Steinbeck IV, 34.

6. Steinbeck IV, 34.

7. Steinbeck IV, *In Touch*, 71.

8. Steinbeck IV, "Importance of Being Stoned," 58.

9. Critical race theorist Nikhil Singh shows how the idea of policing the decolonizing world grew out of an earlier era of continental settlement in which the state treated the American Indian Wars not as wars but as a form of policing. Indians were not "legitimate" adversaries, the settler state believed; they could not wage war. "If the U.S. era of continental settlement progressively translated war into policing and frontiers into borders," Singh writes, "the globalization of the U.S. realm translated policing into war and projected the frontier beyond the nation, so that it became possible to think of war at home and police in the world" (*Race and America's Long War*, 55–56).

10. "Drug War on GIs." See also "Red China Exports Opium."

11. Reiss, *We Sell Drugs*, 11. Reiss argues that from the 1940s to the 1960s the United States used economic sanctions, war, and international governing bodies to define the boundaries of licit drug trafficking, boundaries that, she writes, "were

rooted not in scientific objectivity but in the political economy and cultural politics of US drug control" (10). Her research reveals how drugs functioned as a mechanism of social control as well as a means of creating new markets for American drug manufacturers.

12. For more on the origins of the drug wars, see Frydl, *Drug Wars in America*; Murakawa, *First Civil Right*; and Reiss, *We Sell Drugs*.

13. Nixon, "Special Message on Control of Narcotics."

14. "81% See Law Breakdown."

15. The rise of law-and-order rhetoric in the 1960s has been attributed to a white backlash to civil rights reform, but political scientist Vesla Weaver suggests that it also stemmed from the efforts of conservative elites to redefine black civil rights as a "crime problem." She refers to that effort as a "frontlash," in which "losers in a conflict become the architects of a new program, manipulating the issue space and altering the dimensions of the conflict in an effort to regain their command of the agenda" ("Frontlash," 236). See also Alexander, *New Jim Crow*; and Parenti, *Lockdown America*.

16. Nixon, "Toward Freedom from Fear," 13.

17. Kuzmarov, *Myth of the Addicted Army*, 6.

18. Waters, "My Lai GIs."

19. "Fresh Disclosures," 32.

20. Smith, "Senators Told G.I.'s Smoked Marijuana."

21. "Fresh Disclosures," 32.

22. "Viet Cong."

23. Sociologist William Petersen introduced the idea of Asian Americans as model minorities in a 1966 *New York Times* article, in which he observed that Japanese Americans had a lower incidence of "social pathology" than other ethnic groups, despite living in "neighborhoods characterized by overcrowding, poverty, dilapidated housing, and other 'causes' of crime." Although Japanese Americans are "surrounded by ethnic groups with high crime rates," he wrote, alluding to black communities, "they have been exceptionally law abiding" ("Success Story").

24. Murphy and Steele, "World Heroin Problem," 18.

25. Steele, "Our Most Dangerous Epidemic," 48.

26. "New Withdrawal Costs," 11.

27. Alsop, "Worse Than My Lai," 108. See also "GI Heroin Epidemic"; and "GI's Other Enemy," 26, 31.

28. Steele, "Our Most Dangerous Epidemic," 46.

29. Buckley, "U.S. and Heroin."

30. Reston, "Nixon, Drugs and the War."

31. *Drug Abuse in the Military*, 212.

32. Ethnic studies scholar Lisa Cacho identifies how racial criminalization renders those deemed illegal aliens, gang members, or terrorists "criminal by being,

unlawful by presence, and illegal by status." It makes them unable, whatever their behavior, to be lawful, which, Cacho stresses, "is always the absolute prerequisite for political rights, legal recognition, and resource distribution" (*Social Death*, 8).

33. Nixon, "Remarks about Drug Abuse."

34. Nixon.

35. Gilmore, *Golden Gulag*, 28.

36. Nixon, "If Mob Rule Takes Hold."

37. Nixon, "War in Vietnam."

38. Kuzmarov also identifies a relation between Vietnamization and the drug wars, noting how the Nixon administration escalated its effort to regulate narcotics in Southeast Asia for the health of its soldiers and to enhance the image of the South Vietnamese government, which had done little to control, and in some cases had facilitated, the drug trade in the region (*Myth of the Addicted Army*, 131).

39. Agamben, *State of Exception*, 21.

40. Nixon, "International Narcotics Control."

41. Parenti, *Lockdown America*, 14–18; Weaver, "Frontlash," 243, 260.

42. Murakawa, *First Civil Right*, 10. See also Hinton, *War on Poverty*.

43. Steinbeck IV, "Importance of Being Stoned," 34.

44. Nixon, "Special Message on Drug Abuse."

45. Quoted in Kuzmarov, *Myth of the Addicted Army*, 110.

46. "Trying to Help the GI Addicts," *Life*, July 23, 1971, 26.

47. Nixon, "Special Message on Control of Narcotics"; and "Drug Abuse Act."

48. Nixon, "Drug Abuse Act."

49. Reed, "Black Pathology Biz."

50. Reed, "Should Harvard Teach *The Wire*?"

51. Reed, "Neo-HooDoo."

52. Reed, "Conversation with Ishmael Reed," 12.

53. Literary scholar Henry Louis Gates described Reed's novel in 1988 as a revisionist riff on black literature that satirizes the idea of an "'always already' black signified" (*Signifying Monkey*, 218). Scholars since have followed Gates's lead, examining how Reed "resignifies" the detective novel, science fiction, and Harlem Renaissance modernism.

54. Reed, *Mumbo Jumbo*, 213–14, 218.

55. Reed, 17.

56. Reed, 154.

57. Muhammad, *Condemnation of Blackness*, 13.

58. Reed, *Mumbo Jumbo*, 64.

59. Reed's novel echoes, with some ironic distance, the third worldism of the Bandung era, from which emerged new, transnational Afro-Asian connections based on shared anticolonial and antiracist struggles. That sense of identification with Vietnamese among black writers could at times, as cultural historian Bill Mullen observes, devolve into a kind of "cultural fetishization" and "lead to

reifying definitions of culture" that are part of what he calls the Afro-Orientalist tradition (*Afro-Orientalism*, xx, xxvii).

60. For more on the anti-imperial politics of the Black Panthers, see Singh, *Black Is a Country*, 193–211.

61. Newton, "To the National Liberation Front," 180, 181.

62. Gómez, letter to the draft board, 287, 289.

63. Revolutionary Caucus, "Statement," n.p.

64. Literary scholars Frederick Aldama and Marcial González both argue that Acosta's decision to write a novel rather than a memoir destabilizes the truth claims of "ethnic-identified autobiography" and enacts a "dereifying function" (Aldama, *Postethnic Narrative Criticism*, 64; González, *Chicano Novels*, 79).

65. Acosta, *Revolt of the Cockroach People*, 200.

66. Of the antiwar Chicano movement, historian Lorena Oropeza writes, "Opposition to the war forced movement participants to break apart narrow conceptions of citizenship and national belonging that had privileged whiteness, masculinity, and military service" (*¡Raza Sí! ¡Guerra No!*, 82).

67. Acosta, *Revolt of the Cockroach People*, 65, 69–70.

68. Acosta, 110.

69. Acosta, 34.

70. Acosta, 136.

71. Rodríguez, *Forced Passages*, 47.

72. Thompson, "Strange Rumblings in Aztlan," 36.

73. McCoy, preface to *Politics of Heroin*, x.

74. McCoy, *Politics of Heroin in Southeast Asia*.

75. *International Narcotics Control*, 703.

76. McCoy, *Politics of Heroin*, 222.

77. McCoy, 52.

78. Hersh, "C.I.A. Aides."

79. Colby, "CIA Responds."

80. McCoy, "Author's Response," 118.

81. Colby, "Agency's Brief," 116.

Chapter Four

1. Bush, "Human Rights Day Proclamation."

2. Bush, "Allied Armed Forces."

3. Bush, "American Legislative Exchange Council."

4. Reagan, "Peace."

5. Fukuyama, "End of History?," 4.

6. Bush, "Address on the Persian Gulf Crisis."

7. Feminist scholar Caren Kaplan argues that the introduction of aerial images of other countries did not bring those countries closer but instead made them

seem all the more distant and distinct from the United States. The images that came out of the Gulf War readied Americans to see the later wars in Iraq and Afghanistan as foreign and remote. "For many people living in the United States during the televisual era, their first view of Afghanistan or Iraq had been the 'flashes of light' that signal the commencement of war—tracer fire in Baghdad at the start of the First Persian Gulf War captured in the fledgling network CNN's broadcast," Kaplan writes. "Rarely, if ever, has the United States been viewed in a similar fashion" (*Aerial Aftermaths*, 28). Visual technologies have figured the Middle East again and again as, unlike Western Europe and the United States, an otherworld and a legitimate target for war from above. For more on how the armed forces used GPS to sell Americans on the idea of a live, clean war in the Persian Gulf, see Kaplan, "Precision Targets," 702–5.

8. Media scholars have shown how the Bush administration, with the assistance of television media, strove to represent the Gulf War as the inverse of the Vietnam War. Feminist scholars Susan Jeffords and Lauren Rabinovitz, for example, write, "For the United States to wage a new war, the public memory of the old war would have to be overturned or erased" ("Seeing through History," 20).

9. Quoted in Sweeney, *Military and the Press*, 163–64.

10. Jordan, "Bombing of Baghdad," 538.

11. Truman, "Situation in Korea."

12. Carter, "Universal Declaration of Human Rights."

13. Atanasoski, *Humanitarian Violence*, 74.

14. Reagan, "Peace."

15. Espiritu, *Body Counts*, 101.

16. See, for example, Allen, *Until the Last Man Comes Home*; Chong, *Oriental Obscene*; Hagopian, *Vietnam War in American Memory*; and Nguyen, *Gift of Freedom*.

17. On the three-worlds model of Cold War containment and integration, see Klein, *Cold War Orientalism*, 24–28; and Medovoi, *Rebels*, 10–12.

18. Bush, "News Conference on the Persian Gulf Conflict."

19. Kaplan identifies how military, industrial, media, and entertainment interests converged in the Gulf War to sell Americans on the idea of a clean war in the Middle East and a new consumer technology, GPS. "If the 'witnessing' came from the missiles themselves, the point of view was singular, unidirectional, and heavily censored in favor of orchestrated displays of precision," she writes. "In effect, in the coverage of the Persian Gulf war the U.S. public watched an extended commercial for GPS" ("Precision Targets," 705).

20. *Wag the Dog*.

21. Shimko, *Iraq Wars*, 2.

22. Žižek, "NATO as the Left Hand of God?," 36.

23. Bush and Scowcroft, *World Transformed*, 315.

24. Bush, "Address on the Persian Gulf Crisis,"

25. Oreskes, "Poll Finds Strong Support."

26. Baker III, *Politics of Diplomacy*, 336.

27. Quoted in Sweeney, *Military and the Press*, 163–64.

28. Quoted in Jamieson and Waldman, *Press Effect*, 15–16.

29. Bush, "Fundraising Luncheon for Clayton Williams."

30. MacArthur, "Remember Nayirah." See also MacArthur, *Second Front*. Mac-Arthur's account was later corroborated by *60 Minutes*, the *Columbia Journalism Review*, and Human Rights Watch. See Safer, "Nayirah"; Rowse, "Support for War"; and "Kuwait's 'Stolen' Incubators."

31. Safer, "Nayirah."

32. See Manheim, *Strategic Public Diplomacy*, 7.

33. Manheim, 50–51.

34. Bush, "Fundraising Luncheon for Clayton Williams."

35. MacArthur, *Second Front*, 64–65.

36. MacArthur, 66.

37. Bush, "Open Letter."

38. The incubator story contributed to a broader cultural inversion of how Americans remembered the atrocities their soldiers committed against Vietnamese civilians. "The basic technique," historian Bruce Franklin writes, "was to take images of the war that had become deeply embedded in America's consciousness and change them into their opposite" (*M.I.A.*, 133), by transferring atrocities committed by the United States and their allies to their enemies.

39. Of Bush's decision to declare Hussein the new Hitler and then decline to remove him, historian Lloyd Gardner writes, "The administration had hoped that Saddam Hussein would be overthrown from within, but when this did not happen, and when the dictator suppressed rebelling Kurds and Shiites, the humanitarian argument went the other way" (*Long Road to Baghdad*, 89).

40. Safire, "Bush's Bay of Pigs." For a thorough account of the criticism of the Bush administration's decision not to enter Baghdad, see Robinson, *CNN Effect*, 68–69.

41. Bernstein, "Will the Gulf War Produce Enduring Art?"

42. Baudrillard, *Gulf War Did Not Take Place*, 63.

43. Baudrillard, 32.

44. *Three Kings*.

45. Bush, "News Conference on the Persian Gulf Conflict."

46. The use of a mother and her child to elicit humanitarian affect is a familiar convention of human rights activism that visual culture scholar Wendy Kozol identifies as the militarization of transnational motherhood. The focus on a mother and her child in humanitarian visual culture, she writes, mobilizes "supposedly universal ideals about gender, maternal care, vulnerability, and innocence" meant to "invite the spectator to recognize the humanity, not the ethnic difference, of these women and children" (*Distant Wars Visible*, 45).

47. Bush, "Assistance for Iraqi Refugees."

48. This isn't to suggest that humanitarian feeling is a bad thing. But it is critical, as ethnic studies scholar Randall Williams writes, that we not assume humani-

tarianism to be antithetical to imperialism but recognize how "the contemporary human rights regime obscures the dialectic between (imperial) violence and (international) law" (*Divided World*, xxi).

49. Pease, *New American Exceptionalism*, 47.

50. The inclusion of a black officer, Chief, in the gold heist also reflects how the armed forces had by the time of the Gulf War embraced a multicultural ethic that undermined the liberal belief that good television coverage could end a war by revealing it as brutal and racist. Instead, CNN showed distant aerial images of bombed areas and intimate shots of America's new look, multiracial fighting men and women. "The public representations of the Gulf War did not focus solely on images of technical mastery and precision bombing," cultural historian Melani McAlister writes. "Many news reports also emphasized the changing character of the U.S. armed forces that were winning the war, highlighting the racial diversity of the new military" (*Epic Encounters*, 250).

51. Hall, "Long Civil Rights Movement," 1234.

52. Atanasoski, *Humanitarian Violence*, 145.

53. Bush's war also contributed to a "remasculinization" of national culture that began in the Reagan years. The Gulf War reinscribed masculine values that, some believed, had been wounded by the defeat in Vietnam. But Bush, unlike the "hard body" heroes of 1980s action-adventure movies, "would struggle throughout his presidency to straddle the images of himself as a man who 'cares' about people and as a tough commander-in-chief," feminist scholar Susan Jeffords writes (*Hard Bodies*, 95). This incoherence in the president's embodiment of masculine norms reflected the inconsistencies in the disembodied masculine values that structured the war in the Persian Gulf. Bush imagined his government as the father but also the policeman of the region. For more on the gender politics of the Gulf War, see Chong, *Oriental Obscene*; Jeffords, *Remasculinization of America*; and Lipsitz, *Possessive Investment in Whiteness*.

54. For a detailed account of the post–Cold War racialization of religious difference, see Atanasoski, *Humanitarian Violence*, 12–13.

55. Bronner, "Historians Note Flaws"; George H. W. Bush, "Fundraising Luncheon for Clayton Williams."

56. Davis, "In L.A., Burning All Illusions," 564.

57. Jordan, "Truth of Rodney King," 42.

58. Jordan, "Big-Time Coward," 12.

59. Jordan, "Gulf War," 553.

60. Jordan, "Bombing of Baghdad," 536–37.

61. Jordan, 537–38.

Chapter Five

1. Gallagher, "Where's the Great Novel?"

2. Gallagher.

3. Kakutani, "Human Costs."

4. Gallagher, "Where's the Great Novel?"

5. Quoted in Gallagher.

6. Gallagher.

7. Cultural historian Donald Pease argues, for example, that President Bush's declaration of war unsettled how Americans related to their government by confronting them with disavowed histories of settler colonial and racial violence that alienated them from a belief in their own "radical innocence" (*New American Exceptionalism*, 158).

8. Khalili, *Time in the Shadows*, 5.

9. US Department of the Army, *Counterinsurgency*, 3-8, A-7. Citations from the field manual here and elsewhere refer to the manual's own pagination by chapter and page number.

10. Sarah Sewall, the director of the Carr Center for Human Rights Policy at Harvard University, declared the 2006 counterinsurgency field manual to be advancing a "radical message" ("Radical Field Manual," xxvii) by asking American soldiers and marines to assume more risk in order to secure local civilians.

11. Birtle, *U.S. Army Counterinsurgency Doctrine*, 62.

12. Singh, *Race and America's Long War*, 73.

13. "Letter to *New York Age*," 280, 281.

14. US Department of the Army, *Counterinsurgency*, AB-1. For more on how the American Indian Wars formed American counterinsurgency doctrine, see Khalili, *Time in the Shadows*, 16–19.

15. Kilcullen, "Countering Global Insurgency," 613–14.

16. Bacevich, *Washington Rules*, 192.

17. Petraeus, "American Military and the Lessons of Vietnam," 305.

18. Marshall, "Some Thoughts on Military Revolutions."

19. Rumsfeld, "New Kind of War."

20. Rumsfeld, "21st Century Transformation."

21. Of the short-lived Office of Force Transformation, investigative journalist Christian Parenti observed, a year after its dissolution, "The RMA looks like the last bubble of the nineties, and Iraq is where it bursts" ("Planet America," 890).

22. Crane, "United States," 63.

23. Power, "Our War on Terror."

24. Ephron, "Conrad Crane," 63.

25. US Department of the Army, *Counterinsurgency*, 1-3.

26. Nagl, *Counterinsurgency Lessons*, 11. Like other historical and instructional studies of irregular war, including Field Manual 3-24, Nagl's book found a wider audience with civilian readers and liberal intellectuals as the military transitioned to counterinsurgency operations in the Middle East. The University of Chicago Press republished his book, with the original title and subtitle reversed, in 2005.

27. Nagl, "Evolution and Importance of Field Manuel 3-24," xviii.

28. Crane, "United States," 67.

29. Crane, 61.

30. Petraeus, "Learning Counterinsurgency," 45.

31. Petraeus, Carr, and Abercrombie, "Why We Need FISTs," 3.

32. US Department of the Army, *Counterinsurgency*, 1-27.

33. US Department of the Army, 1-19.

34. US Department of the Army, 2-12.

35. Petraeus and Amos, foreword to *Counterinsurgency*.

36. Gregory, "Rush to the Intimate," 9. Gregory identifies the publication of Field Manual 3-24 as part of a broader "cultural turn" in the counterterror wars. Petraeus, Crane, and their writing team hid how "nonkinetic" activities facilitated lethal ones, but they also redirected Americans' attention to images of their soldiers getting to know, rather than torturing, Muslims in the Middle East. The "legal and ethical entailments [of the new doctrine] were front and centre," Gregory writes.

37. Kilcullen, "Twenty-Eight Articles," 138.

38. Sewall, "Radical Field Manual," xxx.

39. Sewall, xxvii, xxix.

40. US Department of the Army, *Counterinsurgency*, 1-28.

41. Kilcullen, "Countering Global Insurgency," 613. Visual culture scholar Nicholas Mirzoeff suggests that Kilcullen's and other strategists' accounts of Lawrence as a proto-counterinsurgent may be based more on actor Peter O'Toole's turn as the military officer in the 1962 film *Lawrence of Arabia* than on Lawrence's actual actions and writing. "By figuring itself as Lawrence," Mirzoeff writes, "counterinsurgency blends the reflected glamour of Hollywood heroism with the colonial trope of going native, that is to say, of adopting the practices of the local culture in order to defeat it" ("War Is Culture," 1739–40).

42. Packer, "Knowing the Enemy," 64.

43. Packer, 64.

44. US Department of the Army, *Counterinsurgency*, 3-6–7.

45. McFate, "Anthropology and Counterinsurgency," 24, 28.

46. McFate, "Understanding Adversary Culture," 48.

47. McFate and Jackson, "DOD's Cultural Knowledge Needs," 21.

48. US Department of the Army, *Counterinsurgency*, 3-8, 5-10.

49. Historian Vicente Rafael shows, for example, how counterinsurgency is waged through language, with military theorists embracing foreign languages and translation as tools of counterinsurgent war. "Counterinsurgency [is] both the process and the effect of a certain conversion," he writes. "Conversion in this sense entails the translation of things and humans into a 'standing reserve,' that is, into parts of larger technosocial assemblages for the disposal of a colonizing power" (*Motherless Tongues*, 123). Counterinsurgency does not end war. It turns all things into the material of war, making war itself all the more difficult to isolate and define.

50. US Department of the Army, *Counterinsurgency*, 1-15.

51. US Department of the Army, A-7.

52. The norms on which counterinsurgency is founded come through in the revised field manual's reliance on medical-scientific analogies. Insurgent ideology is, the authors suggested, like a cancer, and counterinsurgents are like "surgeons cutting out cancerous tissues while keeping other vital organs intact." The field officer must "cut off the sources of recuperative power" by isolating an insurgency from unaffiliated civilians and, having starved it of resources, "let it die." Counterinsurgent forces are not part of the "tissues" or "organs" but are charged with operating on them, distinguishing the healthy from the cancerous, the normal from the deviant (US Department of the Army, 1-23).

53. US Department of the Army, 5-11.

54. Gioia, preface to *Operation Homecoming*, xv.

55. Weber, "Endowment Chairman."

56. Weber.

57. US Department of the Army, *Counterinsurgency*, 5-11.

58. Quoted in National Endowment for the Arts, "Operation Homecoming," 4.

59. Mark McGurl, *Program Era*, 56, 61. McGurl traces the entangled histories of institutional creative writing and the veteran-writer back to the end of World War II. The GI Bill led to the formation of some of the first creative writing programs, which, McGurl writes, encouraged their veteran-students, with Ernest Hemingway as their model, to convert "war trauma into graceful literary understatement" and undertake "a subtle transition from the silent suffering of trauma into the controlled pathos of literary recollection" (61).

60. Cultural historian Elliott Colla writes that Operation Homecoming and other war-minded arts initiatives—part of what he sees as a larger "military-literary complex"—must be acknowledged as efforts to "forget the many other stories that could be told about war" and to "recreate in letters the very privileges and power that armed soldiers always have in relation to unarmed civilians" ("Military-Literary Complex").

61. Kakutani, "Soldiering amid Hyacinths"; Tobar, "Haunting Iraq War Novel"; and Samet, "War Lies."

62. Powers, "Conversation."

63. Powers, *Yellow Birds*, 11.

64. Powers, 13.

65. Powers, 10.

66. Powers, 13.

67. Powers, 37.

68. Powers, 182, 224.

69. Literary scholar Bruce Robbins observes that American novels, even those that announce their engagement with the broader world, tend to make no more than "mercifully short visits" to non-Western countries that they imagine as

museums of "extreme suffering." The American novel has, he argues, subscribed to an unwritten rule that "history abroad will never be less than atrocity, and atrocity abroad can then serve as the motivating event behind a 'coming to America' story" ("Worlding of the American Novel," 1099). Robbins's argument also holds for "return to America" stories in which a veteran comes home bearing hard knowledge of that violent outside world.

70. Klay, "Failure of Imagination."

71. National Book Foundation, "Phil Klay."

72. Klay, "Transcending the Archetypes of War."

73. Klay, *Redeployment*, 15.

74. Klay, 176–79.

75. Klay, 199–200.

76. Klay, 196.

77. Nguyen, *Nothing Ever Dies*, 221.

78. Kilcullen, *Accidental Guerilla*, xiv, 38.

79. Kilcullen, 38.

80. Robinson, "Novel about the Iraq War."

81. Gallagher, "Hut Next Door."

82. Gallagher, *Youngblood*, 23.

83. Gallagher, "Sex, War, and Writing."

84. Gallagher, *Youngblood*, 70–72.

85. Gallagher has acknowledged his novel's indebtedness to Stone's film, telling an interviewer that he "wanted to play with that Tom Berenger from *Platoon* stereotype that is embedded in war literature, particularly post–Vietnam War literature" ("Matt Gallagher's New Novel").

86. Gallagher, *Youngblood*, 320–21.

87. Gallagher, "Where's the Great Novel?"

88. Mirzoeff writes, reflecting on the field manual's curious rise to best-seller status, "Counterinsurgency is explicitly a cultural and political war, fought as much in the United States as it is in Iraq or elsewhere" (*Right to Look*, 293). The white veteran-novelist may, long after serving in a counterinsurgent war abroad, contribute to a counterinsurgent war at home.

89. US Department of Defense, Administrative Review Board Proceedings.

90. Ethnic studies scholar Naomi Paik writes that the years since World War II have witnessed a "seeming paradox" in which "the expansion of rights discourses" has occurred alongside "an expanding imprisonment regime" (*Rightlessness*, 3). That contradiction makes sense, she suggests, when considering how the state has constructed the categories of the rightless and the inhuman as a constitutive outside to the righted and the human.

91. Kaplan, "Where Is Guantánamo?," 851.

92. Slahi, *Guantánamo Diary*, 192.

93. Rumsfeld, "Guantanamo Bay Facts."

94. Slahi, *Guantánamo Diary*, 264–65.

95. Slahi, 55–60, 301–7, 359–61. Journalist Jess Bravin details a lie-detection examination administered to Slahi on October 31, 2004, in which the detainee denied involvement in or special knowledge of the millennium plot and 9/11 attacks. All the results showed either "No Deception Indicated" or "No Opinion" (*Terror Courts*, 110).

Epilogue

1. Savage, "Rules for Airstrike Killings."

2. Obama, "National Defense University."

3. White House, "Procedures for Approving Direct Action."

4. Savage and Shane, "Death Toll from Airstrikes."

5. Quoted in DeYoung, "Newly Declassified Document."

6. White House, "Procedures for Approving Direct Action."

7. White House.

8. Obama, "National Defense University."

9. Anthropologist Joseph Masco argues that since the onset of the nuclear age, fear has been the affective engine behind the growth of the federal government. "The campaign to normalize threat is the flip side of identifying and articulating new kinds of dangers, allowing new forms of governance to be pursued as a necessary counterformation," he writes, describing terror as "a primary national resource" since the Cold War (*Theater of Operations*, 7, 3).

10. White House, "Procedures for Approving Direct Action."

11. Obama, "Supreme Court Nomination."

12. Rid, *Cyber War Will Not Take Place*, viii.

13. Johnson, "Cyber Attack on Sony."

14. Quoted in Kaplan, "Obama's Way."

15. Obama, "Nobel Lecture."

16. Of Obama, journalist David Sanger wrote at the end of the president's first term, "Quietly, he is attempting to fit [drone and cyber attacks] into a new concept of how the United States can ensure its military predominance around the globe without resorting to the lengthy, expensive, and unpopular wars and occupations that dominated that past decade." His, Sanger concluded, was "a strategy of confrontation and concealment" (*Confront and Conceal*, xvii).

17. Panetta, "Press Briefing."

18. Murphy, "Modern Medal."

19. Veterans of Foreign Wars, "New Medal Ranking."

20. DeYoung, "Distinguished Warfare Medal"; J. E., "Distinguished Warfare Medal."

21. Wood and Harbaugh, "Limits of Armchair Warfare."

22. A closer look at the criteria for combat-service medals reveals the extent to which war, by the state's own measure, has defined all of the twentieth and twenty-first centuries. "These criteria cause wartime to swallow much of American history," legal historian Mary Dudziak writes. "In the smaller conflicts recognized by veterans groups and honored with military campaign medals [such as those in Lebanon, Grenada, and Panama], American military personnel traveled to other nations with their military units, wearing uniforms and bearing arms. . . . It is only through forgetting the small wars that so much of American history is remembered as peacetime" (*War Time*, 28, 31).

23. Hagel, "Distinguished Warfare Medal."

24. Veterans of Foreign Wars, "Distinguished Warfare Medal."

25. US Department of Defense, "Military Decorations Review Results."

26. Delmont, "Drone Encounters," 194.

27. Quoted in Bonnington and Ackerman, "Apple Rejects App."

28. Quoted in Meyer, "New iPhone App."

29. Kelley, "NYU Student"; Bowcott, "Drone Strikes."

30. For detailed accounts of the hack of Sony Pictures, see Elkind, "Hack of the Century"; Kaplan, *Dark Territory*, 268–72; and Seal, "Sony's Hacking Saga."

31. US Federal Bureau of Investigation, "Update on Sony Investigation."

32. Obama, "Year-End Press Conference."

33. Johnson, "Cyber Attack on Sony."

34. See Kaplan, *Dark Territory*, 269. National security writer Kim Zetter identified holes in the government's attribution of the Sony hack to North Korea. See "Evidence Is Flimsy."

35. Seal, "Sony's Hacking Saga."

36. Rand Corporation, "How Hollywood Affects Global Policy."

37. Bennett, email message, June 25.

38. Lynton, email message, June 25.

39. Psaki, press briefing.

40. Bennett, email message, June 26.

41. *Interview*.

42. Hong, "Stranger Than Fiction."

43. Carr, "Hacking at Sony."

44. Quoted in Phillips, "Activists to Send DVDs."

45. Korns, "Cyber Operations," 97.

46. Quoted in Chernus, *Eisenhower's Atoms for Peace*, 44.

47. Ridge, "Press Briefing."

48. Singer, "Do Drones Undermine Democracy?"

49. Du Bois, "Peace Is Dangerous," 3, 5, 6.

50. Obama, "Nobel Lecture."

Bibliography

"81% in a Poll See Law Breakdown." *New York Times*, September 10, 1968.

Acheson, Dean. *Present at the Creation: My Years in the State Department*. New York: W. W. Norton, 1969.

Acosta, Oscar Zeta. *The Revolt of the Cockroach People*. New York: Vintage, 1989. First published 1973 by Straight Arrow.

Agamben, Giorgio, *State of Exception*. Translated by Kevin Attell. Chicago: University of Chicago Press, 2005.

Aldama, Frederick Louis. *Postethnic Narrative Criticism: Magicorealism in Oscar "Zeta" Acosta, Ana Castillo, Julie Dash, Hanif Kureishi, and Salman Rushdie*. Austin: University of Texas Press, 2003.

Alexander, Michelle. *The New Jim Crow: Mass Incarceration in the Age of Colorblindness*. New York: New Press, 2010.

Algren, Nelson. "The Catch." Review of *Catch-22*, by Joseph Heller. *Nation*, November 4, 1961, 357–58.

Allen, Michael J. *Until the Last Man Comes Home: POWs, MIAs, and the Unending Vietnam War*. Chapel Hill: University of North Carolina Press, 2009.

Alsop, Stewart. "Worse Than My Lai." *Newsweek*, May 24, 1971, 108.

American Battle Monuments Commission. "Korean War Memorial." https://www.abmc.gov/about-us/history/korean-war-memorial.

Anderson, Carol. *Eyes Off the Prize: The United Nations and the African American Struggle for Human Rights, 1944–1955*. Cambridge: Cambridge University Press, 2003.

Atanasoski, Neda. *Humanitarian Violence: The U.S. Deployment of Diversity*. Minneapolis: University of Minnesota Press, 2013.

Bacevich, Andrew J. *Washington Rules: America's Path to Permanent War*. New York: Metropolitan, 2010.

Baker, James A., III. *The Politics of Diplomacy: Revolution, War and Peace, 1989–1992*. New York: Putnam, 1995.

Baldwin, Hanson W. "Forrestal Faces Trials." *New York Times*, September 21, 1947.

———. *The Price of Power*. New York: Harper, 1947.

Ball, W. MacMahon. "Some Questions on Korea." *Nation*, July 5, 1952, 14.

Baudrillard, Jean. *The Gulf War Did Not Take Place*. Translated by Paul Patton. Bloomington: Indiana University Press, 1995.

Bennett, Bruce. Email message to Michael Lynton. June 25, 2014. *WikiLeaks*. https://wikileaks.org/sony/emails/emailid/139029.

———. Email message to Michael Lynton. June 26, 2014. *WikiLeaks*. https://wikileaks.org/sony/emails/emailid/139029.

Berlant, Lauren. *Cruel Optimism*. Durham, NC: Duke University Press, 2011.

Bernstein, Richard. "Will the Gulf War Produce Enduring Art?" *New York Times*, June 9, 1991.

Birtle, Andrew J. *U.S. Army Counterinsurgency and Contingency Operations Doctrine, 1860–1941*. Washington, DC: US Army Center of Military History, 1998.

Bonnington, Christina, and Spencer Ackerman. "Apple Rejects App That Tracks U.S. Drone Strikes." *Wired*, August 30, 2012. https://www.wired.com/2012/08/drone-app/.

Bourne, Randolph S. "The State." In *War and the Intellectuals: Collected Essays, 1915–1919*, 65–104. New York: Harper Torchbooks, 1964.

Bowcott, Owen. "Drone Strikes Threaten 50 Years of International Law, Says UN Rapporteur." *Guardian*, June 21, 2012.

Bravin, Jess. *The Terror Courts: Rough Justice at Guantanamo Bay*. New Haven, CT: Yale University Press, 2013.

Brickner, Richard P. "Unrequired Reading." *New York Times Book Review*, February 27, 1966.

Bronner, Ethan. "Historians Note Flaws in President's Speech." *New York Times*, March 26, 1999.

Bryan, C. D. B. "The Different War." Review of *Dispatches*, by Michael Herr. *New York Times Book Review*, November 20, 1977.

Buck, Pearl S. *American Unity in Asia*. New York: John Day, 1942.

Buckley, Tom. "U.S. and Heroin: It's Always a Dead End on 'Scag Alley.' " *New York Times*, June 6, 1971.

Bush, George W. "President Bush Announces Major Combat Operations in Iraq Have Ended." May 1, 2003. *WhiteHouse.gov*. https://georgewbush-whitehouse.archives.gov/news/releases/2003/05/20030501-15.html.

Bush, George H. W. "Address Before a Joint Session of the Congress on the Persian Gulf Crisis and the Federal Budget Deficit." September 11, 1990. American Presidency Project. http://www.presidency.ucsb.edu/ws/?pid=18820.

———. "Open Letter to College Students on the Persian Gulf Crisis." January 9, 1991. American Presidency Project. http://www.presidency.ucsb.edu/ws/?pid=19205.

———. "The President's News Conference on the Persian Gulf Conflict." March 1, 1991. American Presidency Project. http://www.presidency.ucsb.edu/ws/?pid =19352.

———. "Remarks at a Fundraising Luncheon for Gubernatorial Candidate Clayton Williams in Dallas, Texas." October 15, 1990. American Presidency Project. http://www.presidency.ucsb.edu/ws/?pid=18931.

———. "Remarks at a Republican Campaign Rally in Manchester, New Hampshire." October 23, 1990. American Presidency Project. http://www.presidency .ucsb.edu/ws/?pid=18955.

———. "Remarks on Assistance for Iraqi Refugees and a News Conference." April 16, 1991. American Presidency Project. http://www.presidency.ucsb.edu /ws/?pid=19479.

———. "Remarks on Signing the Human Rights Day, Bill of Rights Day, and Human Rights Week Proclamation." December 10, 1990. American Presidency Project. http://www.presidency.ucsb.edu/ws/?pid=19145.

———. "Remarks to Allied Armed Forces Near Dhahran, Saudi Arabia." November 22, 1990. American Presidency Project. http://www.presidency.ucsb.edu/ws /?pid=19088.

———. "Remarks to the American Legislative Exchange Council." March 1, 1991. American Presidency Project. http://www.presidency.ucsb.edu/ws/?pid=19351.

———. "Remarks to Veterans Service Organizations." March 4, 1991. American Presidency Project. http://www.presidency.ucsb.edu/ws/?pid=19356.

———, and Brent Scowcroft. *A World Transformed*. New York: Knopf, 1998.

Cacho, Lisa Marie. *Social Death: Racialized Rightlessness and the Criminalization of the Unprotected*. New York: New York University Press, 2012.

Calder, John. "Martin Esslin: Illuminating Writer and Radio Drama Producer." *Guardian*, February 27, 2002.

Camus, Albert. *The Myth of Sisyphus and Other Essays*. Translated by Justin O'Brien. New York: Vintage, 1991. First published in English 1955 by Knopf.

———. *The Rebel: An Essay on Man in Revolt*. Translated by Anthony Bower. New York: Vintage, 1991. First published in English 1956 by Knopf.

Carr, David. "How the Hacking at Sony over *The Interview* Became a Horror Movie." *New York Times*, December 21, 2014.

Carter, Jimmy. "Universal Declaration of Human Rights Remarks at a White House Meeting Commemorating the 30th Anniversary of the Declaration's Signing." December 6, 1978. American Presidency Project. http://www.presi dency.ucsb.edu/ws/?pid=30264.

Casualties of War. Directed by Brian De Palma. Columbia, 1989.

Chernus, Ira. *Eisenhower's Atoms for Peace*. College Station: Texas A&M University Press, 2002.

Cho, Grace M. *Haunting the Korean Diaspora: Shame, Secrecy, and the Forgotten War*. Minneapolis: University of Minnesota Press, 2008.

Chong, Sylvia Shin Huey. *The Oriental Obscene: Violence and Racial Fantasies in the Vietnam War*. Durham, NC: Duke University Press, 2011.

Chow, Rey. *The Age of the World Target: Self-Referentiality in War, Theory, and Comparative Work*. Durham, NC: Duke University Press, 2006.

Civil Rights Congress. *We Charge Genocide: The Historic Petition to the United Nations for Relief from a Crime of the United States Government against the Negro People*. New York: Civil Rights Congress, 1951.

Clinton, Bill. "Remarks at the Dedication Ceremony for the Korean War Veterans Memorial." July 27, 1995. American Presidency Project. http://www.presidency.ucsb.edu/ws/?pid=51662.

Colby, W. E. "The Agency's Brief." *Harper's*, October 1972, 116–18.

———. "The CIA Responds." *Washington Star*, July 5, 1972.

Colla, Elliott. "The Military-Literary Complex." *Jadaliyya*, July 8, 2014. http://www.jadaliyya.com/pages/index/18384/the-military-literary-complex.

Crane, Conrad. "United States." In *Understanding Counterinsurgency: Doctrine, Operations, and Challenges*, edited by Thomas Rid and Thomas Kearney, 59–72. New York: Routledge, 2010.

Cumings, Bruce. Preface to *The Hidden History of the Korean War, 1950–1951*, by I. F. Stone, xi–xx. New York: Little, Brown, 1988.

Daugherty, Tracy. *Just One Catch: A Biography of Joseph Heller*. New York: St. Martin's, 2011.

Davis, Mike. "In L.A., Burning All Illusions." In *Voices of a People's History of the United States*, edited by Howard Zinn and Anthony Arnove, 560–64. 2nd ed. New York: Seven Stories, 2009.

Delmont, Matt. "Drone Encounters: Noor Behram, Omer Fast, and Visual Critiques of Drone Warfare." *American Quarterly* 65, no. 1 (2013): 193–202.

DeYoung, Karen. "Newly Declassified Document Sheds Light on How President Approves Drone Strikes." *Washington Post*, August 6, 2016.

———. "Senators Ask Chuck Hagel to Downgrade New Distinguished Warfare Medal." *Washington Post*, March 11, 2013.

Doloff, Steven. "What the Hell Kind of Name Is Yossarian?" *Notes and Queries* 60, no. 2 (2013): 302–4.

Drug Abuse in the Military: Hearing Before the Subcommittee on Drug Abuse in the Military of the Committee on Armed Services. 92nd Cong. (1972).

Du Bois, W. E. B. "Fifty Years After." In *The Souls of Black Folk*, 207–8. New York: Oxford University Press, 2007.

———. "Peace Is Dangerous." New York: National Guardian, 1951.

———. *The Souls of Black Folk: Essays and Sketches*. Chicago: McClurg, 1903.

Dudziak, Mary L. *Cold War Civil Rights: Race and the Image of American Democracy*. Princeton, NJ: Princeton University Press, 2000.

———. *War Time: An Idea, Its History, Its Consequences*. New York: Oxford University Press, 2012.

Duong, Lan P. *Treacherous Subjects: Gender, Culture, and Trans-Vietnamese Feminism*. Philadelphia: Temple University Press, 2012.

Elkind, Peter. "Inside the Hack of the Century." *Fortune*, July 2015. http://fortune.com/sony-hack/.

Ephron, Dan. "Conrad Crane: With Iraq in Flames, a Historian Rethinks the Way We Fight the Enemy." *Newsweek*, December 25, 2006, 63.

Espiritu, Yen Le. *Body Counts: The Vietnam War and Militarized Refuge(es)*. Berkeley: University of California Press, 2014.

Esslin, Martin. "The Theatre of the Absurd." *Tulane Drama Review* 4, no. 4 (1960): 3–15.

Feng, Peter X. *Identities in Motion: Asian American Film and Video*. Durham, NC: Duke University Press, 2002.

Ferguson, Roderick A. "The Distributions of Whiteness." *American Quarterly* 66, no. 4 (2014): 1101–6.

———. *The Reorder of Things: The University and Its Pedagogies of Minority Difference*. Minneapolis: University of Minnesota Press, 2012.

Foucault, Michel. *"Society Must Be Defended": Lectures at the Collège de France, 1975–1976*. Translated by David Macey. New York: Picador, 2003.

Franklin, H. Bruce. *M.I.A., or, Mythmaking in America*. Rev. and expanded ed. New Brunswick: Rutgers University Press, 1993.

"Fresh Disclosures on Drugs and GI's." *U.S. News and World Report*, April 6, 1970, 32–33.

Frydl, Kathleen J. *The Drug Wars in America, 1940–1973*. Cambridge: Cambridge University Press, 2013.

Fukuyama, Francis. "The End of History?" *National Interest*, Summer 1989, 3–18.

Full Metal Jacket. Directed by Stanley Kubrick. Warner Bros., 1986.

Gallagher, Matt. "Authors Matt Gallagher and Lea Carpenter Talk Sex, War, and Writing." Interview by Lea Carpenter. *Playboy*, August 29, 2016. http://www.playboy.com/articles/author-matt-gallagher-interview-with-lea-carpenter.

———. "The Hut Next Door." *New York Times*, May 3, 2011. http://opinionator.blogs.nytimes.com/2011/05/03/the-hut-next-door/.

———. "Where's the Great Novel about the War on Terror?" *Atlantic*, June 14, 2011. http://www.theatlantic.com/entertainment/archive/2011/06/wheres-the-great-novel-about-the-war-on-terror/240233/.

———. "Why Matt Gallagher's New Novel About the Iraq War Matters Now." Interview by Rebecca Bengal. *Vogue*, March 18, 2016. http://www.vogue.com/13417898/youngblood-matt-gallagher-interview-iraq-war-invasion-anniversary/.

———. *Youngblood*. New York: Atria, 2016.

Gardner, Lloyd C. *The Long Road to Baghdad: A History of U.S. Foreign Policy from the 1970s to the Present*. New York: New Press, 2008.

Gates, Henry Louis, Jr. *The Signifying Monkey: A Theory of African-American Literary Criticism*. New York: Oxford University Press, 1988.

Gerdau, Axel. "Obama's Speech on Counterterrorism." *New York Times* video, 59:36. May 23, 2013. http://www.nytimes.com/video/us/politics/100000002242 352/president-obama-on-counterterrorism.html.

"GI Heroin Epidemic Reported in Vietnam." *Los Angeles Times*, April 20, 1971.

"The GI's Other Enemy: Heroin." *Newsweek*, May 24, 1971, 26, 31.

Gilmore, Ruth Wilson. *Golden Gulag: Prisons, Surplus, Crisis, and Opposition in Globalizing California*. Berkeley: University of California Press, 2007.

Gioia, Dana. Preface to *Operation Homecoming: Iraq, Afghanistan, and the Home Front, in the Words of U.S. Troops and Their Families*, edited by Andrew Carroll, xi–xv. New York: Random House, 2006.

Gómez, Manuel. Letter to the draft board of Temescal, California. In *Viva La Raza! The Struggle of the Mexican-American People*, by Elizabeth Sutherland Martínez and Enriqueta Longeaux y Vásquez, 287–89. New York: Doubleday, 1974.

González, Marcial. *Chicano Novels and the Politics of Form: Race, Class, and Reification*. Ann Arbor: University of Michigan Press, 2008.

Gregory, Derek. " 'The Rush to the Intimate': Counterinsurgency and the Cultural Turn." *Radical Philosophy*, no. 150 (2008): 8–23.

Gussow, Mel. "Martin Esslin, Drama Theorist, Dies at 83." *New York Times*, June 5, 2002.

Hagel, Chuck. "Distinguished Warfare Medal." Memorandum. US Department of Defense, April 15, 2013.

Hagopian, Patrick. *The Vietnam War in American Memory: Veterans, Memorials, and the Politics of Healing*. Amherst: University of Massachusetts Press, 2009.

Halberstam, David. *The Coldest Winter: America and the Korean War*. New York: Hyperion, 2007.

———. "Two Who Were There View *Platoon*." *New York Times*, March, 8, 1987.

Hall, Jacquelyn Dowd. "The Long Civil Rights Movement and the Political Uses of the Past." *Journal of American History* 91, no. 5 (2005): 1233–63.

Hall, Stuart, Chris Critcher, Tony Jefferson, John Clarke, and Brian Roberts. *Policing the Crisis: Mugging, the State, and Law and Order*. London: Macmillan, 1978.

Hammond, Paul Y. "NSC-68: Prologue to Rearmament." In *Strategy, Politics, and the Defense Budgets*, edited by Warner R. Schilling, Hammond, and Glenn H. Snyder, 271–378. New York: Columbia University Press, 1962.

Harris, Cheryl I. "Whiteness as Property." *Harvard Law Review* 106, no. 8 (1993): 1707–91.

Hass, Kristin Ann. *Sacrificing Soldiers on the National Mall*. Berkeley: University of California Press, 2013.

Heller, Joseph. "Catch-18." *New World Writing*, no. 7 (1955): 204–14.

———. *Catch-22*. New York: Simon and Schuster, 2011. First published 1961 by Simon and Schuster.

————. "An Impolite Interview with Joseph Heller." By Paul Krassner. In *Conversations with Joseph Heller*, edited by Adam J. Sorkin, 6–29. Jackson: University Press of Mississippi, 1993.

————. *"Playboy* Interview: Joseph Heller." By Sam Merrill. In *Conversations with Joseph Heller*, edited by Adam J. Sorkin, 144–76. Jackson: University Press of Mississippi, 1993.

Hemingway, Ernest. *A Farewell to Arms.* 1929. New York: Scribner, 2014. First published 1929 by Scribner's.

————. Letter to F. Scott Fitzgerald. December 15, 1925. In *Ernest Hemingway Selected Letters, 1917–1961,* edited by Carlos Baker, 176–77. New York: Scribner, 1981.

Herr, Michael. *Dispatches.* New York: Vintage, 1991. First published 1977 by Knopf.

————. Foreword to *Full Metal Jacket: The Screenplay,* by Stanley Kubrick, Herr, and Gustav Hasford, v–vii. New York: Knopf, 1987.

Hersh, Seymour M. "C.I.A. Aides Assail Asia Drug Charge." *New York Times,* July 22, 1972.

Hinson, Hal. "Vietnam: The Movies' Coming of Age." *Washington Post,* July 5, 1987.

Hinton, Elizabeth. *From the War on Poverty to the War on Crime: The Making of Mass Incarceration in America.* Cambridge, MA: Harvard University Press, 2016.

Hogan, Michael J. *A Cross of Iron: Harry S. Truman and the Origins of the National Security State, 1945–1954.* Cambridge: Cambridge University Press, 1998.

Homberger, Eric. "Joseph Heller." *Guardian,* December 14, 1999.

Hong, Christine. "Pyongyang Lost: Counterintelligence and Other Fictions of the Forgotten War." In *American Literature and Culture in an Age of Cold War: A Critical Reassessment,* edited by Steven Belletto and Daniel Grausam, 135–62. Iowa City: University of Iowa Press, 2012.

————. "Stranger Than Fiction: *The Interview* and U.S. Regime-Change Policy Toward North Korea." *Asia-Pacific Journal: Japan Focus* 12, no. 4 (2015). http://apjjf.org/2014/12/52/Christine-Hong/4244.html.

————, and Henry Em, eds. "The Unending Korean War." Special issue, *Positions: Asia Critique* 23, no. 4 (2015).

Horne, Gerald. *Black Revolutionary: William Patterson and the Globalization of the African American Freedom Struggle.* Urbana: University of Illinois Press, 2013.

Hughes, Langston. "Memo to Non-White Peoples." In *The Collected Poems of Langston Hughes,* edited by Arnold Rampersad and David Roessel, 456–57. New York: Knopf, 1994.

International Narcotics Control: Hearing Before the Committee on Appropriations. 92nd Cong. (1972).

The Interview. Directed by Seth Rogen and Evan Goldberg. Columbia, 2014.

J. E. "Lower the Precedence of the New Distinguished Warfare Medal." Petition. *WhiteHouse.gov*, February 14, 2013. https://web.archive.org/web/2013030602 5627/https://petitions.whitehouse.gov/petition/lower-precedence-new-distin guished-warfare-medal/5KdnkBBN.

Jamieson, Kathleen Hall, and Paul Waldman. *The Press Effect: Politicians, Journalists, and the Stories That Shape the Political World.* New York: Oxford University Press, 2003.

Jeffords, Susan. *Hard Bodies: Hollywood Masculinity in the Reagan Era.* New Brunswick, NJ: Rutgers University Press, 1994.

———. *The Remasculinization of America: Gender and the Vietnam War.* Bloomington: Indiana University Press, 1989.

Jeffords, Susan, and Lauren Rabinovitz. "Seeing through History: The War for the Past." In *Seeing through the Media: The Persian Gulf War,* edited by Jeffords and Rabinovitz, 19–24. New Brunswick, NJ: Rutgers University Press, 1994.

Johnson, Lyndon B. "Statement by the President Following the Signing of Law Enforcement Assistance Bills." September 22, 1965. American Presidency Project. http://www.presidency.ucsb.edu/ws/index.php?pid=27270.

———. "Statement by the President on Establishing the President's Commission on Law Enforcement and Administration of Justice." July 26, 1965. American Presidency Project. http://www.presidency.ucsb.edu/ws/index.php?pid=27110.

Johnson, Jeh. "Statement by Secretary Johnson on Cyber Attack on Sony Pictures Entertainment." US Department of Homeland Security, December 19, 2014. https://www.dhs.gov/news/2014/12/19/statement-secretary-johnson-cyber -attack-sony-pictures-entertainment.

Johnston, Andrew M. *Hegemony and Culture in the Origins of NATO Nuclear First Use, 1945–1955.* New York: Palgrave, 2005.

Jordan, June. "The Big-Time Coward." In *Affirmative Acts: Political Essays,* 11–15. New York: Anchor, 1998.

———. "The Bombing of Baghdad." In *Directed by Desire: The Collected Poems of June Jordan,* 535–39. Port Townsend, WA: Copper Canyon, 2007.

———. "June Jordan Speaks Out against the 1991 Gulf War." In *Voices of a People's History of the United States,* edited by Howard Zinn and Anthony Arnove, 553–55. 2nd ed. New York: Seven Stories, 2009.

———. "The Truth of Rodney King." In *Affirmative Acts: Political Essays,* 42–51. New York: Anchor, 1998.

Kakutani, Michiko. "Human Costs of the Forever Wars, Enough to Fill a Bookshelf." *New York Times,* December 25, 2014.

———. "Soldiering amid Hyacinths and Horror." Review of *The Yellow Birds,* by Kevin Powers. *New York Times,* September 6, 2012.

Kaplan, Amy. *The Anarchy of Empire in the Making of U.S. Culture.* Cambridge, MA: Harvard University Press, 2002.

———. "'Left Alone with America': The Absence of Empire in the Study of American Culture." In *Cultures of United States Imperialism*, edited by Kaplan and Donald E. Pease, 3–21. Durham, NC: Duke University Press, 1993.

———. "Where Is Guantánamo?" *American Quarterly* 57, no. 3 (2005): 831–58.

Kaplan, Caren. *Aerial Aftermaths: Wartime from Above*. Durham, NC: Duke University Press, 2018.

———. "Precision Targets: GPS and the Militarization of U.S. Consumer Identity." *American Quarterly* 58, no. 3 (2006): 693–714.

Kaplan, Fred. *Dark Territory: The Secret History of Cyber War*. New York: Simon and Schuster, 2016.

———. "Obama's Way." *Foreign Affairs*, January/February 2016. https://www.for eignaffairs.com/articles/2015–12–07/obamas-way.

Kelley, Michael B. "The NYU Student Tweeting Every Reported Drone Strike Has Revealed a Disturbing Trend." *Business Insider*, December 12, 2012. http:// www.businessinsider.com/us-drone-tweets-reveal-double-tap-plan-2012–12.

Kennedy, Paul P. "Police Restrain House Georgian from Attacking a Negro Witness." *New York Times*, August 5, 1950.

Keppel, F. P. Foreword to *An American Dilemma: The Negro Problem and Modern Democracy*, by Gunnar Myrdal, v–viii. New York: Harper, 1944.

Khalili, Laleh. *Time in the Shadows: Confinement in Counterinsurgencies*. Stanford, CA: Stanford University Press, 2013.

Kilcullen, David J. *The Accidental Guerilla: Fighting Small Wars in the Midst of a Big One*. New York: Oxford University Press, 2009.

———. "Countering Global Insurgency." *Journal of Strategic Studies* 28, no. 4 (2005): 597–617.

———. "'Twenty-Eight Articles': Fundamentals of Company-level Counterinsurgency." *Military Review* 86, no. 3 (2006): 134–39.

Kim, Jodi. *Ends of Empire: Asian American Critique and the Cold War*. Minneapolis: University of Minnesota Press, 2010.

King, Martin Luther, Jr. "A Time to Break the Silence." In *Testament of Hope: The Essential Writings and Speeches of Martin Luther King, Jr.*, 231–44. New York: HarperCollins, 1991.

Klay, Phil. "After War, a Failure of Imagination." *New York Times*, February 8, 2014.

———. *Redeployment*. New York: Penguin, 2014.

———. "Transcending the Archetypes of War: An Interview with Phil Klay." By Matt Gallagher. *Paris Review*, March 4, 2014. http://www.theparisreview .org/blog/2014/03/04/transcending-the-archetypes-of-war-an-interview-with -phil-klay/.

Klein, Christina. *Cold War Orientalism: Asia in the Middlebrow Imagination, 1945–1961*. Berkeley: University of California Press, 2003.

"Korea: The 'Forgotten' War." *U.S. News and World Report*, October 5, 1951, 21.

Korns, Stephen W. "Cyber Operations: The New Balance." *Joint Forces Quarterly*, no. 54 (2009): 97–102.

Kozol, Wendy. *Distant Wars Visible: The Ambivalence of Witnessing*. Minneapolis: University of Minnesota Press, 2014.

"Kuwait's 'Stolen' Incubators: The Widespread Repercussions of a Murky Incident." *Middle East Watch*, February 6, 1992.

Kuzmarov, Jeremy. *The Myth of the Addicted Army: Vietnam and the Modern War on Drugs*. Amherst: University of Massachusetts Press, 2009.

LaFeber, Walter. *America, Russia, and the Cold War, 1945–1992*. 7th ed. New York: McGraw-Hill, 1993.

Lederer, William J., and Eugene Burdick. *The Ugly American*. New York: W. W. Norton, 1999. First published 1958 by W. W. Norton.

Lee, Alfred McClung. *Race Riots Aren't Necessary*. Chicago: American Council on Race Relations, 1945.

Lehmann-Haupt, Christopher. "Trying to Novelize Vietnam." Review of *Stringer*, by Ward Just; and *Sweet Reason*, by Robert Littell. *New York Times*, February 20, 1974.

"Letter to *New York Age*, May 17, 1900." In *"Smoked Yankees" and the Struggle for Empire: Letters from Negro Soldiers, 1898–1902*, edited by Willard B. Gatewood, Jr., 279–81. Urbana: University of Illinois Press, 1971.

Lipsitz, George. *The Possessive Investment in Whiteness: How White People Profit from Identity Politics*. Rev. ed. Philadelphia: Temple University Press, 2006.

Lowe, Lisa. *The Intimacies of Four Continents*. Durham, NC: Duke University Press, 2015.

Lynd, Robert S. "Prison for American Genius." Review of *An American Dilemma: The Negro Problem and Modern Democracy*, by Gunnar Myrdal. *Saturday Review of Literature*, April 22, 1944, 5–7, 27.

Lynton, Michael. Email message to Bruce Bennett. June 25, 2014. *WikiLeaks*. https://wikileaks.org/sony/emails/emailid/139029.

MacArthur, John R. "Remember Nayirah, Witness for Kuwait?" *New York Times*, January 6, 1992.

———. *Second Front: Censorship and Propaganda in the 1991 Gulf War*. Rev. ed. Berkeley: University of California Press, 2004. First published 1992 by Hill and Wang.

Manheim, Jarol B. *Strategic Public Diplomacy and American Foreign Policy: The Evolution of Influence*. New York: Oxford University Press, 1994.

Marshall, Andrew W. "Some Thoughts on Military Revolutions." Memorandum for the record. US Department of Defense, August 23, 1993.

Marshall, S. L. A. "Fashioned in Battle." Review of *Breakthrough on the Color Front*, by Lee Nichols. *New York Times Book Review*, February 14, 1954.

Masco, Joseph. *The Theater of Operations: National Security Affect from the Cold War to the War on Terror*. Durham, NC: Duke University Press, 2014.

May, Ernest R., ed. *American Cold War Strategy: Interpreting NSC 68.* New York: Bedford, 1993.

McAlister, Melani. *Epic Encounters: Culture, Media, and U.S. Interests in the Middle East, 1945–2000.* Berkeley: University of California Press, 2001.

McCoy, Alfred W. "The Author's Response." *Harper's,* October 1972, 118–20.

———. *The Politics of Heroin in Southeast Asia.* New York: Harper and Row, 1972.

———. Preface to *The Politics of Heroin: CIA Complicity in the Global Drug Trade,* ix–xxvi. 2nd rev. ed. Chicago: Lawrence Hill, 2003.

McFate, Montgomery. "Anthropology and Counterinsurgency: The Strange Story of Their Curious Relationship." *Military Review* 85, no. 2 (2005): 24–38.

———. "The Military Utility of Understanding Adversary Culture." *Joint Force Quarterly,* no. 38 (2005): 42–48.

———, and Andrea Jackson. "An Organizational Solution for DOD's Cultural Knowledge Needs." *Military Review* 85, no. 4 (2005): 18–21.

McGurl, Mark. *The Program Era: Postwar Fiction and the Rise of Creative Writing.* Cambridge, MA: Harvard University Press, 2009.

Medovoi, Leerom. *Rebels: Youth and the Cold War Origins of Identity.* Durham, NC: Duke University Press, 2005.

Melamed, Jodi. *Represent and Destroy: Rationalizing Violence in the New Racial Capitalism.* Minneapolis: University of Minnesota Press, 2011.

Melley, Timothy. *Empire of Conspiracy: The Culture of Conspiracy in Postwar America.* Ithaca, NY: Cornell University Press, 2000.

Meyer, Robinson. "A New iPhone App Catalogues and Maps U.S. Drone Killings." *Atlantic,* February 11, 2014. http://www.theatlantic.com/technology/archive/2014/02/a-new-iphone-app-catalogues-and-maps-us-drone-killings/283713/.

Mimura, Glen M. *Ghostlife of Third Cinema: Asian American Film and Video.* Minneapolis: University of Minnesota Press, 2009.

Mirzoeff, Nicholas. *The Right to Look: A Counterhistory of Visuality.* Durham, NC: Duke University Press, 2011.

———. "War Is Culture: Global Counterinsurgency, Visuality, and the Petraeus Doctrine." *PMLA* 124, no. 5 (2009): 1737–46.

Muhammad, Khalil Gibran. *The Condemnation of Blackness: Race, Crime, and the Making of Modern Urban America.* Cambridge, MA: Harvard University Press, 2010.

Mullen, Bill V. *Afro-Orientalism.* Minneapolis: University of Minnesota Press, 2004.

Murakawa, Naomi. *The First Civil Right: How Liberals Built Prison America.* New York: Oxford University Press, 2014.

Murphy, Morgan F., and Robert H. Steele. "The World Heroin Problem: Report of Special Study Mission." Washington, DC: Government Printing Office, 1971.

Murphy, Heather. "A Modern Medal Is Met with Modern Protest." *New York Times,* February 22, 2013.

Myrdal, Gunnar. *An American Dilemma: The Negro Problem and Modern Democracy*. New York: Harper, 1944.

Nagl, John A. *Counterinsurgency Lessons from Malaya and Vietnam: Learning to Eat Soup with a Knife*. Westport, CT: Praeger, 2002.

———. "The Evolution and Importance of Army/Marine Corps Field Manual 3–24, *Counterinsurgency*." Foreword to *Counterinsurgency*, Field Manual 3–24, by US Department of the Army, xiii–xlviii. Chicago: University of Chicago Press, 2007.

National Book Foundation. "2014 National Book Award Winner, Fiction: Phil Klay." http://www.nationalbook.org/nba2014_f_klay.html.

National Endowment for the Arts. "Operation Homecoming: Writing the Wartime Experience." *NEA Arts* 3, no. 4 (2006): 3–5.

New York Times Editorial Board. "The End of a Perpetual War." *New York Times*, May 23, 2013.

Newfield, Jack. "The New Left." *Boston Globe*, December 10, 1967.

Newton, Huey P. "Reply to William Patterson: September 19, 1970." In *To Die for the People: The Writings of Huey P. Newton*, 163–77. New York: Vintage, 1972.

———. "To the National Liberation Front of South Vietnam." In *To Die for the People: The Writings of Huey P. Newton*, 178–81. New York: Vintage, 1972.

Nguyen, Mimi Thi. *The Gift of Freedom: War, Debt, and Other Refugee Passages*. Durham, NC: Duke University Press, 2012.

Nguyen, Viet Thanh. *Nothing Ever Dies: Vietnam and the Memory of War*. Cambridge, MA: Harvard University Press, 2016.

Nichols, Lee. *Breakthrough on the Color Front*. New York: Random House, 1954.

———. "The Military's Secret War against Racism." Foundation for Economic Education, July 1, 1990. https://fee.org/articles/the-militarys-secret-war-against-racism/.

Nitze, Paul H. "The Grand Strategy of NSC-68." In *NSC 68: Forging the Strategy of Containment*, edited by S. Nelson Drew, 7–16. Washington, DC: National Defense University Press, 1994.

Nixon, Richard. "Address to the Nation on the War in Vietnam." November 3, 1969. American Presidency Project. http://www.presidency.ucsb.edu/ws/?pid=2303.

———. "Annual Message to the Congress on the State of the Union." January 22, 1970. American Presidency Project. http://www.presidency.ucsb.edu/ws/index.php?pid=2921.

———. "If Mob Rule Takes Hold in U.S.: A Warning from Richard Nixon." *U.S. News and World Report*, August 15, 1966, 64–65.

———. "Remarks about an Intensified Program for Drug Abuse Prevention and Control." June 17, 1971. American Presidency Project. http://www.presidency.ucsb.edu/ws/?pid=3047.

———. "Remarks on Signing the Comprehensive Drug Abuse Prevention and Control Act of 1970." October 27, 1970. American Presidency Project. http://www.presidency.ucsb.edu/ws/?pid=2767.

———. "Remarks to the Washington Conference on International Narcotics Control." September 18, 1972. American Presidency Project. http://www.presidency.ucsb.edu/ws/?pid=3578.

———. "Special Message to the Congress on Control of Narcotics and Dangerous Drugs." July 14, 1969. American Presidency Project. http://www.presidency.ucsb.edu/ws/?pid=2126.

———. "Special Message to the Congress on Drug Abuse Prevention and Control." June 17, 1971. American Presidency Project. http://www.presidency.ucsb.edu/ws/?pid=3048.

———. "Toward Freedom from Fear." New York: Nixon for President Committee, 1968.

Norman, Michael. "*Platoon* Grapples with Vietnam." *New York Times*, December 21, 1986.

Obama, Barack. "Keynote Address at the 2004 Democratic National Convention." July 27, 2004. American Presidency Project. http://www.presidency.ucsb.edu/ws/?pid=76988.

———. "Nobel Lecture: A Just and Lasting Peace." December 10, 2009. *Nobelprize.org*. https://www.nobelprize.org/nobel_prizes/peace/laureates/2009/obama-lecture_en.html.

———. "Obama's Speech against the Iraq War." October 2, 2002. National Public Radio. http://www.npr.org/templates/story/story.php?storyId=99591469.

———. "Remarks by the President at the National Defense University." May 23, 2013. *WhiteHouse.gov*. http://www.whitehouse.gov/the-press-office/2013/05/23/remarks-president-national-defense-university.

———. "Remarks by the President in a Conversation on the Supreme Court Nomination." April 8, 2016. *WhiteHouse.gov*. https://www.whitehouse.gov/the-press-office/2016/04/08/remarks-president-conversation-supreme-court-nomination.

———. "Remarks by the President in Address to the Nation on the End of Combat Operations in Iraq." August 31, 2010. *WhiteHouse.gov*. https://obamawhitehouse.archives.gov/the-press-office/2010/08/31/remarks-president-address-nation-end-combat-operations-iraq.

———. "Remarks by the President in Year-End Press Conference." December 19, 2014. *WhiteHouse.gov*. https://www.whitehouse.gov/the-press-office/2014/12/19/remarks-president-year-end-press-conference.

O'Brien, Justin. "Nobel Prize–Winner Camus: A Man Committed Yet Aloof." *New York Times Book Review*, December 8, 1957.

O'Brien, Tim. "How to Tell a True War Story." *Esquire*, October 1987, 208–15.

———. "Responsibly Inventing History: An Interview with Tim O'Brien." By Brian C. McNerney. *War, Literature, and the Arts* 6, no. 2 (1994): 1–26.

Oreskes, Michael. "Poll Finds Strong Support for Bush's Goals, but Reluctance to Start a War." *New York Times*, October 1, 1990.

Oropeza, Lorena. *¡Raza Sí! ¡Guerra No!: Chicano Protest and Patriotism during the Viet Nam War Era*. Berkeley: University of California Press, 2005.

Packer, George. "Knowing the Enemy." *New Yorker*, December 18, 2016. http://www.newyorker.com/magazine/2006/12/18/knowing-the-enemy.

Paik, A. Naomi. *Rightlessness: Testimony and Redress in U.S. Prison Camps since World War II*. Chapel Hill: University of North Carolina Press, 2016.

Panetta, Leon. "Press Briefing by Secretary Panetta from the Pentagon." February 13, 2013. US Department of Defense. http://archive.defense.gov/transcripts/transcript.aspx?transcriptid=5190.

Parenti, Christian. *Lockdown America: Police and Prisons in the Age of Crisis*. London: Verso, 1999.

———. "Planet America: The Revolution in Military Affairs as Fantasy and Fetish." In *Exceptional State: Contemporary U.S. Culture and the New Imperialism*, edited by Ashley Dawson and Malini Johar Schueller, 88–104. Durham, NC: Duke University Press, 2007.

Patner, Andrew. *I. F. Stone: A Portrait*. New York: Pantheon, 1988.

"Patterson Is Jailed for Contempt Again." *New York Times*, November 20, 1954.

Patterson, William L. Foreword to *We Charge Genocide: The Historic Petition to the United Nations for Relief from a Crime of the United States Government against the Negro People*, by Civil Rights Congress, vii–xi. New York: International Publishers, 1971.

———. *The Man Who Cried Genocide*. New York: International Publishers, 1971.

Pearson, Richard. "*Catch-22* Author Joseph Heller Dies." *Washington Post*, December 13, 1999.

Pease, Donald E. *The New American Exceptionalism*. Minneapolis: University of Minnesota Press, 2009.

Petersen, William. "Success Story, Japanese-American Style." *New York Times*, January 9, 1966.

Petraeus, David H. "The American Military and the Lessons of Vietnam: A Study of Military Influence and the Use of Force in the Post-Vietnam Era." PhD diss., Princeton University, 1987.

———. "Learning Counterinsurgency: Observations from Soldiering in Iraq." *Military Review* 86, no. 1 (2006): 45–55.

———, and James F. Amos. Foreword to *Counterinsurgency*, Field Manual 3–24, by US Department of the Army. Washington, DC: Department of the Army, 2006.

———, Damian P. Carr, and John C. Abercrombie. "Why We Need FISTs: Never Send a Man When You Can Send a Bullet." *Field Artillery*, May–June 1997, 3–5.

Phillips, Catherine. "Activists to Send DVDs of *The Interview* to North Korea by Balloon." *Newsweek*, December 17, 2014. http://www.newsweek.com/activists-send-interview-north-korea-balloon-292767.

Phillips, John. Foreword to *Small Wars Manual*, by US Marine Corps. Washington, DC: Department of the Navy, 1987.

Phillips, Kimberley. *War! What Is It Good For? Black Freedom Struggles and the U.S. Military from World War II to Iraq*. Chapel Hill: University of North Carolina Press, 2012.

Pierce, Jennifer. *Racing for Innocence: Whiteness, Gender, and the Backlash against Affirmative Action*. Stanford, CA: Stanford University Press, 2012.

Platoon. Directed by Oliver Stone. Orion, 1986.

Plummer, Brenda Gayle. *Rising Wind: Black Americans and U.S. Foreign Affairs, 1935–1960*. Chapel Hill: University of North Carolina Press, 1997.

Power, Samantha. "Our War on Terror." *New York Times Book Review*, July 29, 2007.

Powers, Kevin. "Conversation: Kevin Powers, Author of *The Yellow Birds*." Interview by Jeffrey Brown. *PBS NewsHour*, PBS, October 4, 2012. http://www.pbs.org/newshour/art/conversation-kevin-powers-author-of-the-yellow-birds/.

———. *The Yellow Birds*. New York: Little, Brown, 2012.

Pratt, John Clark. "Yossarian's Legacy: *Catch-22* and the Vietnam War." In *Fourteen Landing Zones: Approaches to Vietnam War Literature*, edited by Philip K. Jason, 88–110. Iowa City: University of Iowa Press, 1991.

President's Committee on Civil Rights. *To Secure These Rights: The Report of the President's Committee on Civil Rights*. Washington, DC: Government Printing Office, 1947.

Psaki, Jen. Press briefing. December 17, 2014. US Department of State. https://www.state.gov/r/pa/prs/dpb/2014/12/235370.htm.

Purdum, Todd S. "War in Korea, Fast Receding, Gets Memorial." *New York Times*, July 28, 1995.

Rafael, Vicente L. *Motherless Tongues: The Insurgency of Language amid Wars of Translation*. Durham, NC: Duke University Press, 2016.

Rampersad, Arnold. *The Life of Langston Hughes*. Vol. 2, *1941–1967, I Dream a World*. 2nd ed. New York: Oxford University Press, 2002.

Rand Corporation. "How Hollywood Affects Global Policy." *Rand Blog*, November 27, 2012. http://www.rand.org/blog/2012/11/how-hollywood-affects-global-policy.html.

"Reagan Gets Idea from *Rambo* for Next Time." *Los Angeles Times*, July 1, 1985.

Reagan, Ronald. "Peace: Restoring the Margin of Safety." August 18, 1980. *Ronald Reagan Presidential Library*. http://www.reagan.utexas.edu/archives/reference/8.18.80.html.

"Recent Books." *Foreign Affairs*, October 1952, 167.

"Red China Exports Opium to Make Dope Addicts of Our Boys in Asia!" *Nation*, January 9, 1954, 12.

"Red Chinese Accused of Drug War on GIs." *Washington Post*, April 27, 1952.

Reddy, Chandan. *Freedom with Violence: Race, Sexuality, and the US State*. Durham, NC: Duke University Press, 2011.

Reed, Ishmael. "The Black Pathology Biz." *Nation*, November 20, 1989, 597–98.
———. "A Conversation with Ishmael Reed." Interview by Fred Beauford. *Black Creation* 4 (1973): 12–15.
———. *Mumbo Jumbo*. New York: Scribner, 1996. First published 1972 by Doubleday.
———. "Neo-HooDoo." *Los Angeles Free Press*, September 18, 1972, 42.
———. "Should Harvard Teach *The Wire*? No, It Relies on Clichés about Blacks and Drugs." *Boston Globe*, September 10, 2010.
Reiss, Suzanna. *We Sell Drugs: The Alchemy of US Empire*. Berkeley: University of California Press, 2014.
Reston, James. "Nixon, Drugs and the War." *New York Times*, June 2, 1971.
Revolutionary Caucus. "Statement of the Revolutionary Caucus at Denver's Chicano Youth Liberation Conference." *El Pocho Ché* 1, no. 1 (1969): n.p.
Rid, Thomas. *Cyber War Will Not Take Place*. New York: Oxford University Press, 2013.
Ridge, Tom. "Press Briefing by Homeland Security Director Tom Ridge, FBI Director Bob Mueller, Deputy Postmaster General John Nolan, and Director of Bacterial and Mycotic Disease for the CDC Mitch Cohen." November 2, 2001. American Presidency Project. http://www.presidency.ucsb.edu/ws/index.php?pid=79202.
Robbins, Bruce. "The Worlding of the American Novel." In *The Cambridge History of the American Novel*, edited by Leonard Cassuto, Clare Virginia Eby, and Benjamin Reiss, 1096–1106. Cambridge: Cambridge University Press, 2011.
Robinson, Piers. *The CNN Effect: The Myth of News, Foreign Policy, and Intervention*. New York: Routledge, 2002.
Robinson, Roxana. "A Novel about the Iraq War from a Soldier Who Was There." Review of *Youngblood*, by Matt Gallagher. *Washington Post*, January 22, 2016.
Rodríguez, Dylan. *Forced Passages: Imprisoned Radical Intellectuals in the U.S. Prison Regime*. Minneapolis: University of Minnesota Press, 2006.
Rosenberg, Carol. "Tracking the Hunger Strike." *Miami Herald*, 2013. http://media.miamiherald.com/static/media/projects/gitmo_chart/.
Rovere, Richard. "History in the Stone Age: Hidden 'Facts' and Fiction of the War in Korea." *New York Post*, May 11, 1952.
Rowe, John Carlos. *Literary Culture and U.S. Imperialism: From the Revolution to World War II*. New York: Oxford University Press, 2000.
Rowse, Arthur E. "How to Build Support for War." *Columbia Journalism Review* 31, no. 3 (1992): 28–29.
Rumsfeld, Donald H. "Guantanamo Bay Facts." Memorandum to Eric Edelman. September 1, 2006. *The Rumsfeld Papers*. http://library.rumsfeld.com/doclib/sp/2252/2006-09-01%20To%20Eric%20Edelman%20re%20Guantanamo%20Bay%20Facts-%20Memo%20Attachment.pdf.
———. "A New Kind of War." *New York Times*, September 27, 2001.

————. "Secretary Rumsfeld Speaks on '21st Century Transformation' of U.S. Armed Forces." January 31, 2002. *DefenseLink.mil.* http://defenselink.mil/speeches /2002/s20020131-secdef.html.

Safer, Morley. "Nayirah." *60 Minutes.* CBS, January 19, 1992.

Safire, William. "Bush's Bay of Pigs." *New York Times*, April 4, 1991.

Said, Edward. *Culture and Imperialism.* New York: Vintage, 1994. First published 1993 by Knopf.

Samet, Elizabeth. "War Lies." Review of *The Yellow Birds*, by Kevin Powers. *New Republic*, September 9, 2012. https://newrepublic.com/article/106975/war-lies.

Sanger, David E. *Confront and Conceal: Obama's Secret Wars and Surprising Use of American Power.* New York: Crown, 2012.

Savage, Charlie. "U.S. Releases Rules for Airstrike Killings of Terror Suspects." *New York Times*, August 6, 2016.

————, and Scott Shane. "U.S. Reveals Death Toll from Airstrikes Outside War Zones." *New York Times*, July 1, 2016.

Schlund-Vials, Cathy J. *War, Genocide, and Justice: Cambodian American Memory Work.* Minneapolis: University of Minnesota Press, 2012.

Schwartz, Barry, and Todd Bayma. "Commemoration and the Politics of Recognition: The Korean War Veterans Memorial." *American Behavioral Scientist* 42, no. 6 (1999): 946–67.

Seal, Mark. "An Exclusive Look at Sony's Hacking Saga." *Vanity Fair*, March 2015. http://www.vanityfair.com/hollywood/2015/02/sony-hacking-seth-rogen-evan -goldberg.

Seed, David. *The Fiction of Joseph Heller: Against the Grain.* New York: St. Martin's, 1989.

Sewall, Sarah. "A Radical Field Manual." Introduction to *Counterinsurgency*, Field Manual 3–24, by US Department of the Army, xi–xliii. Chicago: University of Chicago Press, 2007.

Shenker, Israel. "Joseph Heller Draws Dead Bead on the Politics of Gloom." *New York Times*, September 10, 1968.

Shimko, Keith L. *The Iraq Wars and America's Military Revolution.* Cambridge: Cambridge University Press, 2010.

Simon and Schuster. "Happy Birthday *Catch-22*." Advertisement. *New York Times*, October 15, 1962.

Singer, Peter W. "Do Drones Undermine Democracy?" *New York Times*, January 21, 2012.

Singh, Nikhil Pal. *Black Is a Country: Race and the Unfinished Struggle for Democracy.* Cambridge, MA: Harvard University Press, 2004.

————. *Race and America's Long War.* Berkeley: University of California Press, 2017.

Slahi, Mohamedou Ould. *Guantánamo Diary.* New York: Little, Brown, 2015.

Sloane, Charles F. "Dogs in War, Police Work and on Patrol." *Journal of Criminal Law and Criminology* 46, no. 3 (1955): 385–95.

Smethurst, James Edward. *The Black Arts Movement: Literary Nationalism in the 1960s and 1970s*. Chapel Hill: University of North Carolina Press, 2005.

Smith, Robert M. "Senators Told G.I.'s in Songmy Unit Smoked Marijuana Night before Incident." *New York Times*, March 25, 1970.

Sparrow, James T. *Warfare State: World War II Americans and the Age of Big Government*. New York: Oxford University Press, 2011.

Steele, Robert H. "Our Most Dangerous Epidemic." *Nation's Business*, July 1971, 46–48.

Steinbeck, John, IV. "The Importance of Being Stoned in Vietnam." *Washingtonian*, January 1968, 33–35, 56–60.

———. *In Touch*. New York: Knopf, 1969.

———, and Nancy Steinbeck. *The Other Side of Eden: Life with John Steinbeck*. Amherst, NY: Prometheus, 2001.

Stern, Richard G. "Bombers Away." Review of *Catch-22*, by Joseph Heller. *New York Times Book Review*, October 22, 1961.

"Stigmatizing Witness Admitted by Lanham." *New York Times*, April 10, 1951.

Stone, I. F. *The Hidden History of the Korean War, 1950–1951*. New York: Little, Brown, 1988. First published 1952 by Monthly Review Press.

———. "Is the Way We Treat Negroes 'Genocide'?" *Daily Compass*, December 20, 1951.

———. "That Familiar Chill on the Brink of Peace." *I. F. Stone's Weekly*, April 4, 1953, 43.

Stone, Oliver, and Richard Boyle. *Oliver Stone's* Platoon *and* Salvador: *The Original Screenplays*. New York: Vintage, 1987.

Straight, Michael. "A Fictive Report." *New Republic*, June 2, 1952, 21.

Sturken, Marita. *Tangled Memories: The Vietnam War, the AIDS Epidemic, and the Politics of Remembering*. Berkeley: University of California Press, 1997.

The Supplemental Appropriations Bill for 1951: Hearings Before Subcommittees of the Committee on Appropriations. 81st Cong. (1950).

Surname Viet Given Name Nam. Directed by Trinh T. Minh-ha. Women Make Movies, 1989.

Sweeney, Michael S. *The Military and the Press: An Uneasy Truce*. Evanston: Northwestern University Press, 2006.

Szalay, Michael. *Hip Figures: A Literary History of the Democratic Party*. Stanford, CA: Stanford University Press, 2012.

Thompson, Hunter S. "Strange Rumblings in Aztlan." *Rolling Stone*, April 29, 1971, 30–37.

Thompson, Nicholas. *The Hawk and the Dove: Paul Nitze, George Kennan, and the History of the Cold War*. New York: Henry Holt, 2009.

Three Kings. Directed by David O. Russell. Warner Bros., 1999.

Tobar, Hector. "Kevin Powers' Haunting Iraq War Novel." Review of *The Yellow Birds*, by Kevin Powers. *Los Angeles Times*, November 10, 2012.

Trinh, T. Minh-ha. "All-Owning Spectatorship." In *When the Moon Waxes Red: Representation, Gender, and Cultural Politics*, 81–105. New York: Routledge, 1991.

Truman, Harry S. "Annual Message to the Congress on the State of the Union." January 6, 1947. American Presidency Project. http://www.presidency.ucsb.edu /ws/?pid=12762.

———. "Executive Order 9981: Establishing the President's Committee on Equality of Treatment and Opportunity in the Armed Services." July 26, 1948. American Presidency Project. http://www.presidency.ucsb.edu/ws/index.php ?pid=60737.

———. "The President's News Conference." June 29, 1950. American Presidency Project. http://www.presidency.ucsb.edu/ws/index.php?pid=13544.

———. "Presidential Directive to the Secretaries of State and Defense." In *NSC 68: Forging the Strategy of Containment*, edited by S. Nelson Drew, 32–33. Washington, DC: National Defense University Press, 1994.

———. "Radio and Television Address to the American People on the Situation in Korea." July 19, 1950. Harry S. Truman Library and Museum. https://tru manlibrary.org/publicpapers/index.php?pid=861.

———. "Radio and Television Report to the American People on the Situation in Korea." September 1, 1950. American Presidency Project. http://www.presi dency.ucsb.edu/ws/?pid=13561.

———. "Statement by the President upon Signing the National Security Act Amendments of 1949." August 10, 1949. American Presidency Project. http:// www.presidency.ucsb.edu/ws/?pid=13268.

"Trying to Help the GI Addicts." *Life*, July 23, 1971, 20–27.

United Nations General Assembly. "Universal Declaration of Human Rights." December 10, 1948. http://www.un.org/en/universal-declaration-human-rights/.

United Nations Human Rights Office of the High Commissioner. "IACHR, UN Working Group on Arbitrary Detention, UN Rapporteur on Torture, UN Rapporteur on Human Rights and Counter-Terrorism, and UN Rapporteur on Health Reiterate Need to End the Indefinite Detention of Individuals at Guantánamo Naval Base in Light of Current Human Rights Crisis." May 1, 2013. https://web.archive.org/web/20140701210358/http://www.ohchr.org/EN /NewsEvents/Pages/DisplayNews.aspx?NewsID=13278.

US Commission of Fine Arts. Minutes. July 26, 1989. *Internet Archive*. https://archive .org/details/cfaminutes26july1989.

US Department of Defense. Administrative Review Board Proceedings for ISN 760. December 15, 2005. http://www.dod.mil/pubs/foi/Reading_Room/Detainee _Related/ARB_Transcript_Set_8_20751–21016.pdf.

———. "Military Decorations and Awards Review Results." January 7, 2016. https://www.defense.gov/Portals/1/Documents/Military-Decorations-and-Awards -Review-Results.pdf.

US Department of State. *Foreign Relations of the United States, 1950: National Se-curity Affairs; Foreign Economic Policy*. Vol. 1. Washington, DC: Government Printing Office, 1977.

US Department of the Army. *Counterinsurgency*. Field Manual 3-24. Washington, DC: Department of the Army, 2006.

———. *Counterinsurgency*. Field Manual 3–24. Chicago: University of Chicago Press, 2007. First published 2006 by US Department of the Army.

US Federal Bureau of Investigation. "Update on Sony Investigation." December 19, 2014. https://www.fbi.gov/news/pressrel/press-releases/update-on-sony -investigation.

US Marine Corps. *Small Wars Manual*. Washington, DC: Government Printing Office, 1940.

US National Security Council. "NSC 68." In *NSC 68: Forging the Strategy of Con-tainment*, edited by S. Nelson Drew, 33–97. Washington, DC: National Defense University Press, 1994.

Veterans of Foreign Wars. "VFW Statement on Distinguished Warfare Medal." April 15, 2013. http://www.vfw.org/news-and-publications/press-room/archives /2013/4/vfw-statement-on-distinguished-warfare-medal.

———. "VFW Wants New Medal Ranking Lowered." February 14, 2013. https://www.vfw.org/news-and-publications/press-room/archives/2013/2/vfw -wants-new-medal-ranking-lowered.

"Viet Cong Reportedly Smoke No Marijuana." *Los Angeles Times*, August 19, 1970.

Von Eschen, Penny M. *Race against Empire: Black Americans and Anticolonial-ism, 1937–1957*. Ithaca, NY: Cornell University Press, 1997.

———. *Satchmo Blows Up the World: Jazz Ambassadors Play the Cold War*. Cam-bridge, MA: Harvard University Press, 2004.

Wag the Dog. Directed by Barry Levinson. New Line, 1997.

Washington, Mary Helen. *The Other Blacklist: The African American Literary and Cultural Left of the 1950s*. New York: Columbia University Press, 2014.

Waters, Robert. "My Lai GIs Smoked Pot, Claims Veteran." *Hartford Courant*, March 25, 1970.

Weaver, Vesla M. "Frontlash: Race and the Development of Punitive Crime Pol-icy." *Studies in American Political Development* 21, no. 2 (2007): 230–65.

Weber, Bruce. "Endowment Chairman Coaxes Funds for the Arts." *New York Times*, September 7, 2004.

Weheliye, Alexander G. *Habeas Viscus: Racializing Assemblages, Biopolitics, and Black Feminist Theories of the Human*. Durham, NC: Duke University Press, 2014.

Wheeler, John. *Touched with Fire: The Future of the Vietnam Generation*. New York: Franklin Watts, 1984.

White House. "Procedures for Approving Direct Action against Terrorist Tar-gets Located Outside the United States and Areas of Active Hostilities."

May 22, 2013. https://www.justice.gov/oip/foia-library/procedures_for_approv
ing_direct_action_against_terrorist_targets/download.

White, Walter. "Time for a Progress Report." *Saturday Review of Literature*, September 22, 1951, 9–10, 38–41.

Williams, Randall. *The Divided World: Human Rights and Its Violences*. Minneapolis: University of Minnesota Press, 2010.

Winant, Howard. "Behind Blue Eyes: Contemporary White Racial Politics." In
The New Politics of Race: Globalism, Difference, Justice, 50–68. Minneapolis:
University of Minnesota Press, 2004.

———. *The World Is a Ghetto: Race and Democracy since World War II*. New York:
Basic Books, 2001.

Witkin, Richard. "Antiwar Slate to Oppose Johnson in State Primary." *New York
Times*, September 21, 1967.

Wong, Martin. "A Gang of Four." *Giant Robot*, no. 10 (1998): 70–71.

Wood, Jacob, and Ken Harbaugh. "The Limits of Armchair Warfare." *New York
Times*, May 20, 2014.

"Writers Try to Make Sense of the Vietnam-Book Boom." *New York Times*, August 4, 1987.

X [George Kennan]. "The Sources of Soviet Communism." *Foreign Affairs* 25,
no. 4 (1947): 566–82.

Young, Ken. "Revisiting NSC 68." *Journal of Cold War Studies* 15, no. 1 (2013):
3–33.

Zetter, Kim. "The Evidence That North Korea Hacked Sony Is Flimsy." *Wired*,
December 17, 2014. https://www.wired.com/2014/12/evidence-of-north-korea
-hack-is-thin/.

Žižek, Slavoj. "NATO as the Left Hand of God?" In *Law, Justice, and Power: Between Reason and Will*, edited by Sinkwan Cheng, 25–45. Stanford, CA: Stanford University Press, 2004.

Index

absurdism, 61–71; Camus on individual rebellion and, 63–67, 70, 71, 216n17, 216n20; in Heller's *Catch-22*, 62–64, 66–71; in Vietnam War films of the 1980s, 77–78. *See also* antiwar stories

Abu Ghraib, 158

Acheson, Dean, 31, 33, 35–40, 49

Acosta, Oscar Zeta, 25–26, 107–8, 113–18, 222n64

Adamov, Arthur, 66–67

Adams, Eddie, 128

Afghanistan, 8; Americans of color serving in, 15; Civil War in, 182; delegitimization of enemies in, 8; Obama's policies in, 189, 190–91. *See also* war on terror

"After War, a Failure of Imagination" (Klay), 175

Agamben, Giorgio, 104, 208n31

Aldama, Frederick, 222n64

Algren, Nelson, 67

al-Qaeda, 4, 24, 182

Alsop, Stewart, 99

American Anthropological Association, 169

American Battle Monuments Commission, 55–56

American Council on Race Relations, 22

American Dilemma, An (Myrdal), 10–12, 14, 15

American Hero (Beinhart), 145

American Indian Wars, 152, 160–61, 219n9

American Sniper (film), 23

Amnesty International, 137

Amos, Deborah, 155, 157, 165

Anderson, Carol, 214n69

Anslinger, Harry, 95

antiwar activism: in the Cold War, 200–201; on cyber war, 191–92; of draft resisters, 60, 70; of the Gulf War, 151–53; of the Vietnam War, 53, 61–63, 69–70, 125–26, 132, 152

antiwar liberalism, 60, 87; Camus's absurdism and, 63–67, 70, 216n17, 216n20; in Heller's *Catch-22*, 71–76, 217n46; of humanitarian wars, 132, 154–55; Trinh on contradictions of, 64; of the Vietnam War, 53, 61–64, 69–70, 147. *See also* racial regime of defense; white moral enlightenment

antiwar stories, 60–91, 87; absurdism in, 61–71, 216n17, 216n20; *Catch-22* as, 60–64, 66–76; documentary approach to, 82–87; of humanitarian wars, 126–27, 131, 139–50, 152–53; indictment of state violence in, 71; *MASH* as, 29, 61, 68; of the Vietnam War, 15, 17–18, 26–27, 60–64, 76–85, 88–91, 219n70; white moral enlightenment in, 63–64, 66–67, 87, 90–91. *See also* war stories

Apocalypse Now (film), 60, 216n3

Appeal to the World, An (Du Bois), 50

Armstrong, Louis, 214n78

Asian Americans: as model minorities, 97–98, 220n23; as term, 25–26

Atanasoski, Neda, 128, 148–49, 209n42

Atkinson, Rick, 162

Atwater, Lee, 108

Awlaki, Abdulrahman, al- 5

Bacevich, Andrew, 161
Baker, James, 133
Baldwin, Hanson, 7
Balkan Wars of the 1990s: Holocaust nar-
    rative of, 149–50; as humanitarian wars,
    123, 128, 131, 148–50, 154, 165; white
    Muslims of, 148–49
Bandung Conference, 221n59
Bat*21 (film), 77
Baudrillard, Jean, 138–39
Beckett, Samuel, 66–67
Begley, Josh, 193–94
Beinhart, Larry, 145
Benjamin, Medea, 5–6
Bennett, Bruce, 197–98
Berlant, Lauren, 24
Bigelow, Kathryn, 87
bin Laden, Osama, 155, 157, 184
biopolitics, 8–9
black internationalism, 13–14, 111–12,
    214n78, 215n84, 221n59
Black Panther Party for Self-Defense, 27,
    111–12, 116, 211n85
Black Popular Front, 209n47
Black Thunder (Bontemps), 109
Blackwill, Robert, 32
bloodless wars, 131. See also cyber war;
    smart war technologies
"Bombing of Baghdad, The" (Jordan), 152–53
Bontemps, Arna, 109
Born on the Fourth of July (film), 77
Bosnia. See Balkan Wars of the 1990s
Boston Marathon bombing, 193
Bourne, Randolph, 6
Bradley, Omar, 4
Bradley, Tom, 150–51
Bravin, Jess, 230n95
Breakthrough on the Color Front (Nichols),
    42–43
Bretton Woods agreement, 102
Brickner, Richard, 68
Bridges at Toko-Ri, The (Michener), 15, 29,
    156–57
Bronze Star, 192
Brown Berets, 116
Buck, Pearl S., 10
Bunche, Ralph, 11, 50
Burdick, Eugene, 16, 24–25, 27
Bush, George H. W., 58, 165; Gulf War of,
    123–46, 149–54, 215n93, 224nn38–39;

on humanitarian wars, 129–32; Iraq
    policies of, 144; masculine values of,
    225n53; Panama invasion by, 151; refusal
    to overthrow Hussein of, 137–40, 145;
    revised Vietnam War narrative of, 123–
    25, 128–32, 145–47, 151, 223n8; Rodney
    King beating and, 127, 143–45, 150–54;
    Willie Horton ad of, 108
Bush, George W., 4, 21, 32, 145; declaration
    of war on terror by, 158, 208n31, 226n7;
    "Mission Accomplished" declaration of,
    10. See also Iraq War; war on terror
Buzzell, Colby, 155

C (combat) device, 193
Cacho, Lisa, 220n32
Camus, Albert, 63–67, 70, 71, 85, 216n20
Caputo, Philip, 77
Carabatsos, James, 77
Carnegie Corporation, 10–12
Carr, David, 199
Carr Center for Human Rights Policy (Har-
    vard), 162–63, 226n10
Carroll, Andrew, 171
Carter, Ash, 193
Carter, Jimmy, 128
Casualties of War (film), 18, 63, 77, 79
Catch-22 (Heller), 60–64, 66–76, 217n45;
    antiwar absurdism in, 61–63, 66–71,
    216n20; critical reception of, 67–68; as
    critique of Vietnam War, 60–62, 67–71,
    77, 87; white outsider liberalism of,
    71–76, 217n46; Yossarian's enactment of
    blackness in, 75, 217n48
Catcher in the Rye (Salinger), 216n17
Cebrowski, Arthur, 162
Central American wars, 20–21
Central Intelligence Agency (CIA), 7;
    drone-strike reviews by, 186; drug traf-
    ficking by, 118–22; torture conducted
    by, 196
Charlie Hebdo shootings, 199
Chaucer, Geoffrey, 103
Cheney, Dick, 124, 161
Chicano movement, 112–17, 222n66
Childress, Alice, 13–14
Chinese Civil War, 127
Chong, Sylvia, 87
Chow, Rey, 34
Citizens for a Free Kuwait (CFK), 134

Civil Rights Act of 1964, 145
Civil Rights Congress, 48–53
civil rights era: collapse of Jim Crow in, 2, 10, 23; criminalization of race in, 96, 105–7; internationalized freedom struggles of, 48–49; limited accomplishments of, 144–45; Nixon's law-and-order agenda and, 96–97, 105, 220n15; Patterson's *We Charge Genocide* of, 48–54; reconstitution of white racial domination in, 17, 18, 210n58
Clausewitz, Carl von, 8–9, 26, 90
Clinton, Bill: Balkan Wars of, 131, 149–50; dedication of the Korean War Memorial by, 54–55, 58–59; humanitarian wars of, 123, 165; Lewinski scandal of, 145
Clinton, Hillary, 186
CNN: Gulf War coverage on, 125–26, 130–31, 138, 146, 150, 154, 222n7; Nayirah al-Sabah's testimony on, 137
Code Pink, 5
Colby, William, 121
Coldest Winter, The (Halberstam), 28–29
Cold War, 2–4, 25; agency panic of, 217n46; anticommunist basis of, 9, 30, 41–44, 47, 54, 65, 94–95, 127, 216n17; antiwar absurdism of, 61–71, 216n17; antiwar movement against, 200–201; decolonializing nations of, 10, 12, 37, 42, 65, 70, 74; delegitimization of enemies/legitimation of violence in, 6–7, 37–38, 213n29; depictions of universality of liberalism in, 36–37, 65, 71; designation of Asia as key site of, 40–42, 47–48; dissolution of the Soviet Union and, 124–26, 154; as existential struggle, 35–36; hot wars of, 28; human rights narrative of, 127; Kennan's "Long Telegram" on, 33, 212n27; Nixon's drug war and, 102–3; nuclear arms race of, 30, 33, 36, 38; postcolonial challenges of, 2, 207n6, 207n8, 211n75; racial break of, 207n5; racial liberalism of, 10–14, 21, 57–58, 111, 189–90, 209n42, 213n47; racial regime of, 3–4, 9, 13, 36–38, 47–54, 59, 200–201, 212n27, 212n29, 214n69, 214n78; Reagan's re-escalation of, 21, 77, 126; US containment doctrine of, 31, 38–43; US national security state in, 30–43, 47–48, 73, 127, 189; victory of liberal democracy in,

124–26, 129–30. *See also* Korean War; post–Cold War era; Vietnam War
Colla, Elliott, 228n60
Colombia, 124
combat service medals, 192, 231n22
Combined Arms Center, 162
Commission of Fine Arts, 55–56
Comprehensive Drug Abuse Prevention and Control Act of 1970, 101
Connally, Tom, 46, 51
Coppola, Francis Ford, 60
Counterinsurgency field manual, 21, 158–59, 163–71, 226nn9–10, 226n26, 227n36; broad popularity of, 229n88; medical-scientific analogies in, 228n52
counterinsurgent wars, 21, 157–64, 201; Army/Marine Corps Field Manual on, 158–59, 163–71, 226nn9–10, 226n26, 227n36, 228n52, 229n88; history of, 159–64; humanitarian and moral ethos of, 158, 160, 166–67; Human Terrain System program in, 168–69; intellectual approach to, 164, 179; militarization of cultural knowledge in, 159, 164–71, 180, 227n49; as policing, 21, 160–61; psychological operations of, 177–78; racial regime/normative white perspectives in, 158–61, 167, 169–71, 174; war stories of, 171–81. *See also* war on terror
counterterror wars. *See* war on terror
Courage Under Fire (film), 138
Crane, Conrad, 158–59, 163–64, 166, 168–71
creative writing programs, 172–73, 228n59
crime wars, 9, 19, 23, 124; federal agencies formed for, 22–23, 105; Nixon's law-and-order agenda and, 19, 23, 94–97, 101, 220n15. *See also* counterinsurgent wars; drug wars
Cruse, Harold, 111
Cuba, 20–21, 160
Cumings, Bruce, 48
cyber war, 4–5, 186–201; civilian victims of, 187; delegitimization of enemies in, 196–99; Distinguished Warfare Medal for, 190–93; Drones+ and Metadata+ reports of, 193–94; humanitarian framing of, 188–89; on Iran's nuclear facilities, 196; as the new normal, 199–201; on North Korean networks, 196–97; North Korea's hack of Sony Pictures as, 190, 194–99;

cyber war (*cont.*)
  Obama's expansion of, 4–5, 186–90,
    230n16; racial regime of defense of,
    190; *R* (remote) device award for, 193;
    signature strikes of, 194; in US pres-
    idential election of 2016, 189–90

Dang Van Quang, 120
DarkSeoul, 195–97
Daugherty, Tracy, 87
Davis, Angela, 111
Davis, Edward, 117
Davis, Mike, 151
declarations of war, 2
Deer Hunter, The (film), 147
defense. *See* permanent war
Delmont, Matt, 193
Demme, Jonathan, 125–26, 138
Democratic National Committee, 190
De Palma, Brian, 18, 26–27
Department of Defense: counterinsurgency
  doctrine of, 159; creation of, 2–3, 7,
  18–19, 70; drone-strike reviews by, 186;
  racial liberalism of, 13; restructuring in
  1949 of, 7–8. *See also* permanent war
Diary of Anne Frank, The (film), 149
Dispatches (Herr), 60–61
Distinguished Warfare Medal, 190–93
Dodd, Thomas, 97–98, 107
Dog Soldiers (R. Stone), 138
Doloff, Steven, 217n45
Dominican Republic, 20–21, 160
Drones+ reports, 193–94
Drug Enforcement Agency (DEA), 95,
  104–5
drug wars, 3, 9, 19, 93–122, 124, 201, 207n8;
  addicted American soldiers and, 92–100,
  103, 105–7, 118–20, 221n38; communist
  rationale for, 95, 117–21; crime rates
  and, 99–100; criminalization of race and,
  96, 100–108, 110–11, 115–19, 220n32;
  drug czars of, 101, 106–7; drugs targeted
  in, 95, 219n11; federal agencies created
  for, 95, 100, 104–5; incarceration and,
  96, 102–3; under Johnson, 96, 104; medi-
  calization of addiction and treatment
  in, 106–7, 116; militarization of, 101,
  105; Nixon's declaration of war in, 94,
  100–101, 107, 110; Nixon's law-and-order
  agenda and, 94–103, 220n15; Omnibus

Crime Control and Safe Streets Act and,
  96; as policing, 95, 116–18, 122, 219n9;
  racial basis of, 93–96, 99–118; right–left
  consensus on, 105–7; war stories of,
  107–18, 221n53, 221n59, 222n64. *See also*
  Vietnam War
Du Bois, W. E. B., 111; antiwar activism
  of, 200–201; black internationalism of,
  13–14, 111, 214n78; *Encyclopedia of the
  Negro* project of, 11; NAACP petition
  to the UN by, 50; on the racial regime of
  the Cold War, 3–4, 6
Dudziak, Mary, 9, 231n22
Duncan, Patrick Sheane, 77
Duong, Lan, 219n70
Dylan, Bob, 68

Edelman, Eric, 183–84
84 Charlie MoPic (film), 77
Eisenhower, Dwight D., 213n47
Ellsberg, Daniel, 118
Espiritu, Yen Le, 128–29
Esslin, Martin, 63, 66–67
ethnic cleansing, 148–49

Fear and Loathing in Las Vegas (H. S.
  Thompson), 117
Feis, Robert, 31
Feng, Peter, 219n70
Ferguson, Roderick, 17, 218n55
fifth domain. *See* cyber war
Fire and Forget (ed. Gallagher and Scran-
  ton), 156
Fitzgerald, F. Scott, 15
Fordism, 216n17
Forrestal, James, 7
Foucault, Michel, 8–9
Franco, James, 194, 196
Frank, Anne, 149
Franklin, Bruce, 224n38
Frazier, E. Franklin, 12
From Here to Eternity (Jones), 67–68
Fukuyama, Francis, 124, 130
Full Metal Jacket (film), 60, 62, 77, 83–85,
  87–88, 216n3; deracinated racism of,
  83–84; documentary approach to, 83, 88;
  Southeast Asian characters in, 84–85

Gallagher, Matt, 155–59, 172–73, 176, 178–
  81, 229n84

Galula, David, 161, 178
Gardens of Stone (film), 63, 77
Gardner, Lloyd, 224n39
Gates, Henry Louis, 221n53
gender and war, 88–91, 219n70
genocide, 48–54, 148–50
Geolocation Cell, 194
George, Walter, 51
GI Bill, 228n59
Gillespie, Dizzy, 214n78
Gilmore, Ruth Wilson, 102
Gioia, Dana, 171–72
"God Bless the USA" (Greenwood), 139
Going after Cacciato (O'Brien), 68
Goldberg, Evan, 197
Goldwater, Barry, 97
Gómez, Manuel, 113
González, Marcial, 222n64
Good Earth, The (Buck), 10
Good Morning, Vietnam (film), 77
Gordon, Howard, 197
Greenwood, Lee, 139
Gregory, Derek, 166, 227n36
"Guantánamo Bay: The Facts" (Rumsfeld), 183–84
Guantánamo Bay prison: detainee hunger strike at, 1, 5–6, 208n15; interrogation methods at, 182–85
Guantánamo Diary (Slahi), 159, 181–85
Gulf War, 123–46, 149–54; antiwar activism of, 151–53; Baudrillard's essays on, 138–39; Bush's case for, 132–38, 141–42, 149–50, 154, 224nn38–39; CNN's coverage of, 125–26, 130–31, 138, 146, 150, 154, 222n7; failure to overthrow Hussein in, 137–40, 145, 224n39; film satires of, 126–27, 131, 138–50; humanitarian rationale for, 123–32, 137, 149–50; international liberal consensus of, 125, 129–30; Jordan's "The Bombing of Baghdad" on, 152–53; masculine values of, 225n53; multicultural military ethic of, 225n50; multicultural nationalism of, 215n93; Nayirah al-Sabah's incubator story and, 126, 132–37, 146, 224n38; NSC authorization of, 136; oil as motivator for, 132–33, 154; racial regime of, 142–45, 149, 152–54; Rodney King beating and, 127, 143–45, 150–54; smart war technologies of, 130–31, 150, 161–62, 222n7, 223n19;

UN Security Council hearings on, 136; US deaths in, 131; Weinberger–Powell doctrine in, 126. *See also* Iraq
"Gulf War Did Not Take Place, The" (Baudrillard), 138–39
"Gulf War Will Not Take Place, The" (Baudrillard), 138–39
"Gulf War, The: Is It Really Taking Place?" (Baudrillard), 138–39

Haeberle, Robert, 137
Hagel, Chuck, 192–93
Haiti, 20–21, 109–12, 160
Halberstam, David, 28–29, 80–81
Hall, Stuart, 210n74
Hamburger Hill (film), 63, 77
Hamilton, John, 192
Hammond, Paul, 39
Harbaugh, Ken, 192
Harding, Warren, 108–9
Harrington, Ollie, 14
Harris, Cheryl, 210n62
Harris Act of 1914, 104
Hasford, Gustav, 62, 69, 83, 216n3
Hass, Kristin, 215n89
Heaven and Earth (film), 77
Heller, Joseph, 16, 60–81, 87, 216n17, 217n45; antiwar liberalism of, 71–77, 85, 217n46; antiwar movement celebrity of, 61–63, 69–70; World War II service of, 87. *See also* *Catch-22* (Heller)
Helms, Richard, 121
Hemingway, Ernest, 15–16, 31–32, 228n59
heroin addiction, 98–102, 105–7; treatment methods for, 101, 106–7; in Vietnam, 98–102. *See also* drug wars
Herr, Michael, 60–61, 76, 87, 216n3; *Catch-22* and, 61, 71; on Jung's concept of the shadow, 85; on realist filmmaking, 83; on white soldiers as agents of freedom, 73, 75
Hersh, Seymour, 120
Hidden History of the Korean War, The (I. F. Stone), 43–48
high cultural pluralism, 172
Hill and Knowlton, 134–36
Hillenkoetter, Roscoe, 45–46
Hinson, Hal, 77–78
Ho Chi Minh, 141
Holliday, George, 143–45

Hong, Christine, 46–47, 198
Horton, Willie, 108
"How to Tell a True War Story" (O'Brien), 31–32
Huberman, Leo, 44
Hughes, Langston, 14, 209n47
humanitarian wars, 3, 9, 54, 123–54, 165, 201, 207n8; anticommunism and, 127; antiwar liberalism of, 132; antiwar satires of, 126–27, 131, 138–50; of Clinton, 123; defense of liberal democracy in, 126–30; domestic police brutality and, 127; end of Vietnam syndrome in, 123–32, 139, 144–45; humanitarian crises created by, 130–31; portrayal of Islam in, 149; racial regime of defense of, 131–32, 142–45, 149, 152–54, 224n48; revised Vietnam War narratives and, 123–32, 145–49, 151, 223n8; visual imagery of, 224n46. See also Balkan Wars of the 1990s; Gulf War
human rights, 13; expanded imprisonment regime and, 229n90; liberal antiracism of, 142–45, 153; militarization of, 7, 8, 31, 126–32, 141–42, 191; police brutality and, 127; post–Cold War consensus on, 125–26, 129–32, 138, 141; UN Universal Declaration of, 13, 49, 123, 149–50, 214n69; US posture as defender of, 127, 132
Human Rights Day, 123
Human Terrain System, 168–69
Humphrey, Hubert, 43, 213n47
Hurt Locker, The (film), 15, 87
Hussein, Saddam, 125, 132–42, 144–45, 149, 224n39. See also Gulf War
Husserl, Edmund, 65

Ice Cube, 143–44
identity politics, 216n17
"If Mob Rule Takes Hold in U.S." (Nixon), 102–3
Immigration and Nationality Act of 1965, 98
"The Importance of Being Stoned in Vietnam" (Steinbeck), 92–94, 97, 105
In Country (film), 77
Ingersoll, John, 121
institutional racism. See segregation and Jim Crow
Interview, The (film), 190, 194–99

In the Company of Soldiers (Atkinson), 162
intranational violence: in Catch-22, 72, 76; in Full Metal Jacket, 84; in Platoon, 81–82; of World War II, 51–52, 149–50
Ionesco, Eugène, 66–67
Iraq: invasion of Kuwait by, 125; Islamic State in, 1–2; oil reserves of, 132–33, 154; protection of minority communities in, 142, 145. See also Gulf War
Iraq War, 1, 5, 8, 10, 145; Abu Ghraib scandal of, 158; Americans of color serving in, 15; delegitimization of enemies in, 8; Obama's attempts to end, 10, 189; Petraeus's counterterrorism work in, 173, 178–79. See also war on terror
Islam, 149, 183–84
Islamic State, 1–2
Israel, 196

Jackson, Michael, 142–43
Jackson, Robert, 51–52
Jaffe, Jerome, 101, 106–7
James, C. L. R., 111
Jarhead (Swofford), 125–26, 138
Jeffords, Susan, 223n8, 225n53
"Je Suis Charlie" movement, 199
Jim Crow. See segregation and Jim Crow
Johnson, Jeh, 190, 196
Johnson, Louis, 38
Johnson, Lyndon B., 93; drug enforcement policies of, 96, 104; immigration policies of, 98; on professionalization of police, 22–23; war on crime of, 19, 23, 104, 105
Joint Chiefs of Staff, 7
Jones, James, 67–68, 70
Jordan, June, 127, 151–53
Jung, Carl, 85
Junger, Sebastian, 155

Kaboom (Gallagher), 155
Kakutani, Michiko, 156
Kaplan, Amy, 182, 207n8, 223n19
Kaplan, Caren, 222n7
Kennan, George, 33–34, 212n27
Kennedy, John F., 16, 191
Keppel, Frederick, 10–11
Kerry, John, 5
Khalili, Laleh, 158
Khien Lai, 88–91
Kierkegaard, Søren, 65

Kilcullen, David, 158–59, 163–68, 171, 178–80
Kim, Jodi, 212n27, 219n70
Kim Il-sung, 141
Kim Jong-il, 197
Kim Jong-un, 194–99
Kim Young-sam, 54, 58–59
King, Martin Luther, Jr., 26, 152
King, Robert, 198
King, Rodney, 127, 143–45, 150–54
Klay, Phil, 87, 156, 159, 172, 175–78, 181
Korean War, 4, 8, 28–32, 37–59, 141; absence of ending of, 30–32, 54–55, 58–59; Americans of color serving in, 15; armistice agreement of, 28, 30, 56; delegitimization of enemies in, 6–7, 8, 19, 30–31, 40; duration of fighting in, 28, 46; as "forgotten" war, 28–30, 46, 54, 58, 212n3; humanitarian rationale for, 127; I. F. Stone's account of, 32, 43–48, 214n57; Korean motivations for, 30; *MASH* and, 29, 61, 68; origins of, 38–39, 45–47, 214n57; Patterson's *We Charge Genocide* and, 48–54; racialized rationale for, 41–43, 47–54, 59, 213n47; revised small-war narrative of, 54–57, 215n89; US national security state and, 38–43, 45, 47–48; US spending on, 39–40; Veterans Memorial of, 54–59. *See also* Cold War
Korean War Veterans Memorial, 54–59, 215n89; multiracial statues of, 57–58; significance of number "thirty-eight" in, 54–56
Korns, Stephen, 199
Kosovo. *See* Balkan Wars of the 1990s
Kubrick, Stanley, 26–27, 60, 68, 83–87, 216n3. See also *Full Metal Jacket* (film)
Kuzmarov, Jeremy, 97, 221n38

LaFeber, Walter, 31
Lambie, James, 199
Lanham, Henderson, 52
Lantos, Tom, 133–36
Laos, 124
Laotian Fragments, The (Pratt), 69
Law Enforcement Assistance Act of 1965, 22–23, 101
Law Enforcement Assistance Administration (LEAA), 105, 106, 118
Lawrence, T. E., 161, 164, 167, 178–79

Learning to Eat Soup with a Knife (Nagl), 164
Lederer, William, 16, 24–25, 27
Lee, Alfred McClung, 22
Lehmann-Haupt, Christopher, 69
Lemkin, Raphael, 51
Levinson, Barry, 126–27, 145–50, 152. See also *Wag the Dog* (film)
liberal internationalism, 39–40
liberalism, 12–13; absurdism and, 64–67, 216n17, 216n20; universalism ascribed to, 36–37, 65, 71, 114, 189; white soldiers as defenders of, 66, 71–76. *See also* antiwar liberalism; racial liberalism
Libya, 190
Lin, Maya, 55, 129
Lincoln, Abraham, 103
Literary Culture and U.S. Imperialism (Rowe), 207n6
Logan, Rayford, 50
"Long Telegram" (Kennan), 33, 212n27
Los Angeles International Airport bomb plot, 182
Los Angeles Police Department (LAPD), 127, 143–45, 150–54
Lovett, Robert, 33
Lowe, Lisa, 12
Lynd, Robert, 11
Lynton, Michael, 195, 197–99

MacArthur, Douglas, 44, 48
MacArthur, John, 134, 224n30
Mailer, Norman, 67–68, 70
Mai Thu Van, 88
Manchurian Candidate, The (film), 29, 125–26, 138
marijuana, 93–94, 97–98, 105
Marshall, Andrew, 161–62
Marshall, S. L. A., 43, 213n47
Masco, Joseph, 230n9
MASH, 29, 61, 68
Mauritani, Abu Hafs, al-, 182
McAlister, Melani, 215n93, 225n50
McCarthy, Eugene, 70
McCarthy, Joseph (McCarthyism), 14, 44, 209n47
McCoy, Alfred, 118–22
McFate, Montgomery, 163, 168–71
McGurl, Mark, 172, 228n59
Medovoi, Leerom, 65, 216n17

Melamed, Jodi, 41–42, 209n42
Melley, Timothy, 217n46
"Memo to Non-White Peoples" (Hughes), 14, 209n47
Metadata+ reports, 193–94
Mexico, 124
Meyer, Cord, 120
Michener, James, 15, 156
Milošević, Slobodan, 149
Mimura, Glen, 219n70
Mirzoeff, Nicholas, 229n88
model minorities, 97–98, 220n23
Muhammad, Khalil Gibran, 110–11
Mullen, Bill, 221n59
multiculturalism, 79, 172, 218n55
Mumbo Jumbo (Reed), 107–13, 221n53, 221n59
Murakawa, Naomi, 105
Murphy, Michael, 98–99, 107
Myrdal, Gunnar, 11–12, 14, 15
Myth of Sisyphus, The (Camus), 63, 64–66

Nagl, John, 158–59, 163–64, 170–71, 226n26
Naked and the Dead, The (Mailer), 67–68
"Napalm Girl" (Ut), 128, 130, 137, 146–47
National Association for the Advancement of Colored People (NAACP), 50
National Counterterrorism Center, 186–88
National Liberation Front (NLF), 97–98, 112, 114
National Military Establishment (NME), 7
National Security Act of 1947, 2, 7–8, 39, 189; 1949 amendments to, 7–8, 39, 189; unified armed forces under, 7
National Security Agency (NSA), 1, 196–97
National Security Council, 7; containment doctrine (NSC 68) of, 31–43; drone-strike reviews by, 186–87; racialization of the non-Western world by, 36–38; warnings about Asia by, 40, 47–48
Nayirah. *See* al-Sabah, Nayirah
"Neo-HooDoo" (Reed), 108
Newfield, Jack, 68
"New Kind of War, A" (Rumsfeld), 162
Newton, Huey, 27, 112, 211n85
Ngo Du, 120
Nguyen, Mimi, 73
Nguyen, Viet Thanh, 178, 211n75
Nguyen Cao Ky, 119–20
Nguyen Van Thieu, 120

Nicaragua, 20–21, 160
Nichols, Lee, 42–43, 54, 58, 213n47
Nitze, Paul, 31, 33–43; on Kennan's views, 33–34; on military integration, 54; on peaceful role of preventive war, 34–38, 47; on the Soviet Union, 35–38
Nixon, Richard, 94–118; declaration of war on drugs by, 94, 100–101, 107, 110; drug enforcement infrastructure of, 100, 104–5, 107; economic policies of, 102; law-and-order agenda of, 19, 23, 94–97, 101, 102–3, 220n15; Vietnamization policy of, 103–4, 118, 221n38. *See also* drug wars
Nobel Peace Prize, 190–91, 201
normalcy of war, 10, 37, 87, 199–201, 208n31; Herr's recognition of, 61; nuclear weapons and, 199–200; politics by other means and, 8–9, 26–27, 90; role of fear in, 230n9; war on terror and, 87
Norris, Chuck, 77
North Korea: human rights offenses by, 199; outlaw state designation of, 6–7; Sony Pictures hack by, 190, 194–99
NSC 68, 31–43; containment doctrine of, 31–38; cost estimate of, 38–39; Korean War and, 38–43; racialization of the non-Western world in, 36–38
nuclear arms race, 30, 34–36, 38; hydrogen bomb program of, 33; normalcy of, 199–200

Obama, Barack, 1–6, 27, 158, 186–201; Afghanistan policies of, 189, 190–91; anti-war candidacy of, 1, 5, 189–90; on ending the Iraq War, 10, 189; on ending the war on terror, 1–3, 5, 24, 188–89; Guantá-namo policies of, 5–6; Nobel lecture of, 190–91, 201; on North Korea's hack of Sony, 195–96, 198; personal background of, 5; Presidential Policy Guidance on drone strikes of, 4–5, 186–90, 230n16. *See also* cyber war; war on terror
O'Brien, Tim, 15, 16, 23, 62, 68–69, 75; on *Catch-22*, 71; on telling true war stories, 31–32, 55
Ochs, Phil, 68
Office of Drug Abuse Law Enforcement (ODALE), 104–5
Office of Force Transformation, 162, 226n21

Office of Law Enforcement Assistance, 22–23, 105
Off Limits (film), 77
Omnibus Crime Control and Safe Streets Act of 1968, 96, 101
Operation Homecoming anthology, 171–72, 181, 228n60
Oropeza, Lorena, 222n66

Packer, George, 163
Paik, Naomi, 208n15, 229n90
Pakistan, 4, 187, 190, 193
pan-Africanism, 111–12
pan-Asian activism, 25
Panetta, Leon, 191–93
Parenti, Christian, 226n21
Pascal, Amy, 195
Patterson, William, 13–14, 32, 48–54; black internationalism of, 214n78, 215n84; blacklisting of, 50; interrogations and trials of, 52
Pease, Donald, 143–44, 226n7
permanent war, 1–10, 27, 200–201, 207n8; bloodless wars of, 131; construction of new racial categories in, 13–14; counterinsurgency doctrine in, 158–64; defense as basis of, 2–3; delegitimization of enemies in, 4–8, 20–21, 23, 30–31, 38, 40, 196–99; economic benefits of, 53; the fifth domain of, 186–90; First Amendment defense of, 198–99; health of the state under, 6–10; national security state in, 30–43, 45, 47–48, 73, 127, 189; as normal, 10, 37, 61, 87, 199–201, 208n31, 230n9; as policing, 19–23, 95, 210n62, 210n67, 210n74; as politics by other means, 8–9, 26–27, 90; presidential power and, 104; pursuit of peace through, 34–38, 47, 188–89, 191, 213n29; tension between militarism and liberal rights in, 7, 8, 31; war stories of, 26–27. *See also* Cold War; cyber war; drug wars; humanitarian wars; Korean War; racial regime of defense; Vietnam War; war on terror
Perry, William, 161
Persian Gulf War. *See* Gulf War
Petersen, William, 220n23
Petraeus, David, 21; counterinsurgency doctrine of, 158–59, 161–71; Iraq service of, 173, 178–79

Phan Thi Kim Phúc, 130, 137, 146–47
Phan Thi Mao, 79
Philippine–American War, 20–21, 157, 160
Phillips, John, 21
Phillips, Kimberley, 52–53
Pierce, Jennifer, 225n66
Platoon (film), 15, 17–18, 63, 76–83, 87, 147, 180; commercial success of, 76–77; critical reception of, 80–81; documentary style of, 82–83, 88; in Gallagher's *Youngblood*, 180, 229n84; racially diverse cast of, 78–80; white hero of, 78; white moral reckoning with war in, 80–82, 87
Poetry for the People, 154
policing, 19–23; American Indian Wars as, 152, 219n9; Black Panther challenges to, 27, 211n85; counterinsurgency function of, 21, 160–61; criminalization of race and, 20, 96, 100; drug wars as, 95, 116–18, 122, 219n9; human rights violations of, 127, 143–45, 150–54; Korean War as, 56, 95; professionalization and law-and-order policies in, 210n74; property rights as basis of, 19–20, 210n62, 211n75; racial violence of, 21–23, 116–18, 127, 143–45, 150–54, 210n74; training and militarization of, 21–23, 118; Vietnam War as, 95
Policing the Crisis (Hall), 210n74
Politics of Heroin in Southeast Asia, The (McCoy), 118–22
Popular Front, 43
Porter, John Edward, 133–36
post–Cold War era: diversity in the armed forces of, 58, 225n50; humanitarian wars of, 54, 123–54; human rights consensus of, 125–26, 129–32, 138, 141; revised Vietnam War narratives of, 123–32, 145–49, 151, 223n8; revolution in military affairs (RMA) of, 161–62, 165, 226n21. *See also* Balkan Wars of the 1990s; Gulf War; war on terror
Power, Samantha, 163
Powers, Kevin, 156, 159, 172–75, 181
Pratt, John Clark, 62, 69, 77
Preparing for the Possibility of a North Korean Collapse (Bennett), 198
Present at the Creation (Acheson), 33
presidential election of 2016, 186, 189–90
President's Commission on Law Enforcement and Administration of Justice, 19

President's Committee on Civil Rights, 22
Price, Ned, 187
"Procedures for Approving Direct Action
    Against Terrorist Targets," 186–90
Proxmire, William, 119
"Psychological Operations" (Klay), 177–78
Purdum, Todd, 58
Purple Heart, 192

R (remote) device, 193
Rabe, David, 77
Rabinovitz, Lauren, 223n8
racial liberalism, 2, 10–14, 21, 189–90, 209n42;
    criminalization of race and, 110–11; drug
    wars and, 105–7; of humanitarian wars,
    142–45, 152–53; Korean War and, 41–43,
    57–58, 213n47; multiculturalism of, 79,
    172, 218n55, 225n50; Myrdal's advocacy
    of, 10–12, 15; Nixon's law-and-order
    agenda and, 103, 220n15; policing of
    race riots and, 21–23, 210n74; short-
    comings of, 12–14, 153; Southeast Asian
    refugees and, 128–29; of Vietnam-era
    film heroes, 218n66; of the war on ter-
    ror's counterinsurgency doctrine, 166–70.
    See also civil rights era
racial regime of defense, 3–5, 8–10, 23; in
    antiwar stories, 63; in Balkan Wars of
    the 1990s, 148–49; black internationalist
    views of, 13–14, 111–12, 214n78, 215n84,
    221n59; Camus's absurdism and, 66,
    70; of the Cold War, 3–4, 9, 13, 36–38,
    47–54, 59, 200–201, 212n27, 212n29,
    214n69, 214n78; in counterinsurgency
    wars, 158–61, 167, 169–71, 174; crimi-
    nalization of race and, 20, 96, 100–108,
    110–11, 115–19, 220n32; in cyber war,
    190; delegitimization of enemies in, 4–5,
    8, 13, 20–21, 23, 30–31, 53, 196–99; de-
    segregation of the armed forces and, 15,
    42–43, 57–58, 75, 225n50; in drug wars,
    93–122; forced assimilation in, 114–15;
    Foucault on, 9; genocide and, 51–52; in
    the Gulf War, 142–45, 149, 152–54; in
    humanitarian wars, 131–32, 142–45, 149,
    152–54, 224n48; incarceration and, 96;
    in internationalized freedom struggles,
    48–49; in the Korean War, 41–43, 47–54,
    59, 213n47; LAPD beating of Rodney
    King in, 127, 143–45, 150–54; in NSC 68,

36–38; Patterson's We Charge Genocide
    on, 48–54; racialization of communism
    and, 37–38, 41–42, 117–18, 212n29,
    214n69; in the Vietnam War, 25–26, 53–
    54, 63–64, 70–76, 88–91; in the war on
    terror, 181–85. See also segregation and
    Jim Crow; white moral enlightenment
racial enlightenment. See segregation and Jim
    Crow
Rafael, Vicente, 227n49
Rambo: First Blood Part II (film), 77
Rampersad, Arnold, 209n47
Rand Corporation, 197–98
Reagan, Ronald, 128; military actions by,
    77; redistributive racial reforms under,
    86, 218n66; re-escalation of the Cold
    War by, 21, 77, 126; revised Vietnam
    War narrative of, 124, 128–29; on white
    masculinity, 85–86, 225n53
Rebel, The (Camus), 64
Reddy, Chandan, 213n29
Redeployment (Klay), 87, 156, 175–78
Reed, Ishmael, 107–13, 117–18, 221n53,
    221n59; on images of black crime, 108;
    Neo-Hoodooism of, 108–11
Reiss, Suzanna, 95, 219n11
remote war. See cyber war
Ressam, Ahmed, 182
Revolt of the Cockroach People, The
    (Acosta), 25, 107–8, 113–18, 222n64
Rid, Thomas, 190
Ridge, Tom, 200
Robbins, Richard, 171–72, 228n69
Robeson, Paul, 50, 52, 214n78
Rodríguez, Dylan, 117
Rogen, Seth, 194–99
Roosevelt, Eleanor, 13
Roosevelt, Franklin D., 96–97
Roth, Philip, 172
Rovere, Richard, 44
Rowe, John Carlos, 207n6
Rumor of War, A (Caputo), 77
Rumsfeld, Donald, 158, 161–63, 183–84
Russel, Daniel, 198
Russell, David O., 126–27, 139–45, 152. See
    also Three Kings (film)

Sabah, Nayirah, al-, 126, 132–37, 146
Sabah, Saud Nasir, al-, 134–36
Safire, William, 138

Said, Edward, 211n75
"Saigon Execution" (Adams), 128
Salazar, Ruben, 116–17
Salinger, J. D., 216n17
Sanger, David, 230n16
Sartre, Jean-Paul, 64
Schlund-Vials, Cathy, 81
Schwarzkopf, Norman, 131
Scowcroft, Brent, 132
Scranton, Roy, 156
Seale, Bobby, 27
segregation and Jim Crow: collapse of, 2, 10, 23; legal and extralegal violence of, 37, 51–54; Patterson's *We Charge Genocide* on, 48–54; structural geography of, 94. *See also* civil rights era
September 11, 2001 attacks, 162, 208n31. *See also* war on terror
settler colonialism. *See* American Indian Wars
Seven Pillars of Wisdom, The (Lawrence), 164, 179
Sewall, Sarah, 163, 166, 170–71, 174, 226n10
Short-Timers, The (Hasford), 62
Singer, Peter, 200
Singh, Nikhil, 19, 160, 211n85, 213n47, 219n9
Slahi, Mohamedou Ould, 159, 181–85; classification as terrorist of, 182–83; interrogations and torture of, 182–85, 230n95; redacted content in memoir of, 184–85
Sloane, Charles, 20
small wars. *See* policing
Small Wars Manual (Marine Corps), 20–21, 160, 210n67
smart war technologies, 4–5, 130–31, 161–62, 222n7, 223n19. *See also* cyber war
Smethurst, James, 209n47
Snowden, Edward, 1
Somalia: counterinsurgency approach in, 165; cyber war in, 190, 193; humanitarian war in, 123, 131, 149–50, 154
"Some Thoughts on Military Revolutions" (A. Marshall), 161–62
Sony Pictures, 190, 194–99
Souls of Black Folk, The (Du Bois), 3–4
Southeast Asian wars. *See* Vietnam War
Soviet Union, 2, 8, 127, 216n17; dissolution of, 124–26, 154; influence in Asia of, 41; justification of use of force by,

34; Kennan's "Long Telegram" on, 33, 212n27; NSC 68 and Nitze on, 34–39; nuclear weapons program of, 36, 38. *See also* Cold War
Special Action Office for Drug Abuse Prevention (SAODAP), 100, 105, 106
Stalin, Joseph, 2
Stallone, Sylvester, 77
Steele, Robert, 98–100, 107
Steinbeck, John, IV, 92–94, 97, 105, 107
Stone, I. F.: on Jim Crow genocide, 51; on the Korean War, 32, 43–48, 54, 214n57; on the Vietnam War, 53
Stone, Oliver, 85; on the Gulf War, 138; on realist filmmaking, 82–83; Vietnam service of, 78; Vietnam War films of, 17–18, 26–27, 62–63, 69, 75–77, 87, 180. See also *Platoon* (film)
Stone, Robert, 138
"Strange Rumblings in Aztlan" (H. S. Thompson), 117–18
Sturken, Marita, 216n9
Surname Viet Given Name Nam (film), 26–27, 64, 219n70
Sweezy, Paul, 44
Swofford, Anthony, 125–26
Szalay, Michael, 217n48

Taliban, 4, 24
Theatre of the Absurd, The (Esslin), 66–67
Things They Carried, The (O'Brien), 15, 23
third worldism, 221n59
Thompson, Hunter S., 117–18
Thompson, Robert, 161
Three Kings (film), 127, 138–45, 150–52
Thu Van, 88–89
Tobias, Channing, 50
Touched with Fire (Wheeler), 18
transnationalism, 207n8, 228n69
Tran Thi Bich Yen, 89
Trinh T. Minh-ha, 26–27, 64, 88–91, 219n70. See also *Surname Viet Given Name Nam* (film)
Truman, Harry: containment doctrine of, 31, 38–43; defense and intelligence infrastructure of, 2, 7–8, 13, 18–19, 70, 127, 189; on defense of liberal values, 8; defense spending by, 38–40; desegregation of the armed forces by, 15, 42–43, 57–58; on Human Rights Day, 123,

Truman, Harry (*cont.*)
    126; on the Korean War, 40–41, 49–50;
    nuclear weapons program of, 33, 36,
    38; postcolonial policies of, 2, 207n6,
    211n75; on professionalization of police,
    22, 23, 210n67; racial policies of, 3–4, 37,
    49, 213n47. *See also* Cold War; Korean
    War
Trump, Donald: escalation of war on terror
    by, 1–2; 2016 campaign of, 186, 189–90
Tsarnaev, Dzhokhar, 193
Tsarnaev, Tamerlan, 193
2016. *See* presidential election of 2016

Ugly American, The (Burdick and Lederer),
    16–17, 24–25
United Nations: Charter of, 49–50; Com-
    mission on Korea of, 45; Convention on
    Genocide of, 49–52, 51, 54; Office of the
    Commissioner for Human Rights of, 6;
    Universal Declaration of Human Rights
    of, 13, 49, 123, 127, 149–50, 214n69
Ut, Nick, 128, 137, 146–47

Van Fleet, James, 48
Vang Pao, 119
Veterans of Foreign Wars, 192–93
Vietnam (Mai), 88
Vietnam Veterans Memorial, 54, 55, 62, 129
Vietnam War, 15–18, 25–29, 60–91, 141;
    addicted American soldiers of, 92–100,
    103, 105–7, 118–20, 221n38; Americans
    of color serving in, 15, 74, 78–79, 83–84,
    105; antiwar absurdism and, 61–71,
    216n17, 216n20; antiwar films of, 15,
    17–18, 26–27, 60, 62–64, 76–91, 219n70;
    antiwar movement against, 53, 61–63,
    69–70, 125–26, 132, 152; army-supplied
    amphetamines of, 94; *Catch-22* and
    MASH as fables of, 60–63, 66–77, 87,
    217n46; CIA's drug-trafficking allies in,
    118–22; civilian victims of, 74, 78, 79, 84–
    85, 128, 130; counterinsurgency policies
    in, 165; cultural memory of, 62, 128–29,
    216n9; delegitimization of enemies in, 8;
    deteriorating anticommunist consensus
    of, 9, 54, 94–95, 105, 118–19, 127; divisive
    impact of, 28–29; the draft and, 60, 70,
    74, 79; end in US defeat of, 121–22,
    127–28, 161; French colonialism and, 70;

minority group alliances with Southeast
    Asians in, 111–15, 221n59, 222n66; My
    Lai massacre of, 79–80, 81, 93, 97–98,
    114, 128; Nixon's Vietnamization policy
    of, 103–4, 118, 221n38; photographic
    images of, 128, 130, 137, 146–47; as
    policing, 95; racist basis of, 25–26, 53–54,
    63, 70, 88–91; refugees from, 128–29;
    revised narratives of, 123–25, 128–32,
    145–49, 151, 223n8; secret bombings
    of, 118; Tet Offensive of, 92, 97, 101–2;
    Veterans Memorial of, 54–55, 62, 129;
    veterans of, 18, 86–87, 93, 99, 105–6, 172,
    210n58; Vietnam syndrome after, 123–
    32, 139, 144–45. *See also* antiwar stories;
    drug wars
Von Eschen, Penny, 214n78
Voting Rights Act of 1965, 145
Vyshinsky, Andrey, 44

Wag the Dog (film), 127, 131, 138, 145–50,
    152
Wallace, George, 96–97
war on terror, 1–6, 87, 201, 207n8; bin
    Laden's death in, 155, 157, 184; Bush's
    declaration of, 158, 208n31, 226n7; civil-
    ian victims of, 187; counterinsurgency
    doctrine of, 2, 4–6, 24, 157–71; cyber
    war of, 4–5, 186–201; delegitimization of
    enemies in, 4–5, 8; drone attacks of, 4, 5,
    186–87, 190, 193; drone-strike authoriza-
    tion procedures of, 4–5, 186–90; interro-
    gations and torture in, 159, 181–85, 196;
    military awards in, 191–94; military–
    civilian divide of, 155, 157–58, 163–64,
    176, 181; military prisons and black sites
    of, 158, 159, 182–84; multiple sites of,
    155–56; nonfiction accounts of, 155; nor-
    malcy of war and, 87, 199–201; Obama's
    polices for ending of, 1–3, 5, 24, 188–89;
    racial regime of, 158–59, 167, 181–85;
    Trump's escalation of, 1–2; war stories
    of, 155–59, 171–85, 229n85, 229n88.
    See also Guantánamo Bay prison
War Porn (Scranton), 156
war stories, 23–27, 211n75; bridging the
    military–civilian divide with, 176, 181;
    of combat medal recipients' valor, 192;
    combat soldier perspectives in, 31–32;
    by detained and tortured victims, 159,

181–85; of drug wars, 107–18, 221n53, 221n59, 222n64; NSC 68's blueprint for empire as, 32–38; ordinariness of war in, 24–25, 55; of racial and state violence, 25–26; of the war on terror, 155–58, 171–85; white moral culture of, 15–18, 26, 63–64, 87, 90–91, 157–58, 210n58; white veteran-writers of, 156, 159, 172–81, 229n85, 229n88. *See also* antiwar stories

Washington, Mary Helen, 209n47

Watts riots of 1965, 151

We Charge Genocide (Patterson), 48–54

Weheliye, Alexander, 215n84

West, Charles, 97

Wheeler, John, 18

"Where's the Great Novel about the War on Terror?" (Gallagher), 155, 181

White, Walter, 50

white moral enlightenment, 15–20, 26, 87, 90–91, 210n58; antiwar liberalism in, 63–67, 87, 216n17; in *Catch-22*, 69–76, 78–79, 87, 217n46; Cold War apologetics of, 81; in *Full Metal Jacket*, 83–85; in *Platoon*, 80–82; property rights and, 19–20, 210n62; war on terror stories and, 157–58; of white liberal heroes, 16–18, 74–76, 84, 90–91, 218n66

white supremacy. *See* segregation and Jim Crow

Williams, Clayton, 134

Williams, Kayla, 155, 156–57

Williams, Randall, 224n48

Wilson, Woodrow, 109

Winant, Howard, 207n5, 210n58

Wingate, Orde, 161

Wire, The, 108

Wolfowitz, Paul, 161

Wong, Vicci, 26

Wood, Jacob, 192

"World Heroin Problem, The" (Murphy and Steele), 98–100

World War II, 2, 21; atomic bombing of, 34–35; classic fiction of, 67–68, 70; division of Korea and, 30; GI Bill of, 228n59; Heller's *Catch-22* and, 60–64, 66–76; Holocaust of, 51–52, 149–50; national security state of, 31; Nuremberg Trials on, 52, 136; photographic images of, 146–47; racial reforms following, 10, 207n5; racial unrest during, 21–22; segregated armed forces of, 42; unifying purpose of, 28–29; upset of liberal universalism by, 12–13

X, Malcolm, 152

Yellow Birds, The (Powers), 156, 173–75

Yemen, 4–5, 187, 190, 193

Youngblood (Gallagher), 156, 178–81, 229n84

Žižek, Slavoj, 131